THOSE WHO PLAY WITH FIRE

THOSE WHO PLAY WITH FIRE

GENDER, FERTILITY AND TRANSFORMATION IN EAST AND SOUTHERN AFRICA

HENRIETTA L. MOORE   TODD SANDERS   BWIRE KAARE

LONDON SCHOOL OF ECONOMICS MONOGRAPHS ON SOCIAL ANTHROPOLOGY

Volume 69

THE ATHLONE PRESS
London and New Brunswick, N.J.

First published 1999 by
THE ATHLONE PRESS
1 Park Drive, London NW11 7SG
and New Brunswick, New Jersey

© The Contributors, 1999

British Library Cataloguing in Publication Data
A catalogue record for this book is available
from the British Library

ISBN 0 485 19569 0

Library of Congress Cataloging-in-Publication Data

Those who play with fire : gender, fertility and transformation in
East and Southern Africa / editors, Henrietta L. Moore, Todd
Sanders, Bwire Kaare.
    p.   cm. – (London School of Economics. Monographs on Social
Anthropology; no. 69)
  Includes bibliographical references and index.
  ISBN 0-485-19569-0 (cloth)
  1. Rites and ceremonies–Africa, Eastern. 2. Rites and
ceremonies–Africa, Southern. 3. Sex role–Africa, Eastern. 4. Sex
role–Africa, Southern. 5. Body, Human–Symbolic aspects–Africa,
Eastern. 6. Body, Human–Symbolic aspects–Africa, Southern.
7. Africa, Eastern–Social life and customs. 8. Africa, Southern–
Social life and customs. I. Moore, Henrietta L., 1957– II. Sanders.
Todd, 1965– . III. Kaare, Bwire, 1954– . IV. Series:
Monographs on social anthropology: no. 69.
GN658.T46   1999
306'.09676–dc21   99-1220
                                             CIP

Distributed in the United States, Canada and South America by
Transaction Publishers
390 Campus Drive
Somerset, New Jersey 08873

Typeset by Acorn Bookwork, Salisbury, Wilts.

CONTENTS

CONTENTS

NOTES ON CONTRIBUTORS

Astrid Blystad is Associate Professor at the University of Bergen, Norway, in the Department of Public Health and Primary Health Care. Her most recent publications include 'Peril or penalty: AIDS in the context of social change among the Barabaig' in K.-I. Klepp, P.M. Biswalo and A. Talle (eds) *Young People at Risk: Fighting AIDS in Northern Tanzania* (1995), 'La chant qui reveille la terre', in T. Dom (ed.) *Houn-Noukoun: Tambours et Visages* (Paris, 1996) and (with O.B Rekdal) '"We are as sheep and goats": Iraqw and Datooga discourses on fortune, failure and the future' in D.M. Anderson and V. Broch-Due (eds) *'The Poor are not Us': Poverty and Pastoralism in Eastern Africa* (forthcoming).

Vigdis Broch-Due currently holds positions at the School of Oriental and African Studies, London, and the Nordic Africa Institute, Uppsala, where she heads a research programme entitled 'Poverty, Gender and Conflict'. She has written a number of articles on the pastoral Turkana of Kenya, and has co-edited *Carved Flesh/Cast Selves: Gendered Symbols and Social Practices* (Berg, 1993).

Maia Green has been a Lecturer in Anthropology at the University of Manchester since 1994, and has published several articles on conceptual systems among the Pogoro Catholics of southern Tanzania. She is currently co-editing (with F. Cannell) *Words and Things: Power and Transformation in Local Christianities.*

Anita Jacobson-Widding is a Professor at the University of Uppsala. She has published extensively on African cosmology, belief and ritual. Her forthcoming book, *Chapungu: The Bird that*

Never Drops a Feather, explores gender identities in an African context.

Bwire Kaare studied anthropology at the London School of Economics, and is currently Lecturer in Sociology and Research Methods at the Institute of Finance Management, Dar es Salaam, Tanzania. He has conducted research among the Akie and Hadza (both also known as Dorobo) hunter-gatherers of Tanzania. He has written on Hadza relations with the state and the construction of their identities as minority groups in Tanzania.

Deborah Kaspin is Assistant Professor of Anthropology at Yale University. She has published 'A Chewa cosmology of the body', *American Ethnologist*, 23 (1996) and is currently working on a book on Chewa ritual and political history.

Henrietta L. Moore is Professor of Anthropology and Director of the Gender Institute at the London School of Economics and Political Science. Her publications include *Space, Text and Gender* (1986), *Feminism and Anthropology* (1988), *A Passion for Difference* (1994), *Cutting Down Trees: Gender, Nutrition and Change in the Northern Province of Zambia, 1890–1990* (with Megan Vaughan, 1994) and *The Future of Anthropological Knowledge* (1996).

Camilla Power is a Lecturer in Anthropology at the University of East London, in the Department of Sociology and Anthropology. She is currently completing her thesis on cosmetics and gender performance in African initiation ritual, and has published several articles on gender, cosmetics and the evolution of ritual.

Todd Sanders is a postdoctoral Research Fellow at the London School of Economics and Political Science, in the Department of Anthropology and the Gender Institute. His most recent publication, on rainmaking in Tanzania, appeared in *Africa* (vol. 68, 1998). Currently he is writing a book on witchcraft and modernity in East Africa.

Katherine Snyder is Assistant Professor at Queens College, City University of New York, in the Department of Anthropology. Her recent publications include 'Elders' authority and women's protest: the *masay* ritual and social change among the Iraqw of northern Tanzania', *Journal of the Royal Anthropological Institute*, 3 (1997), and 'Agrarian change and the farmers' land-use strategies among the Iraqw of northern Tanzania', *Human Ecology*, 24 (1996).

Ian Watts has recently completed his PhD at University College, University of London, having undertaken research into the archaeology of early modern peoples in southern Africa. He has published (with Camilla Power) a chapter in J. Steel and S. Shennan (eds) *The Archaeology of Human Ancestry* (1996) and 'The woman with the zebra's penis: gender, mutability and performance', *Journal of the Royal Anthropological Institute*, 3 (1997). His most recent publication is a chapter in R. Dunbar, C. Knight and C. Power (eds) *The Evolution of Culture* (1999).

PART I
INTRODUCTION

CHAPTER I

GENDER, SYMBOLISM AND PRAXIS

THEORETICAL APPROACHES

HENRIETTA L. MOORE

In reality – there are no religions which are false. All are true
in their own fashion, all answer, though in different ways, to
the given conditions of human existence (Durkheim 1964: 3).

In many African societies, there is an abiding concern with sexual
morality, with the power of sex and with issues of sexual access
and denial (e.g. Heald 1995; Beidelman 1971). The larger context
for this concern is the relationship between body processes and
social processes, the way that the inner rhythms and functions of
the body have an established set of concordances with social
structures and cosmological understandings (e.g. Devisch 1985a;
1985b; Jacobson-Widding 1991; Kaspin 1996). Such concerns are
mirrored in a wide range of ethnographic studies from all over
the continent, and have formed the basis for structuralist and
symbolist interpretations of a broad spectrum of ritual practices.
An earlier division of intellectual labour within anthropology
characterized a 'French approach' to African systems of thought
as one based on the analysis of ideational systems, as opposed to
a 'British emphasis' on social structure and action (cf. Fortes and
Dieterlen 1965; Karp 1980; B. Morris 1987: chs 3 and 5). The
validity of this division of labour between national traditions has
been considerably eroded, if it was ever actually valid, by recent
studies of African systems of thought and ritual practices (see
Kaspin, ch. 3, this volume). However, Durkheim's legacy in
anthropology – in its most attenuated form – has been to leave
his inheritors with the question of whether categories of thought
are socially derived.[1] There might be few anthropologists at the
present time who would accept this proposition uncritically,

3

but the legacy of Durkheim as percolated through the works of Radcliffe-Brown (1952), Victor Turner (1967; 1969), Douglas (1966; 1970), Lévi-Strauss (1966) and others continues to have a marked influence on theoretical orientations in the discipline. Hence, it is commonplace to find contemporary scholars of Africa asking questions about the relationship between forms of descent and gender symbolism, and enquiring as to how positive symbolic valuations of female fertility or gender complementarity can be related to systems of patrilineal descent and/or to the importance of uterine links within agnatic descent systems (e.g. Devisch 1988; Håkansson 1990; Houseman 1988; Jacobson-Widding 1985; Udvardy 1990).[2]

The studies collected together in this volume present new and recent ethnography on East and Southern Africa which extends and updates our knowledge of gender, ritual and symbolism in the region. The authors utilize recent theories on gender, subjectivity, agency and performance to examine their ethnography and suggest new directions for research. However, while all these studies take fresh theoretical approaches to their material, they nonetheless continue to struggle with aspects of the Durkheimian legacy and thus their contributions should be understood both as an attempt to develop new theoretical perspectives relevant to the changing nature of gender and symbolism in Africa, and as part of the developing historiography of anthropology in Africa.

APPROACHES TO SYMBOLISM AND RITUAL: THE IMPACT OF PHENOMENOLOGY AND PRAXIS THEORY

Approaches to the analysis of symbolism in anthropology are extremely diverse when viewed in terms of their often self-avowed and detailed comparisons – scholars frequently and necessarily clarify their own positions by differentiating them from those of others.[3] But the basic theoretical orientations can be summed up as those which privilege underlying formal patterns or structures (structuralist), those that see social structure as the basis of symbol systems (socio-structuralist/symbolist), and those that prioritize local understandings and practices (phenomenological/experiential). In practice, many writers have developed approaches over time that combine aspects of all three approaches, and frequently adopt the theoretical emphasis most appropriate to the material they are dealing with. The tension between abstract, comparative models and detailed empirical and experiential ethnography is a necessary condition of the domain of enquiry. No set of cultural symbols or ritual practices can be seriously analysed out of context, but neither can the similarities of existential struggle, cognitive capacities and physiological processes be ignored. The latter difficulty explains the prevalence of such terms and phrases as 'the meaning of life', 'primordial unity', 'the ineffable', 'the sacred' and 'the divine' in anthropological writings on ritual and symbolism. Such phrases and terms do not by their nature have clear-cut meanings or standard emotional correlates, and thus when subjected to critique by unsympathetic sceptics almost any writer on religious symbolism can be made to look foolish.

The issue of plausibility is further complicated by the fact that many anthropological explanations of ritual and symbolism exceed local exegesis (cf. Gell 1975; Lewis 1980). This is particularly the case when the explanation is comparative in nature, and in recent years the comparative project of anthropology has been subject to critique on this point as part of the turn away from 'grand theory' and 'grand narratives'.[4] However, the larger principle is that any description of a culture is implicitly comparative because it is simultaneously a description of what it is not (Hastrup 1995: 7). It is axiomatic in anthropology that cultural symbols and rituals – in fact all aspects of culture – must be described in terms of the culture's own epistemological concerns, and in that sense every description must remain faithful to local understandings. However, this is not the same thing as saying that all anthropological explanations can be or should be exact renditions of local exegesis. For one thing, this would ignore the problem of unequal distributions of power and knowledge, and fail to investigate how both of these work in the service of vested interests.

In the study of ritual and symbolism, there are also other theoretical and methodological difficulties. Language may provide a very indirect route to experience, and there are many cultural concerns that cannot be elicited from spoken words (Hastrup 1995: 42). The ability to make links between different cultural domains, different aspects of social experience, is frequently embodied in performance. The experience of engagement with a life-world this provides constructs practical activity as an interpretation of that world without necessarily engaging in philosophical discussion or the construction of articulated all-embracing models. This is why it is misleading to refer to 'folk models' if by this we intend to reduce such models to spoken exegesis (Holy and Stuchlick 1980; Jacobson-Widding and van Beek 1990). To privilege performance in this way is clearly not to imply that local exegesis does not exist or should not be privileged where it does, but simply to point out that not all forms of exegesis are linguistic, if by this we mean sets of articulated propositions (Jackson 1996).[5]

All over East and Southern Africa, gender and ritual symbolism are concerned with a series of tensions embedded in basic sets of oppositions: male/female; cold/hot; sour/sweet; sun/moon; dry/wet; day/night; raw/cooked.[6] These oppositions are connected to elements of the natural world – fire, blood, water, sex – that emphasize the transformative power of symbol systems and their technological relation to the world. 'Those who play with fire' are those engaged in living bodily, social and cosmological worlds constructed in terms of such oppositions. Not all oppositional pairs have equal prominence in all social contexts, and each society constructs and lives out the particularities of its symbolism in a specific way, but the major concern of ritual practice is to manage relations within and between these oppositions – sometimes through harmony, sometimes through mediation and transcendence. What is significant about these oppositions is that they are corporeally embodied and stem from corporeal experiences (McDougall 1977). It is the body that provides the most immediate and physical point of reference for the individual's relation with herself, with others and with the world (Devisch 1985b: 591). The experiences and sensations of the body thus provide concrete images for other processes and forms of connection. In order to ground these assertions, it is necessary to review some of the theoretical assumptions and consequences of recent writing, and provide some ethnographic examples.

The larger context in which symbolic oppositions are powerful and find meaning in East and Southern Africa is a concern with the continuity and maintenance of the social and natural worlds and their relation. In this context, it is ideas about gender and reproduction that both undergrid and encompass the larger set of symbolic oppositions. The bodily engagement with gender distinctions and social and biological reproduction provides a mechanism for the externalization and transposition of symbolic oppositions onto the spatio-temporal structuring of the environment, social structures and relations and the cosmos. The Yaka of Zaire, for example, see gender categories and gender relations as associated with birth, death and the succession of the generations. These processes they liken to various processes of plant growth – rising of sap, flowering, bearing of fruit, and decay. This gives rise to ideas that some foods are appropriate for women and some for men, and links certain colours to the genders. Motifs of death, regeneration and birth are thus intertwined with aspects of the natural world, and these motifs form the basis for the transition rituals of initiation, enthronement and burials/funerals (Devisch 1988; 1993: ch. 2; see also De Boeck 1994b; Stevens 1995). The Yaka case is specific in its particularities, but is otherwise paradigmatic for the region, as its comparison with the ethnography presented in this volume shows.

However, it would be a mistake to see Yaka symbolism as purely a form of representation, or to imagine that anthropological analyses of symbolism and ritual that identify pervasive oppositions that are extended and transposed across many domains are simply idealized or ideational accounts. Recent anthropological accounts of symbolism and ritual in the region (e.g. Devisch 1993; Beidelman 1997; Taylor 1993; Kratz 1994) have emphasized that the sets of oppositions identified in analysis are part of a symbolic logic that underpins a philosophy of social and natural continuity and reproduction that is forged by the demands and requirements of ecology and ways of life. This is a point made forcibly by Kaspin and Broch-Due in their articles in this volume. Symbolism in these contexts is about a concrete relation with a physical world where the fertility of humans, plants and animals has to be managed in ritual as well as in day-to-day activities. Recent work on symbolism and ritual in the region should thus be distinguished markedly from earlier structuralist analyses which dealt with symbols as if they were abstracted from the material realities of day-to-day living. The intimate relationship between knowledge and power, on which the parallel management and regeneration of the natural and social worlds depends, links cosmology to a knowledge of the forces that effect outcomes in the world (Herbert 1993: 1–3; Sanders, this volume; Kaarc, this volume). The social and symbolic manipulation of gender – as the basis for reproduction and continuity – legitimizes and disguises social orders of inequality, distinction and reciprocity (Devisch 1985a: 697; Snyder, this volume; Blystad, this volume; Green, this volume).[7] Symbolism and ritual are thus about the management of a lived world and its material conditions, and not just about its representation, and that process of management is sensuous, physical and practical, and not simply ideational and intellectual.

Thus, this contemporary work – which has been profoundly influenced by praxis theory and phenomenology – should also be distinguished from an earlier anthropology (see Douglas 1970; Leach 1976; Tambiah 1968; 1979) that viewed bodies as representations, and symbols and rituals as means of communication. The main problem with this work is its assumption that symbols and rituals represent, dramatize or enact prior concepts, meanings and codes. The primary focus of enquiry is 'What does this symbol/ritual mean or stand for?' This is true even for those scholars who espouse a performative approach to ritual, where symbols and ritual dramatize or enact key social values, or conflicts between such values or between aspects of social structure (e.g. V. Turner 1967; 1969). Performance theorists might be more concerned with 'what do symbols and ritual do?', but they still approach that question through a hermeneutic of meaning that privileges the linguistic.

The notion of performance has obvious links and continuities with praxis theory in anthropology (Ortner 1984). Praxis theorists emphasize that the world is both structured and structuring, the aim is to mediate, or, at least, comprehend the dialectic between the dichotomies of structure/agency, material/symbolic. In its most useful formulation, praxis theory forces a confrontation with the act itself, and marks a move away from an over-reliance on linguistic interpretation. A focus on acting has necessarily been conjoined with a return to the body, where this concern helps to mediate, but not resolve, a further set of dichotomies between individual/society, subject/object and mind/body. In anthropology, theorists have drawn on the work of Pierre Bourdieu (1977; 1990) and more recently on that of Merleau-Ponty (1962; 1963) as a means of combining praxis theory with phenomenology. The resulting theoretical perspective has some interesting consequences for the analysis of ritual and symbolism, and, in particular, gender.[8]

There are some tensions in melding together the work of Bourdieu and Merleau-Ponty. Bourdieu has little time for phenomenology which he views as a form of naive subjectivism that ignores the historical and cultural conditions under which individuals come to self-consciousness (Bourdieu 1990: 25–6).[9] However, the value of theoretical approaches which draw, to greater or lesser extent, on the writings of these two theorists is a concern with forms of knowledge as incorporated in physical activity. Merleau-Ponty argues that bodily actions are not to be understood as expressing or objectifying meanings originating in the mind. The meaning is in the action itself, and should not be reduced to what can be thought and said (Merleau-Ponty 1962). Michael Jackson's work on the Kuranko develops this perspective and shows that the meaning of body praxis is not always reducible to cognitive and semantic operations, and that body movements can make sense, and make sense of the world, without being intentional in the linguistic sense (Jackson 1989: 123; Blystad, this volume). 'The meaning of practical knowledge lies in what is accomplished through it, not in what conceptual order may be said to underlie or precede it' (Jackson 1996: 34).

Social praxis from a phenomenological viewpoint is concerned with the experience of self as part of the experience of the relation of self and other. Thus, phenomenology is never about individuals acting alone, and the question of consciousness, of subjectivity, is always an issue of intersubjectivity, of relating to others. To live in a life-world is to continually adapt to and be subject to conceptual orders and social discourses, but this is not the same thing as saying that experience is only constrained to, or faithful to, such orders. Experience of the world is the result of a project of physical engagement with the world and can thus never be the result simply of rule-following or subject to final closure.

Bourdieu takes a slightly different approach because, while he is concerned with practical knowledge and with the practical mastery of schemes of perception and action (habitus) learnt through practical engagement with the world, he is less interested in the sensory and intersubjective basis of much bodily knowledge. In many societies in Africa, different kinds of knowledge are associated with different parts of the body and much is made of the sensory and practical acquisition of knowledge (see Broch-Due, this volume). For the Yaka, for example, the ear is how the child learns of the world, and the heart is the centre of moral vision and social responsiveness, while the liver is the seat of negative and inward-turning feelings (Devisch 1993: 139–41). The way that the body is literally orientated towards, and physically engaged with, the world is an important part not only of knowledge acquisition, but of the very understanding of knowledge itself and of its effects on the world, on self and on others. But Bourdieu's interest in the body is more narrowly confined to an analysis of kinaesthetics as a form of mnemonics.

The habitus is defined as a set of generative cognitive and motivating schemes produced within a particular set of material conditions, but for Bourdieu these conditions are those of historically produced social divisions and distinctions linked primarily to productive relations. The schemes comprising the habitus are 'structured structures predisposed to function as structuring structures' for cognition and action (Bourdieu 1990: 53). Practical knowledge of the world is generated through the engagement of the habitus with the world, but this form of practical knowledge is embodied in the knowledge of how to proceed, it does not necessarily come into language. Cultural distinctions and cultural values thus produce and are produced by daily activities, but in a way that is not recognized, or only rarely, by those who carry out those activities. It is possible to

> instil a whole cosmology, through injunctions as insignificant as 'sit up straight' or 'don't hold your knife in your left hand', and inscribe the most fundamental principles of the arbitrary content of a culture in seemingly innocuous details of bearing or physical and verbal manners, so putting them beyond the reach of consciousness and explicit statement (Bourdieu, 1990: 69).

But, in spite of his concern with unthought practical action in the world, Bourdieu's emphasis is still on the logic of the generative schemes (habitus) and thus behind his theory of practical knowledge lies a theory of cognition very close to that of Lévi-Strauss.[10] However, because Bourdieu is less concerned with the individual and more concerned with the conditions for social reproduction, his work incorporates an analysis of the material conditions of existence and maintains an emphasis on ideology, dominance and power that is quite absent from the work of Merleau-Ponty. This materiality is crucial for an understanding of gender, ritual and lived symbolism.

However, what anthropologists have elicited – and the reason they draw together these somewhat divergent theorists – is the potential for understanding symbolism and ritual in a way that integrates social structure and individual experience through an engaged knowledge of the world that is practical, unthought and sensuous. The result of such an approach is a focus on the body and on how the experiences and capacities of the body produce symbols that operate across different cultural domains, setting up homologies among diverse levels and experiences, social categories and values. What is distinctive about the approach is that it does not treat the relationship between embodiment and symbolism as one of semantics, nor does it view the body either as a *tabula rasa* for cultural representations or as an object of representation (see Blystad, this volume).

Bemba initiation and bodily praxis

An example here can be provided through a rethinking of Audrey Richards's analysis of the initiation rite for Bemba girls, *chisungu* (Richards 1982).[11] The *chisungu* ritual involves, like all other initiation rites in Africa, a great deal of practical mimesis, in which symbolic elements relating to several domains of Bemba life are enacted and worked over. The women in charge told Richards that the purpose of the ceremony was to teach the girls and make them clever. The women claimed to be teaching the girls how to bear and bring up children, keep house, manage food supplies and garden. But all Bemba girls know how to cook, garden, collect firewood and so on long before they go into the *chisungu* ceremony. It is clear that they do learn secret words and songs, and primarily they learn the secret songs and multiple meanings associated with the *mbusa*, the 'sacred emblems', which include clay figurines, wall paintings, and small bundles of objects representing the domestic and productive life of the Bemba people. These 'sacred emblems' are shown to the girls on various occasions during the ceremony. They also learn the special language and taboos associated with relations between women and men, and on which the successful fertility of a Bemba marriage, and indeed the fertility of society and the land, depend.

This represents a substantial body of knowledge, but Richards notes that in many of the rituals associated with the month-long rites, the meanings and symbolism employed were not only obscure to her, but also apparently to the participants (Richards

1982: 55). Moreover, the ritual does not have a fixed script: the order and timing of its component parts vary from one occasion to another, the verses of the songs and the dance performances change, and, whilst saying that they are adhering to the way of the ancestors, the performers insist on the ambiguity and multiplicity of meanings. In view of the absence of any formal instruction in the course of the rite, and the fact that on various occasions the initiates were kept out of the thick of activities apparently so that they could not participate or look too closely at what was going on, Richards was puzzled by exactly what the girls were learning, and concluded in characteristic style: 'If any useful information was handed out during the chisungu one would be inclined to think that the candidates themselves would be the last people to have a chance of acquiring it' (Richards 1982: 126).

What Richards did not see was that the bodily praxis of the initiation ritual literally incorporates its moral teachings. The preparation, presentation and handling of the *mbusa* take up much of the time given to the ritual. *Mbusa* literally means 'things handed down' and these objects act as mnemonics for a series of songs and dances appropriate to each object, and for the moral and spiritual precepts contained in the multiple sets of meanings associated with each *mbusa*. In many of the individual rites of the *chisungu*, instructors and initiands use their mouths as much as possible, rather than their hands, to handle the *mbusa* and complete various tasks. During the 'honouring of the mwenge tree', the senior women sing a refrain: 'Pick up what you have, Pick up things with the mouth' (Richards 1982: 93). The concrete nature of the knowledge which is passed from senior women to young girls in the *chisungu* ceremony is embodied in the transfer by mouth from one woman to another, in order of seniority, of the corporate knowledge contained in the *mbusa*, which is literally the 'thing handed down'. In various contexts, the senior women in charge of the ceremony open containers with their mouths to reveal hidden *mbusa* (Richards 1982: 78–80), while the girls acknowledge the truth of the knowledge handed down to them through the mouths of senior women through such acts as opening bundles of firewood with their teeth (Richards 1982: 107), and placing a marriage purification pot on the fire with their mouths (Richards 1982: 77–8).

It is a mistake to underestimate the importance and power of an embodied knowledge which does not require precise linguistic

referents. This does not mean that language and linguistic interpretations are not important in the ritual or that the Bemba do
not use the *mbusa* as straightforward mnemonic devices which
assist initiates and others in remembering various moral precepts.
However, the Bemba make use of bodily metaphors that indicate
how general precepts are to be understood as sensible truths, that
is as a form of knowledge which has a concrete, sensuous relation
to the world through the body. The fact that symbols are concretized in the body in forms which have no direct linguistic referent
accounts perhaps for Audrey Richards's puzzlement about what
the girls were learning and for her assertion that some of the
meanings of the rites were obscure. The ambiguity of meaning
associated with embodied experience is something which can only
be incompletely copied in language, and hence the women's insistence on the multiplicity and fluid nature of the linguistic
meanings associated with the *mbusa*. The *mbusa* act as mnemonics not for the linguistic meanings embodied in verbal exegesis,
but for the physical experiences which make up the lived world of
sexuality, fertility and gaining a living, as well as for the long
reflection on those activities which is the *chisungu* rite.

Thus, what the rite achieves is a physical and symbolic manipulation of the body in relation to the world, and of the world in
relation to the body. The rite becomes part of a lived relation to
the base metaphors of Bemba culture which are themselves
evident in the productive and reproductive relations of Bemba
life. This is what Bourdieu intends when he says that 'the mental
structures which construct the world of objects are constructed in
the practice of a world of objects constructed according to the
same structures' (Bourdieu 1977: 91). This in turn makes sense of
his assertion that 'The mind is a metaphor of the world of
objects which is itself but an endless circle of mutually reflecting
metaphors' (Bourdieu 1977: 91). However, it would be a mistake
to move from this statement to the assumption that the
movement of the body in space or the set of embodied actions of
an initiation rite have a 'meaning' beyond the acts themselves, to
assume, in other words, that the act stands for something else.
The act is not the representation of symbolic principles, but
rather a lived interpretation of them, an interpretation which
does not require a linguistic exegesis or have to enter into discourse. The meaning of the act can be the act.

This explains how homologies and hierarchies are created

among and across diverse levels and domains of experience, social structures and values. Body space is integrated with social and cosmic space by virtue of the fact that they are all constructed in terms of the same symbolic principles. One of the major songs of the *chisungu* ceremony that is sung throughout the rites is one where seniority between senior and junior women, between women and men, and between chiefs and commoners is grounded in the make-up of the human body: *Kuapa takacila kubea* (the armpit is not higher than the shoulder). This statement does not require elaboration or exegesis, it is itself the interpretation, and the evidence for its veracity is given in the body. Statements such as this are verbal correlates of patterns of social interaction and sets of bodily dispositions within a particular environment (Jackson 1989: 147). They are not just metaphors for social relations: they are also the material bases of individual lives. Relations of seniority and respect maintain economic and political life within families, villages and chiefdoms. The Bemba draw on base metaphors in the *chisungu* ritual and elsewhere which refer to practical and bodily activity within their environment. An uninitiated girl, for example, is referred to as a 'weed' or an 'unfired' pot, and this relation of likeness is not a mere figure of speech, because these allusions to domestic and agricultural life disclose real connections between personal maturity and knowledge, and the ability to provide for others (Jackson 1983: 132).

Ritual and quotidian praxis as interpretation

This last point is an important one because it emphasizes that when we speak of body, social and cosmic space as constructed according to the same symbolic principles, we should understand that this process of construction is achieved practically, through physical engagement with the world, and does not have to rely on verbal exegesis or enter into discourse, as noted earlier. This does not mean that symbolic principles or the homologies established among domains cannot become the subject of discourse under specific circumstances. The fact that discursive interpretation and disputation is possible alongside physical engagement is one reason why some individuals are much more knowledgeable – in the sense of intellectually coherent – about symbolism and ritual than are others.[12] However, the homologies established between different levels of experience and different domains of

life are not overdetermining. The repetition and analogical extension of basic symbolic principles, based on the body's orientations
and movements in the world, provide a loose sense of systematicness without ever fixing or defining in any one specific way the
meaning of symbolic contrasts, relations and transformations.[13]
The contrasts, relations and transformations are the result of
daily and ritual practice. I argued in my analysis of domestic
space among the Marakwet of Kenya that the organization of
space has no meaning outside practice, outside the activities of
knowledgeable social actors who invoke meanings, some intended
and some not, through their actions (H.L. Moore 1996: ch. 5). In
this sense to speak of 'structuring structures', 'sets of oppositions', 'dual classification' systems is not necessarily to reduce
social and symbolic systems to some kind of formal taxonomy or
abstract ideational system, whether owned by the ethnographic
subjects or only by the anthropologist. The aim rather is to give
the same weight to embodied action and embodied cognition as a
form of interpretation, as to language and linguistic exegesis (see
Kaare, this volume; Kaspin, this volume; Sanders, this volume).

As a way of comprehending the theoretical shift this entails, we
might usefully term – in a formal sense – many contemporary
analyses of African ritual and symbolism (e.g. De Boeck 1991;
H.L. Moore 1996; Devisch 1993)[14] that draw on aspects of praxis
theory and/or phenomenology 'post-structuralist', in the sense
that the analysis they provide depends upon a prior recognition
of oppositions, symbolic codes or base metaphors – a move that
looks very structuralist – but also emphasizes that constellations
of meaning are only invoked in practice, that signs and symbols
only have meanings in specific contexts, and that those meanings
are not fixed or closed. It is because the interpretations given to
body practices in one context are never entirely separable from
those invoked in others that meanings are implied, but never
fixed. This form of analysis depends upon a play of differences
among certain elements, but one where signification is deferred.[15]
Thus, in ritual and in day-to-day activity, oppositions and
symbolic principles are invoked, brought into play, but never
resolved, never finalized. There is no necessary logical end to the
significations set in motion, but only a processual movement
through them. This does not exclude the processes of disputation,
strategy and violence which are moments when actors seek to
freeze process and impose particular interpretations. The paradox

is that the apparent systematicness of the symbol system comes from its very fluidity, from the fact that everything appears to refer to everything else in an endless process of deferred meaning. Anthropological models, like local exegesis, are just abstractions of this process or attempts to freeze one moment of it. This is one reason why symbolic principles and ritual practices appear so consonant with social structures, with conflicts within and between structures and values, and with vested interests and distributions of power.

Gender symbolism and gender complementarity

A vast literature exists on gender in Africa, and much of it is concerned with the revaluation of women and women's role in society.[16] Topics include the impact of colonialism on women's status and political participation, how women seek to advance their economic and political interests, the impact of poverty and urbanization on women, the changing nature of the sexual division of labour and the effect of development policies, agricultural intensification and the economic organization of households, the changing nature of marriage and kinship ties, and the role of women in ritual and religion. However, in spite of the mass of available material, the cultural construction of gender and sexuality has remained somewhat underdeveloped.[17] It is instructive in this regard to compare the data from Africa with that from New Guinea, for example. Where ideas about femininity and masculinity, and their connection to notions of fertility and social transformation, have been explored in East and Southern Africa it has mostly not been by scholars concerned with gender, but by scholars writing on ritual symbolism and cosmological/ideational systems (e.g. Devisch 1993; Jacobson-Widding 1985; 1991; Beidelman 1993; 1997). This should come as no surprise, since it turns out that it is impossible to write about symbolism, ritual and cosmology in the region without writing about gender. Gender is the key structuring principle and base metaphor of cosmologies and symbol systems, and thus many anthropologists writing on African societies in the period 1930s–1970s were analysing aspects of gender rituals and gender symbolism long before there was any imperative in anthropology to consider gender or re-evaluate the data on women.[18] Much of the early writing focused on initiation where anthropologists at once noted that such rituals make use of male and female symbolism, and that male initiates may be explicitly feminized or associated with feminine powers and symbols in the course of the ritual, while girls may be masculinized or associated with masculine symbols and powerful productive and regenerative forces in the world (e.g. Vansina 1955; V. Turner 1967: ch. 5; Krige 1968; White *et al.* 1958). This breaking down of symbolic classification immediately caught the attention of ethnographers who saw these processes as being at odds with patrilineal and/or patriarchal ideologies and practices in the societies they were studying. The explicit reference to boys as women or wives in initiation (e.g. Vansina 1955; V. Turner 1967) and the wearing of men's clothes and the mimicking of male activities by girls and women during certain rites (cf. Power and Watts 1997; Power and Watts, this volume) led inevitably to a discussion of ritual role reversal and ritual transvestism. Gluckman interpreted such reversals as rituals of rebellion, where women literally rebelled – albeit symbolically – against their inferior status. Kaare (this volume) and Power and Watts (this volume) provide recent ethnography with which to criticize this thesis, thereby extending the earlier criticisms made by Rigby (1968) and Krige (1968), as well as providing alternative interpretations for these apparent processes of reversal.

One issue that the symbolic manipulation of gender roles and cosmological principles raises – and one which demonstrates how pertinent the inherited Durkheimian dilemma remains – is the problem of whether evidence for gender reversal, equality or complementarity in ritual and/or other contexts is really at odds with dominant ideologies of patrilineal and/or patriarchal dominance. There are a number of points to be made here. The first concerns anthropological interpretation or anthropological bias. Broch-Due points out in this volume how myths celebrating the creative force of the female divine have failed to find their way into various anthropological accounts of the Turkana. It is quite clear that in spite of much recuperative ethnography that anthropologists have routinely misunderstood the female nature of the various creative forces associated with cosmological principles and systems in many societies in the region (Burton 1991). The result, in the past, has been to express some disquiet or surprise when female and male principles are revealed as equally powerful and/or as complementary. In her critique of Gluckman, Krige pointed out that the Zulu girls' puberty rite could not be analysed in isolation, but had to be seen as part of a larger ritual cycle associated with fertility, involving rainmaking and the health of animals and crops. Central to these rites was the female deity Inkosazana whom Krige complained had never received serious anthropological attention (Krige 1968: 183; cf. Berglund 1976). More recent ethnography of the region has emphasized both gender complementarity in many ritual contexts, and the importance of seeing individual rites as part of a larger set of ritual practices (cf. Kratz 1994; Werbner 1988). Several writers in this volume stress that initiation rituals have to be seen as part of a larger set of rites associated with fertility, including death rituals (Blystad, Green, Kaspin, Snyder, all in this volume).

The issue of anthropological interpretation is not however restricted to the domain of the cosmological and the divine. This is perhaps unsurprising because the larger problem is one about allowing a western conception of the dualistic nature of the categories 'masculine' and 'feminine' to overdetermine ideas about power, potency, life force and fertility. This difficulty is revealed in a variety of studies in the region through a discussion of kinship. The issue can be neatly summed up as the 'problem of the maternal'. Recent anthropological accounts have seen a resurgence of feminine symbols, women's agency, uterine links, women's reproductive power, and the feminine principles of the cosmological and natural worlds. I use the term 'resurgence' because evidence for all these things can be found in earlier ethnographies of the region concerned with ritual. However, what is of interest is the impact this resurgence/re-evaluation has had on the study of kinship. Societies which were unilineal suddenly appear to acknowledge uterine links or dual lines of descent, and in some cases anthropologists are even unable to agree on the appropriate classification of the descent system (e.g. Feldman-Savelsberg 1995; Stevens 1995; Broch-Due, this volume; Snyder, this volume; Udvardy 1990).

Of course, Wendy James remarked twenty years ago that matrifocal ideas are present even in the most 'notoriously patrilineal societies' (James 1978). She attributed the tendency of anthropologists to overlook this point to an overemphasis on jural structures, but this explanation ignores the paradoxical fact that matrilineal societies have also been subject to the same interpretative bias. Matrilineal societies in the region have frequently been portrayed as subject to specific structural conflicts. The implication here is that descent in the female line – sometimes with resources held or controlled by women – causes understandable conflict with patriarchal ideologies and the desire of men for control over their children. If this is the case, then how do we explain the existence of matrilineal societies? It might be useful here to start with the role of the mother's brother.

The mother's brother is most often portrayed as exemplifying male control and male dominance in matrilineal contexts, but several societies in the region refer to him as the male mother or mother without breasts. De Boeck points out in relation to the Aluund that the avunculate represents the uterine location of the vital life-flow (*mooy*), and that the maternal uncle should be seen as a life-giving body, as the point for the intergenerational transmission of the life-flow that perpetuates the lineage (De Boeck 1994a: 262). It is interesting in this regard that anthropologists habitually refer to this male individual as the mother's brother (a sibling relation) rather than as the mother's son (a parent/child relation); the latter emphasis might arguably be of more relevance to an understanding of matrilineal kinship.

All the societies of the region are concerned with the creative life forces of the world and their manifestation through fertility and reproduction. Yet, anthropologists, with some exceptions, have found it difficult to understand the nature of these life forces.[19] Devisch points out for the Yaka that *ngoongu*, the regenerative forces, are embodied by the chief and metaphorically transferred during various rites from the cosmic to the bodily and social orders. *Ngoongu*, according to Devisch, is a higher-order principle of fertility that comprises genitor, genitrix and ancestor or child: that is, two genders and two generations (Devisch 1988: 263). The important point here is the relationship between gender and generation, and I would argue that the *ngoongu* might be better understood as a principle of fertility embodied within the transformative potential of reproduction. It is the fact of reproduction, and its often precarious nature, that accounts for the focus both on gender and on fertility in the cosmologies, rituals and quotidian practices of many societies in the region (see Broch-Due, this volume; Blystad, this volume). What reproduction introduces is the centrality of the maternal and, in particular, of the maternal body. This body encapsulates and encompasses the regenerative life forces of bodily, social and cosmic continuity, and the maternal must therefore be present in some form in all kinship systems.[20] However, the maternal image is a complex figure and it is probably a mistake to view it as purely 'female' in terms of a fixed dualistic categorization which opposes male and female principles. The maternal body contains both genders, not just because indigenous theories of procreation speak of the mixing of male and female elements to form the foetus in the womb, but also because the maternal body is the only body with the capacity to reproduce both genders. More than this, the maternal body has the capacity, through pregnancy, to become two bodies, to produce the offspring that will guarantee bodily, social and cosmic continuity: future reproduction. In this sense, the maternal encapsulates division in unity, but as a symbol it can no more be reduced to the bodies of actual women than it can be disassociated or disconnected from them. This raises the old question – which I have characterized as one of Durkheim's legacies to anthropology – what is the relationship between the symbolic and the social, and how should we understand it? One way to answer this question is to return to the ethnography and to the way the societies of the region handle the relationship between the social and the symbolic.

Sex and reproduction or cooking and hunting

A focus on reproduction and the maternal body may help to explain the importance of uterine links in all forms of kinship systems (see Snyder, this volume; Broch-Due, this volume),[21] but only when the wider links between sexuality and reproduction are taken into account. A pervasive set of associations between sex and eating are characteristic of the societies of the region. The result is that symbolic ideas concerning reproduction and the maternal body are woven together with quotidian activities and the practical arrangements of managing a household, gaining a living and maintaining social relationships (see Kaspin, this volume; Blystad, this volume; and Broch-Due, this volume). In the ideal Bangangté household economy, the husband provides his wife with meat, oil and salt which she mixes with the ingredients she produces herself (maize, beans and peanuts) to produce a cooked meal (Feldman-Savelsberg 1995: 488–9). The complementary contributions to the reproduction of children and household are further concretized in the associations established between certain objects, practical activities, and parts of the human body.

In the case of the Kaguru, for example, the male centre-post of the house and the female hearthstones next to it symbolize coitus and the complementary contributions of women and men to the maintenance of the household, family and kinship. A similar pairing is evident in the relationships between other paired objects necessary for production and food preparation, and parts of the body. Metaphors for the penis include a spear (*mugoha*), stone pestle (*isago*) or wooden pestle (*mtwango*); a vagina is a stone mortar (*luwala*), wooden mortar (*ituli*), calabash, pot or basket. Euphemisms for sexual intercourse also link human sexuality to the transformation of foodstuffs and the management of modes of livelihood: to pound flour (*kutwanga*), to grind flour (*kusanjila*), to make fire (*kuhegesa*) are all euphemisms for the sexual act (Beidelman 1993: 39–40).

Throughout the region, children are spoken of as the product of cooking or firing, the result of a transformation brought about through fire. Fire is a dominant base metaphor for social transformation and hence the title of this book. Children are frequently said to be cooked in their mother's wombs, a fact which produces a pervasive and seductive culinary symbolism relating to procreation and reproduction (e.g. De Boeck 1994a: 271). Children are the product of the mixing of male and female fluids/substances: the blood/semen of the man and the menstrual blood of the woman (Beidelman 1973: 136). Both these substances carry life itself, part of the vital flow, and consequently a set of common associations links semen and/or the moistness of the vagina (and sometimes blood) with rain, thus establishing an intimate connection between the proper management of human sexuality and the fertility of the human, natural and cosmological worlds (Sanders 1998).

If the maternal body and images of cooking underpin both the female contribution to fertility and childbearing, and the complementarity of the genders in the successful maintenance of life, hunting is an activity that marks the male contribution to life-giving. In this sense it is represented as the symbolic equivalent of giving birth. For the Yaka, for example, fertility involves fermentation or cooking. A man's semen rots in the woman's womb and the odour of sexual intercourse, representing the welding together of life forces, is likened to the smell of the game carcass which, through cooking, will also be transformed into life-giving nourishment (Devisch 1993: 136). Hunting in many societies in the region is associated with mastery of the wild/bush, with the bringing into the social domain of part of the vital force of the natural world (cf. Beidelman 1997: 251; Kaspin, this volume; Power and Watts, this volume; and Blystad, this volume). Hunting, like menstruation and childbirth, sheds blood to bring life. Death and decay are thus part of the process of regeneration (cf. Devisch 1988: 264; Kaspin, this volume). The association of women with prey and men with hunters is represented in many initiation rites (e.g. V. Turner 1967; Richards 1982; Kaspin, this volume), and establish links across domains of production, linking human sexuality to the natural world and the powerful forces of death and regeneration.[22] This explains, amongst other things, the explicit links between death, fertility and initiation rites (see Green, this volume; Sanders, this volume; and Kaspin, this volume). However, Kaspin, Power and Watts (both in this volume), demonstrate that while initiation rites involve aspects of gender complementarity, they also involve moments of symbolic reversal, when what is male is contained in the female, when women no longer bleed, and when women become hunters and men prey. These reversals continue to be of interest to anthropologists and especially given the fact that in day-to-day contexts women are forbidden contact with a man's hunting implements, and hunters themselves must regulate sexual contact with women, and avoid menstruating women.[23]

There are a number of ways of understanding the evident contradictions and apparent reversals in gender symbolism. One is to speak of alternative models. In the case of the Aluund, De Boeck (1991: 40) defines a (male) political model of masculine dominance and female subordination as against a (female) body-linked model of feminine regenerative powers and male dependence. The co-existence of two such models is well supported by the data from many of the societies in the region. An approach based on multiple models of gender certainly moves us away from the idea that relations between the genders can be characterized in a single, monolithic fashion.[24] It also allows us to deal with such questions as whether evidence for gender complementarity or female powers is at odds with patrilineal and/or patriarchal ideologies by asserting that discrepant models co-exist, whilst acknowledging that in certain contexts one may dominate over the other.

However, what the symbolic systems of the region principally alert us to is that gender systems, far from being merely ideational, are in fact technological systems for engagement with the world. What initiation rituals – and indeed rituals of all kinds – do is to bring individuals into relation with others. They present an opportunity to understand one's own experience and relation to the world through understanding that of others. This world is, of course, one in which the human body, its feelings, postures and orientations, extend into the natural and cosmic worlds through physical engagement and linguistic reflection. The body is both the starting point of one's own experience and the origin of a set of culturally constructed imaginative domains (cf. Beidelman 1993). Bodily experiences are thus tied to the imaginative and practical possibilities of being a gendered individual in a specific context. This means that while metaphoric associations can never be fixed or finalized or brought to a point of closure, neither are they completely free of dominant cultural understandings (H.L. Moore 1996).

But, the converse is equally true. Rituals present staged narrative sequences of symbols, opportunities for reflection and enlargement of understanding (cf. Beidelman 1997). Hitherto separate images, sounds, colours, emotions and aspects of life are brought into relation with each other in ways that reveal new connections and understandings. However, each individual experiences these connections for him or herself, and some no doubt reflect on them more than others. Experiences in ritual are powerful and over time, as Bloch (1992: 34) says, they may fade, but they do not disappear completely. Other aspects of life apparently unconnected to the ritual experience may thus take on new significance. Interpretation is a process, not a single event. African societies make this explicit in the way they link knowledge to age, in the way understandings of gender shift over the life course in response to a changing relation to knowledge (see Snyder, this volume; and Green, this volume). Language, like embodied praxis, has no single meaning. The words and songs of many initiation and fertility rites are apparently obscure, highly metaphorized, and not self-evident. It takes experience to understand them because exegesis is a matter of making connections.

Reflections on bodily experiences and their metaphoric transpositions – whether through practice or linguistic exegesis – enlarge one's sense of agency and of self. It is one of the paradoxes of gender that, because it is relational, it is only possible to understand the gender of the other through reflection on one's own gender, and to comprehend one's own gender through engagement with that of the other. This should not surprise us, since this is anyway the paradox of subjectivity. However, what an emphasis on relations and connections alerts us to is a problem with the dualistic classification of gender employed in anthropological analysis. Dominant Western conceptions of gender emphasize the boundedness of gender categories, their difference from each other, and their hierarchical relation. In spite of recent theoretical work in anthropology that emphasizes the cross-cultural variation in gender constructs and categorizations, the implicit assumptions underlying Western concepts of gender are still evident in African ethnography in terms of the way some authors write about 'women's models', 'symbolic reversals' and 'women's power'. The same implicit assumptions underpin questions about how to reconcile gender complementarity with patrilineal and/or patriarchal ideologies. The mistake here is to see gender categories in African societies as discrete and bounded, and as held together in a relationship of dualism such that one must always negate the other.

The problem, as Marilyn Strathern (1988: 64) identified, lies with the assumption of autonomy, with assuming that reflection on masculinity proceeds without any reference to femininity, that privileging agnation does not involve taking a position *vis-à-vis* uterine links and so on. The paradox is that many anthropologists, in asking for example whether evidence of female power is at odds with patrilineal ideology, are effectively reducing the representations of gender to actual women and men, even as their data informs them that the social and the symbolic are not mirror images of each other (Sanders, this volume). Gender symbolism in the contexts discussed in this book, and in the region as a whole, is better understood relationally, as something that manifests itself as division in unity, a fact that accounts, of course, both for the importance of the maternal body – encompassing two genders and two generations – and for the preoccupation with fertility.

GENDER PERFORMANCE AND GENDERED AGENCY

Anthropologists often refer to initiation rituals as events relating to the acquisition of gender identity, where the biological body is transformed into the socially gendered body. This is perhaps just another way of saying that initiation involves the imposition of the signifier onto the body, a fact that is often made concrete through the physical transformation of the body during initiation. In most societies in the region, male initiation is thought to make the boy dry and thereby to distinguish him from female moistness and fluidity. What is evinced is that the biological is somehow never enough; there is always a symbolic form to masculinity – and indeed to femininity – which must be assumed. The paradox this produces is that there is always an important, indeed essential, element to sexuality which is not human, in the straightforward sense that it is symbolic, and thus exceeds individual experience. It is for this reason that the symbolic categories 'woman' and 'man' cannot be reduced to women and men, and that the relation between the social and the symbolic is not isomorphic.

In many African societies, what exceeds the human dimension, and therefore human agency, is associated with the creative powers of the world, with the manifest fact that humans do not control the forces of the natural world. And yet, human society depends on maintaining a relation with that world, one that is productive. The symbolic and cosmological systems of the region represent this problem not just in terms of epistemology, but in terms of ontology. As Sherry Ortner has argued, the relationship between what humanity can achieve and a natural world that sets limits on those achievements must be a universal problem, even if the solutions to that problem vary historically and cross-culturally (Ortner 1996: 179). The ontological nature of the problem can be revealed through an examination of origin myths.

In many societies in the region, human society comes about through human agency which results in two things: the separation of humans from the sphere of the divine (see Broch-Due, this volume; and Kaare, this volume) and the emergence of reproductive human sexuality. Symbolic praxis and interpretation in relation to gender and fertility are thus philosophical reflections on the ontological nature of being, on the origins of gendered difference and human society itself. The severing of the human world from the sphere of the divine, often represented as a severing of a link between them (a strap or rope) provides the first of a series of tropes where one becomes two. Human sexuality arises in the same moment and is often represented as a process involving the killing or banishment of a mythical mother figure (e.g. Maxwell 1983: ch. 2; De Boeck 1994a: 276) and sometimes includes the theft by men from women of the origins of something representing culture or circumcision (e.g. De Boeck 1991; S.F. Moore 1976). What this theft signifies is the imposition of a socially reproductive sexuality onto a previously multiply constituted maternal figure who has the potential to reproduce on her own since she contains both sexes. De Boeck implies that this is repeated in the structural problematic of matriliny, where cross-cousin marriages (a male ego with his mother's brother's daughter) are sometimes preferred because they retain resources and offspring within the lineage, as well as recreating an autonomous maternal 'body' that is not dependent on outsiders for its regenerative capacities. This autonomy is encapsulated in the maternal uncle who becomes wife-giver and wife-receiver, the uterine life-source and the affinal link. However, such marriages may also be problematic because of the heightened possibility of sorcery between uterine kin, and because the uterine womb is enclosed and fails to exchange with others. Thus the Aluund refer to these marriages as 'a dog eating its own placenta' with all the connotations of incest, destruction and auto-consumption this implies (De Boeck 1994a: 263–4).

The management of fertility, like the management of a human world that is separate from the divine sphere yet subject to it, depends on creating gendered differences, revealing the division within unity, and productively supervising the interdependence of the female and the male. This is one reason why rituals and symbolic practice frequently involve the recombining of male and female attributes and categories. In so doing, they recall the 'primordial unity' both as a way of appropriating an aspect of the divine, of the forces beyond human agency, but also as a mechanism for recalling the origins of human society and of gender, the moment when difference is introduced into unity (see Kaare, this volume). For the secret of fertility, and indeed of reproduction, is to be able to make two out of one (gender), and then one out of two (generation) (Sanders 1998). In this sense, African societies are much like those Melanesian societies described by Strathern (1988) and others, where the problem of gender is revealed not as one of construction, but of decomposition (cf. Broch-Due 1993).

What kind of agency does 'performing' gender involve?

What a reflection on the mythic and cosmological origins of gender reveals is that gender is the result of actions, not the origin of them. Current positions in anthropology and feminist theory assert that gender is not simply culturally constructed, but must be performed (Butler 1990; Sanders, this volume; Blystad, this volume; and Power and Watts, this volume). The notion of performance opens up gender, as a construct and as a lived relation, to historical change and cross-cultural variability. But, many writers assume – quite erroneously – that an emphasis on the performative aspects of gender implies a significant degree of voluntarism and free choice, in other words, that individuals can change their gender and make of it what they will. This interpretation is quite at odds with the approach of Judith Butler whose work is most often cited as the origin of performative theory in anthropology (cf. R.C. Morris 1995).

Butler's theoretical work is inspired by psychoanalytic thinking and thus she does not suppose that one can choose to live one's gender as one will because of the role of the unconscious and the importance of unconscious desires. More pertinently, in a psycho-analytic framework, the matrix of sexual difference must be prior to the gendered subject, since to come into subjectivity and language is to be subjected to the imperatives of sexual difference: 'there is no "I" prior to its assumption of sex' (Butler 1993: 99). What this means is that individuals cannot live their genders outside the symbolic framework of sexual difference, and that this is the case however subversive or alternative their construc-tions of gender might be. But this should not be taken to mean that individuals lack agency with regard to the way they live their genders. Butler argues that Western gender systems naturalize the masculine and the feminine as ideal constructions against which, or in terms of which, all individuals experience their bodily selves. In Butler's terms masculine and feminine identifications cannot be fully exhaustive, in the sense that there will always be a gap between the symbolic constructions of female and male, and the experience of being a woman or a man. Since gender identities are never complete, never finished, they cannot be fully stable. They therefore require repetition and this for Butler explains the iterative nature of gender performance (Butler 1993: 187–8).

There are other aspects of Butler's theory that cannot be explored here, but it is worth considering her work in relation to ritual performances and symbolic systems in the African context. Blystad (this volume) and Power and Watts (this volume) explore the connections and disconnections between Butler's notion of performance and the way it has been used in anthropology (cf. V. Turner 1967; 1969; Tambiah 1979). What is evident is that the psychoanalytic emphasis on the gap between the experience of living a gendered identity and the symbolic constructions of gender is essential in any attempt to understand the basic paradox of the relation between the social and the symbolic. It explains why the categories 'female' and 'male' cannot be reduced to actual women and men (see Sanders, this volume). It is also potentially helpful to see ritual performances as instances of what Butler terms the 'discourses of sex',[25] as moments or events, where images and narratives about the nature of gendered identities, the relations between women and men, and the powerful nature of sexuality and fertility are being reiterated and repeated. What is important, however, in the context of the ethnography is that we do not see these reiterations as fixed, closed and determining. The metaphoric extension of gender symbolism across many domains of human experience, and its technological relation to a lived world of practice, means that gender discourses – as they are enacted in rituals – act as a reflection on the capacities of the genders and their interactions. Each individual makes his or her own interpretations based on this reflective performance, and through a process of creative imagination, rather than intellectual exegesis, arrives at an understanding of him or herself and others as gendered individuals. In this sense, practical engagement with gender symbolism in ritual and day-to-day contexts provides possibilities for agency both individual and collective. Groups of women who perform fertility rituals thus identify a space for their collective agency in terms of a gender symbolism that brings their experience of their bodies into close relation with the problem of how to manage the reproduction of the human, natural and cosmological worlds (see Snyder, this volume; Green, this volume; and Blystad, this volume). When African women and men perform operations on their genders a great deal more is at stake than simply gender.

NOTES

1 Both Radcliffe-Brown (1952) and Evans-Pritchard (1956; 1965) were concerned with this point, and both in their own way demonstrated that the relationship between religion and social structure is rarely direct and not always self-evident. Evans-Pritchard (1956: 180–1)

even argued that an understanding of the cultural logic of Nuer religious beliefs would not necessarily be advanced by relating those beliefs to ideas of social order. Needham (1963: xxvi) subsequently refuted any causality between the two domains: 'All that we are permitted to say is that however we may divide the social ideas in question (into "social order" and "symbolic order" for example) they exhibit common principles of order, no sphere of interest being the cause or model of organisation of the other'.

2 'Without resorting to socio-structural determinism one may thus note that the definition of the relative importance of male and female contributions to fertility (human, agricultural or otherwise) seems to correspond to the cognition of principles of descent' (Jacobson-Widding and van Beek 1990: 22).

3 See B. Morris (1987) and Bell (1992) for overviews.

4 But see Hastrup (1995) and H.L. Moore (1997a) for critiques of an oversimplified 'turn away' from theory.

5 It is crucial here to recognize that any emphasis on embodiment in the anthropological analysis of symbolism and ritual comes as a response to an earlier overemphasis on linguistic meanings and interpretation. However, disputation between individuals involved in rituals, reasoned argument and strategic manipulation of symbols are part of analogic and/or intellectual modes of thought that are as powerful in shaping agency and understandings as analogies based on practical engagement and forms of body praxis (cf. Beidelman 1966b; 1993).

6 These are, in fact, the pervasive concerns of societies all over the continent. The literature is far too large to cite in any comprehensive form, but for collections of relevant writings and overviews see Jacobson-Widding, (1991), Jacobson-Widding and Van Beek (1990), Herbert (1993).

7 Binary oppositions almost always involve asymmetrical relationships of dominance and subordination. In anthropology, this insight and its relation to social inequality has been noted by Hertz (1973), Bourdieu (1977), T. Turner (1984). This point has also been extensively discussed by feminist and deconstructionist theorists (cf. Jaggar and Bordo 1988; Hekman 1990; Butler 1990; Nicholson 1990; Braidotti 1991; Irigaray 1985; Cixous and Clement 1986; Derrida 1976).

8 See Jackson (1995; 1996) and Csordas (1994) for overviews.

9 However, Wacquant (1992: 20) claims that Bourdieu is properly speaking better seen as the sociological heir of Merleau-Ponty because he subsumes phenomenology in his work by grounding intersubjectivity in historical conditions through the mechanism of the habitus.

10 Corinne Kratz makes a very similar argument when she criticizes Bourdieu for his lack of interest in emotion (Kratz 1994: 30–4).

11 For a fuller reanalysis of Richards's work, see H.L. Moore (1997b), from which this discussion is abstracted.

12 Beidelman (1973: 153) sums up the main points: 'Initiation and inculcation of symbolic lore are gradual and complicated processes which

not all Kaguru learn equally.... Some ... are uninterested in helping
at further initiations, while others are unable to remember such lore;
thus, we must not expect all Kaguru ... to be comparably versed in
symbolism and although they participate in ... rituals ... some may
be only dimly aware that these have deeper, esoteric meanings.... We
must then picture Kaguru dual symbolic classification as a system of
beliefs grasped in varying degrees by the members of Kaguru society
and not uniformly meaningful to all'.
13 The position taken here is very close to that of Lakoff and Johnson
(Lakoff and Johnson 1980; Lakoff 1987). Lakoff (1987: 267–76)
describes how nonpropositional schemata generate meaning without
the formulation of propositions, and one form of these schemata are
kinaesthetic images drawn from bodily experience, and it is these
images that provide the experiential basis of metaphoric extension.
14 Beidelman (1997) strongly differentiates himself both from phenomenology and post-structuralism, but in many ways his approach is congruent with the other writers referred to here.
15 This is the point of Derrida's grammatology and the value of the
concept of *différence* (Derrida 1976). See Catherine Bell (1992) for an
excellent discussion of the relevance of the Derridean notion of *différence* to the analysis of ritual.
16 See Potash (1989), Stichter and Parpart (1988), Hay and Stichter
(1984), Strobel (1982) for overviews and important collections.
17 Notable exceptions include Shepherd (1987), Llewelyn-Davies (1981),
Nelson (1987), Beidelman (1964; 1966b; 1972; 1980), Kratz (1994),
Herbert (1993).
18 Many of these writers were concerned with initiation rituals, the
transgression of sexual taboos, rain making, procreation theories, and
fertility, examples from the region include Richards (1982), V. Turner
(1967), Krige (1968), Cory (1944; 1960; 1962), Hambly (1935),
Schapera (1978; 1979), Hammond-Tooke (1958), Tucker (1949),
Gluckman (1949), Silberbauer (1963), Brain (1977; 1978), Vansina
(1955), Marwick (1968), Beattie (1960), Evans-Pritchard (1962), White
(1953), White *et al.* (1958), Larson (1979). For references to the early
work on rainmaking, see Sanders (1997).
19 Is it God? The answer to this is not straightforward, but many ethnographers have pointed out that God or the Supreme Being is often
conceived of as very distant from humans and as a transcendent principle. This God is quite distinct from the Christian and Muslim God,
for example. The life force may be a manifestation of the potency of
the divine, but is not reducible to a divine figure (cf. Devisch 1993;
Marshall 1957; White 1948; Brain 1983).
20 This is an extension of Van Baal's (1975: 79) point that there can be
no kinship without motherhood because in the case of the societies of
East and Southern Africa, it might be more accurate to say that
without fertile maternal bodies there can be no society.
21 The nature of these links, their practical efficacy, their symbolic representation and experiential power will clearly vary from one context to
another.

22 This argument is very close to that put forward by Bloch (1992), where he argues that the purpose of rituals is the consumption of an external vitality, but that the result is that living communities are brought into relation with the transcendental.
23 These ideas about hunters and hunting persist in many contexts in spite of the fact there is very little game in most areas and hunting forms a very small part of most present-day rural economies.
24 For further discussion of multiple gender models see H.L. Moore (1994), Meigs (1990), Peletz (1994), Ortner (1996).
25 See H.L. Moore (1994) for a discussion of the application of psychoanalytic and feminist theory to anthropology.

REFERENCES

Beattie, J. (1960) 'On the Nyoro concept of Mahano', *African Studies*, 19 (3): 145–50.
Beidelman, T.O. (1964) 'Pig (*guluwe*): an essay on Ngulu sexual symbolism and ceremony', *Southwestern Journal of Anthropology*, 20: 359–92.
Beidelman, T.O. (1966a) 'Swazi royal ritual', *Africa*, 36 (4): 373–405.
Beidelman, T.O. (1966b) 'Utani: some Kaguru notions of death, sexuality and affinity', *Southwestern Journal of Anthropology*, 22: 354–80.
Beidelman, T.O. (1971) 'Some Kaguru notions about incest and other sexual prohibitions', in R. Needham, (ed.) *Rethinking Kinship and Marriage* (London: Tavistock).
Beidelman, T.O. (1972) 'The filth of incest: a text and comments on Kaguru notions of sexuality, alimentation and aggression', *Cahiers d'Études Africaines*, 12: 164–73.
Beidelman, T.O. (1973) 'Kaguru symbolic classification', in R. Needham (ed.) *Right and Left: Essays on Dual Symbolic Classification* (Chicago: Chicago University Press).
Beidelman, T.O. (1980) 'Women and men in two East African societies', in I. Karp and C. Bird (eds) *Explorations in African Systems of Thought* (Bloomington: Indiana University Press).
Beidelman, T.O. (1993) *Moral Imagination in Kaguru Modes of Thought* (Washington DC: Smithsonian Institution Press).
Beidelman, T.O. (1997) *The Cool Knife: Imagery of Gender, Sexuality, and Moral Education in Kaguru Initiation Ritual* (Washington DC: Smithsonian Institution Press).
Bell, C. (1992) *Ritual Theory, Ritual Practice* (Oxford: Oxford University Press).
Berglund, A.-I. (1976) *Zulu Thought-Patterns and Symbolism* (London: Hurst and Company).
Bloch, M. (1992) *Prey into Hunter: The Politics of Religious Experience* (Cambridge: Cambridge University Press).
Bourdieu, P. (1977) *Outline of a Theory of Practice* (Cambridge: Cambridge University Press).
Bourdieu, P. (1990) *The Logic of Practice* (Cambridge: Polity).
Braidotti, R. (1991) *Patterns of Dissonance* (Cambridge: Polity).

Brain, J.L. (1977) 'Sex, incest and death: initiation rites reconsidered', *Current Anthropology*, 18 (2): 191–208.

Brain, J.L. (1978) 'Symbolic rebirth: the *mwali* rite among the Luguru of eastern Tanzania', *Africa*, 48 (2): 176–88.

Brain, J.L. (1983) 'Basic concepts of life according to the Luguru of eastern Tanzania', *Ultimate Reality and Meaning*, 6 (1): 4–21.

Broch-Due, V. (1993) 'Making meaning out of matter: perceptions of sex, gender and bodies among the Turkana', in V. Broch-Due, I. Rudie and T Bleie (eds) *Carved Flesh/Cast Selves: Gendered Symbols and Social Practices* (Oxford: Berg).

Burton, J.W. (1991) 'Representations of the feminine in Nilotic cosmologies', in A. Jacobson-Widding (ed.) *Body and Space: Symbolic Models of Unity and Division in African Cosmology and Experience* (Uppsala: Acta Universitatis Upsaliensis).

Butler, J.P. (1990) *Gender Trouble* (London: Routledge).

Butler, J.P. (1993) *Bodies that Matter* (London: Routledge).

Cixous, H. and C. Clement (1986) *The Newly Born Woman* (Minneapolis: University of Minnesota Press).

Cory, H. (1944) 'Sukuma twin ceremonies – Mabasa', *Tanganyika Notes and Records*, 17: 34–43.

Cory, H. (1960) 'Religious beliefs and practices of the Sukuma/Nyamwezi tribal group', *Tanganyika Notes and Records* 54: 14–26.

Cory, H. (1962) 'The Sambaa initiation rites for boys', *Tanganyika Notes and Records*, 58/59: 2–12.

Csordas, T.J. (1994) *The Sacred Self: A Cultural Phenomenology of Charismatic Healing* (Berkeley: University of California Press).

De Boeck, F. (1991) 'Of bushbucks without horns: male and female initiation among the Aluund of southwest Zaire', *Journal des Africanistes*, 61 (1): 32–72.

De Boeck, F. (1994a) 'When hunger goes around the land: hunger and food among the Aluund of Zaire', *Man*, 29: 257–82.

De Boeck, F. (1994b) 'Of trees and kings: politics and metaphor among the Aluund of southwestern Zaire', *American Ethnologist*, 21 (3): 451–73.

Derrida, J. (1976) *Of Grammatology* (Baltimore: Johns Hopkins University Press).

Devisch, R. (1985a) 'Polluting and healing among the northern Yaka of Zaire', *Social Science and Medicine*, 21 (6): 693–700.

Devisch, R. (1985b) 'Symbol and psychosomatic symptom in bodily space-time: the case of the Yaka of Zaire', *International Journal of Psychology*, 20 (3–4): 589–616.

Devisch, R. (1988) 'From equal to better: investing the chief among the northern Yaka of Zaire', *Africa*, 58 (3): 261–90.

Devisch, R. (1993) *Weaving the Threads of Life: The Khita Gyn-eco-logical Healing Cult among the Yaka* (Chicago: University of Chicago Press).

Douglas, M. (1966) *Purity and Danger* (Harmondsworth: Penguin).

Douglas, M. (1970) *Natural Symbols* (Harmondsworth: Penguin).

Durkheim, E. (1964) [1915] *The Elementary Forms of the Religious Life* (London: Allen & Unwin).

Evans-Pritchard, E. E. (1956) *Nuer Religion* (Oxford: Clarendon Press).

Evans-Pritchard, E. E. (1962) 'Heredity and gestation as the Azande see them', in *Essays in Social Anthropology* (London: Faber & Faber).

Evans-Pritchard, E. E. (1965) *Theories of Primitive Religion* (London: Oxford University Press).

Feldman-Savelsberg, P. (1995) 'Cooking inside: kinship and gender in Bangangté idioms of marriage and procreation', *American Ethnologist*, 22 (3): 483–501.

Fortes, M. and G. Dieterlen (eds) (1965) *African Systems of Thought* (London: Oxford University Press).

Gell, A. (1975) *The Metamorphosis of the Cassowaries* (London: Athlone).

Gluckman, M. (1949) 'The role of the sexes in Wiko circumcision ceremonies', in *Social Structure* (London: Oxford University Press).

Håkansson, T. (1990) 'The appropriation of fertility: descent and sex among the Gusii', in A. Jacobson-Widding and W. van Beek (eds) *The Creative Communion: African Folk Models of Fertility and the Regeneration of Life* (Uppsala: Acta Universitatis Upsaliensis).

Hambly, W. (1935) 'Tribal initiation of boys in Angola', *American Anthropologist*, 37: 21–33.

Hammond-Tooke, W.D. (1958) 'The attainment of adult status among the Mount Frere Bhaca', *African Studies*, 17: 16–20.

Hastrup, K. (1995) *A Passage to Anthropology: Between Experience and Theory* (London: Routledge).

Hay, M. and S. Stichter (eds) (1984) *African Women South of the Sahara* (New York: Longman).

Heald, S. (1995) 'The power of sex: some reflections on Caldwell's "African sexuality" thesis', *Africa*, 65 (4): 489–505.

Hekman, S. (1990) *Gender and Knowledge: Elements of a Postmodern Feminism* (Cambridge: Polity Press).

Herbert, E. (1993) *Iron, Gender and Power: Rituals of Transformation in African Societies* (Bloomington: Indiana University Press).

Hertz, R. (1973) [1909]. 'The pre-eminence of the right hand: a study in religious polarity', in R. Needham (ed.) *Right and Left: Essays on Dual Symbolic Classification* (Chicago: University of Chicago Press).

Holy, L. and M. Stuchlik (eds) (1980) *The Structure of Folk Models* (London: Academic Press).

Houseman, M. (1988) 'Social structure is where the hearth is: a "woman's place" in Beti society', *Africa*, 58 (1): 51–69.

Irigaray, L. (1985) *Speculum of the Other Woman* (Ithaca, NY: Cornell University Press).

Jackson, M. (1983) 'Thinking through the body: an essay on understanding metaphor', *Social Analysis*, 14: 127–49.

Jackson, M. (1989) *Paths Toward a Clearing: Radical Empiricism and Ethnographic Enquiry* (Bloomington: Indiana University Press).

Jackson, M. (1995) *At Home in the World* (Durham, NC: Duke University Press).

Jackson, M. (1996) 'Introduction: phenomenology, radical empiricism and anthropological critique', in M. Jackson (ed.) *Things As They Are: New Directions in Phenomenological Anthropology* (Bloomington: Indiana University Press).

Jacobson-Widding, A. (1985) *Private Spirits and the Ego: A Psychological Ethnography of Ancestor Cult and Spirit Possession among the Manyika of Zimbabwe*, Working Papers in African Studies, 24, African Studies Programme, University of Uppsala.

Jacobson-Widding, A. (ed.) (1991) *Body and Space: Symbolic Models of Unity and Division in African Cosmology and Experience* (Uppsala: Acta Universitatis Upsaliensis).

Jacobson-Widding, A. and W. van Beek (1990) 'Chaos, order and communion in African models of fertility', in A. Jacobson-Widding and W. Van Beek (eds) *The Creative Communion: African Folk Models of Fertility and the Regeneration of Life* (Uppsala: Acta Universitatis Upsaliensis).

James, W. (1978) 'Matrifocus on African women', in S. Ardener (ed.) *Defining Females: The Nature of Women in Society* (London: Croom Helm).

Jaggar, A. and S. Bordo (eds) (1988) *Gender/Body/Knowledge: Feminist Reconstructions of Being and Knowing* (New Brunswick, NJ: Rutgers University Press).

Karp, I. (1980) 'Introduction', in I. Karp and C. Bird (eds) *Explorations in African Systems of Thought* (Bloomington: Indiana University Press).

Kaspin, D. (1996) 'A Chewa cosmology of the body', *American Ethnologist*, 23 (3): 561–78.

Kratz, C.A. (1994) *Affecting Performance: Meaning, Movement and Experience in Okiek Women's Initiation* (Washington DC: Smithsonian Institution Press).

Krige, E. (1968) 'Girls' puberty songs and their relation to fertility, health, morality and religion among the Zulu', *Africa*, 38 (2): 173–98.

Lakoff, G. (1987) *Women, Fire and Other Dangerous Things* (Chicago: University of Chicago Press).

Lakoff, G. and M. Johnson (1980) *Metaphors We Live By* (Chicago: University of Chicago Press).

Larson, T. (1979) 'Hambukushu girls' puberty rites', *Botswana Notes and Records*, 11: 33–6.

Leach, E. R. (1976) *Culture and Communication* (Cambridge: Cambridge University Press).

Lewis, G. (1980) *Day of Shining Red: An Essay on Understanding Ritual* (Cambridge: Cambridge University Press).

Lévi-Strauss, C. (1966) *The Savage Mind* (London: Weidenfeld and Nicolson).

Llewelyn-Davies, M. (1981) 'Women, warriors, and patriarchs', in S. B. Ortner and H. Whitehead (eds) *Sexual Meanings: The Cultural Construction of Gender and Sexuality* (Cambridge: Cambridge University Press).

McDougall, L. (1977) 'Symbols and somatic structure', in J. Blacking (ed.) *The Anthropology of the Body* (London: Academic).

Marshall, L. (1957) 'N/ow', *Africa*, 27 (3): 232–40.

Marwick, M. (1968) 'Notes on some Cewa rituals', *African Studies*, 27 (1): 3–14.

Maxwell, K. (1983) *Bemba Myth and Ritual* (Frankfurt: Peter Lang).

Meigs, A. (1990) 'Multiple gender ideologies and statuses', in P. Sanday and R. Goodenough (eds) *Beyond the Second Sex* (Philadelphia: University of Pennsylvania Press).

Merleau-Ponty, M. (1962) *The Phenomenology of Perception* (London: Routledge & Kegan Paul).

Merleau-Ponty, M. (1963) *The Primacy of Perception* (Evanston: Northwestern).

Moore, H.L. (1994) *A Passion for Difference: Essays in Anthropology and Gender* (Cambridge: Polity).

Moore, H.L. (1996) *Space, Text and Gender: An Anthropological Study of the Marakwet of Kenya* 2nd edn (New York: Guilford).

Moore, H.L. (1997a) 'Interior landscapes and external worlds: the return of grand theory in anthropology', *Australian Journal of Anthropology*, 8 (2): 125–44.

Moore, H.L. (1997b) 'Sex, symbolism and psychoanalysis', *Differences*, 9 (1): 68–94.

Moore, S.F. (1976) 'The secret of the men: a fiction of Chagga initiation and its relation to the logic of Chagga symbolism', *Africa*, 46: 357–70.

Morris, B. (1987) *Anthropological Studies of Religion: An Introductory Text* (Cambridge: Cambridge University Press).

Morris, R. C. (1995) 'All made up: performance theory and the new anthropology of sex and gender', *Annual Review of Anthropology*, 24: 567–92.

Needham, R. (1963) 'Introduction' in E. Durkheim and M. Mauss *Primitive Classification* (London: Cohen & West).

Nelson, N. (1987) 'Selling her kiosk: Kikuyu notions of sexuality and sex for sale in Mathare Valley, Kenya' in P. Caplan (ed.) *The Cultural Construction of Sexuality* (London: Routledge).

Nicholson, L. (1990) *Feminism/Postmodernism* (London: Routledge).

Ortner, S.B. (1984) 'Theory in anthropology since the sixties', *Comparative Studies in Society and History*, 26: 126–65.

Ortner, S.B. (1996) *Making Gender: The Politics and Erotics of Culture* (Boston: Beacon).

Peletz, M.G. (1994) 'Neither reasonable nor responsible: contrasting representations of masculinity in a Malay society', *Cultural Anthropology*, 9 (2): 135–78.

Potash, B. (1989) 'Gender relations in sub-Saharan Africa' in S. Morgen (ed.) *Gender and Anthropology: Critical Reviews for Research and Teaching* (Washington DC: American Anthropological Association).

Power, C. and I. Watts (1997) 'The woman with the zebra's penis: gender, mutability and performance', *Journal of the Royal Anthropological Institute*, 3: 537–60.

Radcliffe-Brown, A. R. (1952) 'Religion and society' in *Structure and Function in Primitive Society* (London: Cohen & West).

Richards, A. (1982) *Chisungu: A Girl's Initiation Ceremony among the Bemba of Zambia* (London: Tavistock).

Rigby, P. (1968) 'Some Gogo rituals of "purification": an essay on social and moral categories' in E.R. Leach (ed.) *Dialectic in Practical Religion* (Cambridge: Cambridge University Press).

Sanders, T. (1997) 'Rainmaking, gender and power in Ihanzu, Tanzania, 1885–1995'. PhD thesis, London School of Economics.

Sanders, T. (1998) 'Making children, making chiefs: gender, power and ritual legitimacy', *Africa*, 68 (2): 238–62.

Schapera, I. (1978) 'Some Kgatla theories of procreation' in J. Argyle and E. Preston-Whyte (eds) *Social System and Tradition in Southern Africa* (Cape Town: Oxford University Press).

Schapera, I. (1979) 'Kgatla notions of ritual impurity', *African Studies*, 38: 3–15.

Shepherd, G. (1987) 'Rank, gender and homosexuality: Mombasa as a key to understanding sexual options' in P. Caplan (ed.) *The Cultural Construction of Sexuality* (London: Routledge).

Silberbauer, G. B. (1963) 'Marriage and the girls' puberty ceremony of the G/wi bushmen', *Africa*, 33 (1): 12–24.

Stevens, L. (1995) 'Bananas, babies, and women who buy their graves: matrifocal values in a patrilineal Tanzanian society', *Canadian Journal of African Studies*, 29 (3): 454–80.

Stichter, S. and J. Parpart (eds) (1988) *Patriarchy and Class: African Women in the Home and the Workforce* (Boulder: Westview).

Strathern, M. (1988) *Gender of the Gift* (Berkeley: University of California Press).

Strobel, M. (1982) 'Review essay: African women', *Signs*, 7, 109–31.

Tambiah, S.J. (1968) 'The magical power of words', *Man*, 3 (2): 175–208.

Tambiah, S.J. (1979) 'A performative approach to ritual', *Proceedings of the British Academy*, 65, 113–69.

Taylor, C. (1993) *Milk, Honey and Money* (Washington DC: Smithsonian Institution Press).

Tucker, J. (1949) 'Initiation ceremonies for Luimbi boys', *Africa*, 19 (1): 53–60.

Turner, T. (1984) 'Dual opposition, hierarchy and value' in J.-C. Galey (ed.) *Différences, Valeurs, Hiérarchie: Texts Offerts à Louis Dumont* (Paris: Ecole des Hautes Etudes).

Turner, V.W. (1967) *The Forest of Symbols: Aspects of Ndembu Ritual* (Ithaca: Cornell University Press).

Turner, V.W. (1969) *The Ritual Process* (Harmondsworth: Penguin).

Udvardy, M. (1990) 'Kifudu: a female fertility cult among the Giriama' in A. Jacobson-Widding and W. van Beek (eds) *The Creative Communion: African Folk Models of Fertility and the Regeneration of Life* (Uppsala: Acta Universitatis Upsaliensis).

Van Baal, J. (1975) *Reciprocity and the Position of Women* (Assen: Van Gorcum).

Vansina, J. (1955) 'Initiation rituals of the Bushong', *Africa*, 25 (2): 138–53.

Wacquant, L. (1992) 'Toward a social praxeology: the structure and logic of Bourdieu's sociology' in P. Bourdieu and L. Wacquant, *An Invitation to Reflexive Sociology* (Cambridge: Polity).

Werbner, R. (1988) *Ritual Passage, Sacred Journey* (Washington DC: Smithsonian Institution Press).

White, C. (1948) 'The Supreme Being in the beliefs of the Balovale tribes', *African Studies*, 7 (1): 29–35.

White, C. (1953) 'Notes on the circumcision rites of the Balovale tribes', *African Studies* 12, 41–56.

White, C., J. Chinjavata and L. Mukwato (1958) 'Comparative aspects of Luvale female puberty ritual', *African Studies*, 17, 204–20.

PART II
RITUAL SYMBOLS

PERFORMANCES AND NARRATIVES

CHAPTER 2

'DOING GENDER' IN AFRICA

EMBODYING CATEGORIES AND THE CATEGORICALLY DISEMBODIED

TODD SANDERS

INTRODUCTION

The title of this chapter – ' "Doing Gender" in Africa' – is meant to evoke and juxtapose a few different ideas simultaneously, ideas that are not often treated under one heading. For one, it raises the by now commonplace criticism that the social sciences have largely ignored women and gender, in Africa as elsewhere. Yet this general critique rings particularly hollow when levelled against anthropology, given that the discipline has long been concerned with women and women's lives. Nor, for that matter, is it easy to imagine how things could have been otherwise: to the extent that empirical research remains a central tenet of the anthropological enterprise, and to the extent that anthropologists concern themselves with such topics as marriage, kinship, the sexual division of labour, ritual and symbolism, we are bound to find that women and women's tasks comprise an integral part of our works.

Nowhere has this been more apparent than in Africa. Here, in this respect, anthropologists have long been 'doing gender,' if by this we mean exploring the roles of and relationships between women and men in mundane and ritual contexts.[1] It is of course only more recent writings on men and women that use the word 'gender'.

What is more, there is an enormous amount of scholarship focusing extensively or exclusively on African women: women's status and rights (Driberg 1932; Howell 1953; Child 1958; Lewin 1959; Perlman 1966; 1969; Dobkin 1968; Vincent 1979), politically and religiously powerful women (Jaques 1934; Bazeley 1940; Saakse 1952; Rangeley 1952; J.D. White 1977; Cohen 1977; Perrot 1979), women's protests and uprisings (Ritzenthaler 1960; Van Allen 1976; Schwartz 1979; Wells 1983), female deities (Barr 1946), the impact of colonialism on women (Hunter 1933; Culwick 1939; Wentzel 1944; Little 1948; Perlman 1966; Dobkin 1968; Van Allen 1972; 1976), female initiation and other rites (Gluckman 1935, C.M.N. White 1953; Holas 1953; Richards 1956; Jeffreys 1956; Silberbauer 1963; Rigby 1968; Blacking 1969a; 1969b; 1969c; 1969d), inheritance and women's labour (Goody and Buckley 1973; Bujra 1975; Mandeville 1979; Kollehlon 1984), among other topics.[2] And the number of contemporary works that deal with African women and their roles and relationships in society is, if anything, on the rise.[3] One journal, for instance, recently devoted an entire issue to what Hodgson and McCurdy call, in a tongue-in-cheek manner, 'wicked women' – those wayward wives, misfit mothers and disobedient daughters who in one way or another, 'individually or collectively, push the boundaries of "acceptable" behavior' to reconfigure gender roles and relations (Hodgson and McCurdy 1996: 3). Another recent collection of essays focuses on powerful and élite African women, at present and in the past (Kaplan 1997). But whatever the case, it is abundantly clear that in the early and later African ethnographic materials women and gender relations were, in popular parlance, 'always already' there.[4]

Beyond these issues, the chapter's title is perhaps most evocative in its allusion to gender as performance – quite literally, that is, to 'doing gender' (West and Zimmerman 1987) – a movement that has a lengthy history in anthropology but is nonetheless often attributed to the theoretical works of Butler (1990; 1993) and to a lesser extent those of Bourdieu (1977; 1990) and de Certeau (1984).[5] Doing gender, from this point of view, takes issue with the proposition that men and women are distinct categories of being; that their different behaviours and psychological characteristics can be deduced directly from their reproductive functions. Men and women are said to be 'natural' categories, anchored firmly and for ever in their distinctive biological make-ups. Biological differences thus produce social consequences, but never the reverse.

Butler's argument stands this naïve biological determinist view on end, insisting instead that gender is neither a given, nor is it something immanently 'natural', located in people's bodies. Because gender is not given, one of her central concerns is to explain why it appears to be so.

What is it, exactly, that gives gender its ontological status, its apparent naturalness and manifestly mundane character? Like others before her, Butler's answer is performativity. As West and Zimmerman put it, 'a person's gender is not simply an aspect of what one is, but, more fundamentally, it is something that one does, and does recurrently, in interaction with others' (1987: 140). Apparent gender differences, then, are produced through everyday acts and actions, gestures and behaviours. Gender is fixed – that is, made to seem biological and thus natural – through 'an enactment that performatively constitutes the appearance of its own fixity' (Butler 1990: 70). To put it another way, although gender is mutable and highly indeterminate, it takes on a seemingly obvious and therefore natural appearance through daily practices, through the very act of doing gender. In terms of ethnography, this anti-essentialist position has most fruitfully found expression in a Melanesian context (Meigs 1990; Strathern 1988; 1993) and, more recently, in Africa (Broch-Due 1993; Blystad, this volume; Power and Watts, this volume). This approach to doing gender I shall refer to as performing *with* gender, for reasons that will become apparent momentarily.

What the above approaches to doing gender appear to have in common is their focus on men and women and their respective bodies. The first approach attends to women's and men's (or sometimes just women's) everyday social relations and their engagement with(in) the political economy: the differential impact of colonialism, migrant labour and markets on men and women; factors that enable and constrain men's and women's access to social, political and economic resources; power relations between men and women in domestic and public domains; and so on (e.g. Walker 1990; Glaser 1992; Manicom 1992; Chege 1993; Drucker-Brown 1993; Håkansson 1994; Greene 1996; Crehan 1997; Sunseri 1997). By the same token, the embodiment approach to doing gender is also concerned with men and women though, admittedly, in rather different ways. Here the focus has been on individual social identities or, more to the point, gendered subject formation. In this way scholars have been able to demonstrate how African men and women themselves are doing gender by exploring the culturally specific ways that boys are made into

men, girls into women, and how gendered identities and subjectiv-
ities are defined and redefined, negotiated and re-negotiated,
through time (e.g. Kratz 1994; Broch-Due 1993; Blystad, this
volume; Power and Watts, this volume).

Together these approaches have produced extremely valuable
information on and insights into ritual and everyday gender relations, gender identities and the apparent malleability of both in
various African contexts. Yet there are a few points worth
noting. First, as already mentioned, the vast majority of work on
gender in Africa has been concerned with social relations, which
is to say, with men and women and the things they do. Important
though these issues are, such attention has come at the expense of
a more careful consideration of the symbolic, ideational systems
of gender that underlie and inform people's day-to-day behaviours. At worst, scholars have ignored gender ideals by conflat-
ing them with gender practices, incorrectly assuming that one
directly and unproblematically mirrors the other (cf. Durkheim
and Mauss 1963). Of course in the real world the social and the
symbolic can never be fully disentangled, as both realms interpenetrate and mutually inform one another. But this does not mean
we should muddle or ignore the distinction altogether. To do so,
I contend, confuses more than it clarifies. The relationship
between symbolic and social aspects of gender cannot simply be
assumed; rather, it must be problematized.

A second and related point is that if ideational systems of
gender had received greater attention, Africanists would no doubt
have more frequently found – as have others in other ethnographic settings – that gender is not only '"about" men and
women but "about" other things as well' (Strathern 1981: 177).
Gender, in other words, is more than mere bodies. For gender
frequency encapsulates and has something of interest to say, not
only about men and women, but also about more general and
gendered cosmic principles: spirits, seasons, rains and rituals and
a number of everyday practices like cooking, eating, churning
butter, pounding grain, grinding flour, smoking and hunting
(Murray 1975; Moore and Puritt 1977: 59; Brain 1978: 181;
Taylor 1990: 1027; Feldman-Savelsberg 1994; 1995; Emanatian
1996: 203ff; Beidelman 1997: 128; Sanders 1997; 1998).

My general aim in this chapter is to explore, through one particular ritual, a third way of 'doing gender' in Africa. This
approach focuses on ideational systems of gender and the

linkages of these systems to certain ritual practices. By considering gender 'as a traveling sort of trope rather than a reality stuck to the bodies of real women and men' (Rosenthal 1997: 199), I wish to argue that *disembodied gender categories* may be performed, in much the same way as embodied genders. I shall refer to this approach as a performance *of* gender.

Now, at first glance it might seem peculiar, impossible or just plain foolish to argue that people perform disembodied gender categories, that they may be doing gender with little or no desire to link this process with actual physical human shells. What, after all, could gender possibly mean if severed altogether from its 'biological' mooring (cf. Collier and Yanagisako 1987)? And what would be the point of such performances if not literally to engender specific types of persons?

Using data collected amongst the Ihanzu of Tanzania,[6] I intend to show how, through ritual, people engage with the living and with the dead in a gendered, cosmic drama that ultimately reconfigures the cultural universe. More to the point, a ritual assertion of harmonious and complementary gender relations in this world leads to harmonious and complementary gender relations in the spirit world. And this, in turn, ensures that the cosmic channels between this and the other world remain temporarily open, allowing the omnipotent spirits to bring the rain, bridle the powers of witchcraft, and cure the ill. 'Doing gender' in this sense is not about turning boys into men, girls into women, or in any other way engendering bodies. What it is about is the acting-out of idealized cosmic gender categories and specifying the appropriate relationship between them. It is about the management of the gendered aspect of the universe, a process that is conceived of as essential to all people's well-being. By playing on themes of gender difference and complementarity, these performances of gender bring people into a relationship with forces in their natural and social worlds over which they have little control, but nonetheless need to control. Furthermore, as the term 'performance' implies, it is the acting out, the actual *doing*, that is at issue: to reduce the complex ritual symbolism entirely to language would be to miss the point. For the Ihanzu, ritual provides a way of saying the obvious while, at the same time, saying nothing at all.

The following section traces the contours of the Ihanzu cultural imagination. This is followed by an in-depth discussion of one particular ancestral offering, an offering carried out to cure dying livestock. The final section then links the Ihanzu cultural imagination discussed in part one with the ancestral offering discussed in part two and shows how ritual participants are actively doing gender – by which I mean engaging in a performance *of* gender – in order to realign the cosmos and, thus, cure their afflicted animals.

GENDER AND THE IHANZU CULTURAL IMAGINATION

The Ihanzu, a matrilineal Bantu-speaking agricultural people, live in a world permeated by gender. This is not only to state the obvious: that Ihanzu women and men live together and thus constitute, quite literally, the social and cultural universe they inhabit. Much more than this, it is to point out that idealized gender categories provide the Ihanzu with an indigenous model – a cosmic template of sorts – that both structures their world and allows them to act meaningfully upon it.

By 'gender' I mean the cultural construction of male (or masculinity) and female (or femininity), as well as the relationship between them. Defining gender in this way allows us to think beyond men and women as specific types of persons, to create a necessary conceptual space – a space, I might add, that the Ihanzu themselves often inhabit – in which gender is more than mere bodies. For this is clearly the way the Ihanzu imagine their world: filled, as it is, with gendered rulers, rituals, rainstones and even rains. In this respect, in Ihanzu eyes, gender serves as a primary cosmological structuring principle, enabling people to conceive, consider and occasionally contest the ways their social and natural worlds are constructed (cf. Beidelman 1964; 1993; 1997; S.F. Moore 1976). Ihanzu ideas and ideals about male (-*gohá*) and female (-*süngü*) provide an indigenously grounded interpretative framework for making sense of a number of distinct yet interrelated cultural domains. Furthermore, as we shall see presently, Ihanzu gender categories also provide a model that the Ihanzu use *to act* purposively upon their world.

There are, of course, many ways to imagine gender categories and the relationship between them. For instance, some Ihanzu discourses and practices either assert or imply that men are superior to women, that male is dominant over female. Others claim precisely the opposite, that female is superior to male. Still others paint a decidedly egalitarian picture where men and women, male and female, are 'separate but equal' (cf. Shope 1994). Since all these contradictory notions and practices are found in Ihanzu simultaneously, it is not possible to gloss accurately Ihanzu gender relations as simply patriarchal, matriarchal, egalitarian or anything else. As Meigs concisely puts it in the context of New Guinea, 'Probably there is no such thing as a single gender ideology in any society. On a topic like the relationship of males and females, each society undoubtedly has many ways of thinking – complex, subtle, and even contradictory ideological options' (Meigs 1990: 15). In Ihanzu, as has been reported elsewhere, the relative status and power of men and women, male and female, changes markedly from one context to another (Caplan 1989; Holy 1985; Meigs 1990). Thus, the issue of interest becomes one of specifying how varied and conflicting cultural representations of gender are operationalized in practical situations (Bloch 1987; Harrison 1985; Hill 1984; Jacobson-Widding 1990; Kratz 1990; Ortner 1996; Peletz 1994).

In the context of Ihanzu ancestral offerings like the one to be discussed below, women and men emphasize strongly the equality and complementarity of the genders. Here, masculine and feminine are – and indeed must be – equal. For any offering to be successful, so informants claim, male and female must 'cooperate' (*kiunga*) and 'reside together harmoniously' (*wikiĩ ũza palũng'wĩ*). The Ihanzu share a number of more specific notions about the complementarity of male and female that give these rather general claims more definitive shape. These notions are often explained as binary contrasts and are meant to account for the alleged natural differences between the genders.

For instance, it is common knowledge in Ihanzu that male is dry (*-kalamũku*) and female is wet (*-totu*). Men's and women's bodies are often evoked as evidence of this proposition: men are generally lean whereas women are (sometimes) fatty and possess 'birth waters' (*mazĩ a mũmbũ*) and vaginal waters (*mazĩ a nio*) that guarantee their moist make-up.

In a similar fashion, male is said to be active and a leader, while female is passive and a follower. This is explained in different ways. For example, people note that men should normally be served food and beer before women, a rule that is frequently followed on the homestead and less so elsewhere. Another example is the common claim that it is men, and not women, who enter the bush to clear farm plots. This is arduous work and requires a good deal of perseverance, traits that men should ideally possess. Women come later, after the land has been cleared, to farm it. Without their joint co-operation, however, it would be difficult to obtain an adequate harvest. The fact that women may on occasion clear their own plots, or take the initiative and pay men to do it for them, is seldom mentioned. Rather, we are concerned with Ihanzu ideals, and these stress complementarity. The notion of gender complementarity also comes out clearly in people's descriptions of male and female rains. Male rain is said to arrive first and be active while female rain follows and is passive. Male rain is harsh and passes quickly; by 'himself' male rain cannot saturate the land sufficiently. Female rain, on the other hand, though enduring, is somewhat fickle and requires male rain to clear the way before 'she' can do her work. As a general rule, in Ihanzu eyes, both gendered rains are indispensable. They must work together (Sanders 1998). The principle of gender complementarity is found in other realms too, as, for example, when discussing ownership of, and control over, social, political and economic resources.

Ownership of and control over livestock fall roundly into the male domain, men and women seem to agree. Men own nearly all livestock. They inherit it, use it for bridewealth exchanges and make all important decisions concerning its sale and slaughter. To a large extent, livestock is 'men's business' and women are excluded from it. Never mind that practices sometimes belie these beliefs: sheep and goats, for example, are often herded by young girls and women, and women have disposal rights over the milk of their husbands' livestock. Furthermore, some women inherit and own livestock themselves. But, again, our concern here is with Ihanzu cultural ideals – with the ways Ihanzu often *portray* the genders as complementary – and not with the more complicated question of multiple and contradictory notions of gender, or how men and women actually behave in relation to these notions. Overall, in this ideal realm, people see livestock as male-coded.

Just as livestock are thought to make up part of the men's domain, so grain and the products made from it are said to fall within women's domain. Although a man and his wife (or wives) farm their fields jointly, once the grain is harvested and has been safely stowed in the grainstore, a wife gains close to total control over its future allocation within and outside the household. With her grain, a woman must budget from one harvest to the next. She must make decisions about when and how many times to brew and sell beer, the single largest contributor to household income. She must also decide how much she can afford to give to needy neighbours, kin and others, and still have enough to provide for herself, her husband and children. Control over grain is thus a source of women's power and status in Ihanzu. For all these reasons, women are often associated with grain, and especially with the indispensable grain products of everyday life: stiff porridge and beer. Grain and its by-products become symbolically female-coded.

Thus, even basic sustenance strategies are, at some ideational level, often cast in terms of gender complementarity. Men provide the meat; women provide stiff porridge and beer. Indeed, a meal that lacks either meat or stiff porridge is commonly said to be no meal at all. Together male and female can survive and thrive, something that alone would be difficult if not impossible. To reiterate, none of this is to imply that the man and women of Ihanzu are, on balance, equal. They are not. The point, rather, is that people often portray the genders as such, and especially, as we shall see, in certain ritual contexts.

From the foregoing it should be plain that the categories 'male' and 'female' mutually inform and define each other, that one without the other is both a theoretical and practical impossibility (Strathern 1988). It is difficult, if not impossible, for people in Ihanzu to contemplate one gender without the other. And in this ideational context (but not in all), male and female are viewed as equal and complementary. No relative evaluation of gender categories is here implied. What one lacks the other provides, often in abundance. Male and female provide meaning to each other and, when joined, form more than the sum of their parts.

Yet above all else, the point of interest is that even though people's ideas about gender complementarity are often couched in terms of men's and women's bodies, they also go well beyond those bodies to envelop and inform other cultural and cosmic domains. Thus, just as bodies are seen as gendered and complementary, so, too, are subsistence activities, the rains and other things as well. In this respect, ideational gender categories provide an underlying symbolic scheme that cross-cuts and informs many social and cultural domains of the Ihanzu universe.

Clearly, for the people of Ihanzu, gender is good to think (cf. Beidelman 1964; 1993; 1997).

But gender provides the Ihanzu with more than a way of imagining their world: it also provides an indigenous model of transformative processes that is good to act. As I have argued elsewhere (Sanders 1998), a certain 'procreative paradigm' (Herbert 1993) underlies and informs Ihanzu notions of transformation. To unite masculine and feminine elements of a thoroughly gendered universe is to activate the cosmic and divine powers of the Ihanzu social and natural worlds (cf. S.F. Moore 1976). But most important of all for the Ihanzu, to effect any sort of change or transformation – be it to produce iron, pots, babies, rain or, in the case I shall now discuss, to stave off ancestral affliction – masculine and feminine elements must unite as complementary and equal elements.

The following section provides a detailed look at an Ihanzu ancestral offering. The offering's explicit aim is to cure dying cattle. What I will argue is that the offering accomplishes its intended goal by acting out idealized gender categories and specifying the proper relationship between them. Only with the proper performance of the genders – which is to say, joining the genders as equal and complementary units – will their joint powers be realized, the spirits satisfied and the afflicted beasts cured.

IHANZU ANCESTRAL OFFERINGS FOR ILLNESSES[7]

In Ihanzu it is not possible to carry out an ancestral offering before something has actually gone wrong, be it a personal or livestock illness, the failure of the rains or some other catastrophe. Rather, it is only after the fact, when disaster strikes and it has subsequently been divined that clan spirits demand such an offering, that ancestral offerings take place. To follow is an example of one such offering.

Demands from the spirits

In early 1993, the cattle of Chief Omari began dying mysteriously. At a divination session it transpired that his royal clan spirits required an offering – some beer and a black sheep born at night – before they would allow the cattle to recover. The spirits' main complaint, made clear through the chicken oracle, was that they wanted to be able to see the cattle leaving their cattle enclosure each morning as they went out to graze. Since these clan spirits are thought to reside in the north, this meant re-orientating the cattle enclosure door to face that direction. Such requests by the spirits are in no way unusual, and are made of royalty, as in this case, and of commoners alike. Following the divination session, preparations for an offering began almost immediately.[8]

Initiating the offering (kūkūmbīka)

To initiate the offering, which was done on the evening following the divination session, a few 'grandchildren' were summoned to chief Omari's homestead. Grandchildren – they are always classificatory grandchildren and either middle-aged or elderly – orchestrate and play a leading role in all such offerings. They are so called because their paternal grandfather is (or more likely, was) a member of the clan and clan-section of the men or women carrying out the offering. In this case, that means the royal *Anyampanda wa Kirumi* clan-section.

To ensure the ultimate success of offerings it is imperative, Ihanzu stress, that at least one grandson and one granddaughter participate: these two must co-operate (*kiunga*) in all their ritual chores and reside together harmoniously (*wikiī ūza palūng'wī*). Jointly they must initiate each and every phase in the ritual sequence. Once the grandchildren have initiated each activity 'to remove the taboo' (*kūheja miko*), others may on occasion assist them.

On this particular evening, one granddaughter and one grandson came.[9] Following a brief address to the royal spirits, the grandson went into the bush and gathered some cuttings from several ritually significant cool or gentle trees (*mītī nī mīpolo*)[10] and returned them to the chief's homestead. The granddaughter then addressed the spirits while grinding some white sorghum on a grinding stone.[11] Collecting a special long-necked calabash (*mūmbū*) from inside the house, she filled it with water and mixed in the sorghum flour. After this, the grandchildren took some of the fresh tree cuttings and inserted them into the opening in the top of the calabash. After setting the calabash in the homestead's doorway, they addressed, one at a time, the royal clan spirits.

The grandson's address preceded the granddaughter's. Like most addresses throughout the offering, these were brief, stating what was more or less obvious: 'we are initiating an offering'; 'we are cutting some branches for you'; 'we are putting this beer here for you'; and so forth. As we shall see below certain addresses are paid more attention than others.

From beginning to end these preliminary rites took less than an hour. Nonetheless they are essential to the success of any offering since they announce to the spirits, formally and publicly, that an offering is under way. At this point, it remained to collect the sacrificial sheep and the grain to brew the ancestral beer.

The sacrificial sheep and ancestral beer brewing

It is always the responsibility of the clan of the afflicted to come up with the sacrificial animal for an offering. It sometimes takes considerable effort to locate an animal that meets the spirits' demands (its colour, type, when it was born, and so on). When the necessary animal cannot be identified within the clan in question, another may be exchanged for one outside the clan with the appropriate characteristics. For this particular offering, matters were facilitated greatly by the fact that the chief himself had a black sheep born at night on his own compound which he agreed to give for the offering.

Beer, like livestock, forms a necessary part of all Ihanzu ancestral offerings. Unlike in everyday contexts, however, where it is always woman who brew beer, at ancestral offerings the granddaughter and grandson must labour jointly at this task. At each stage in the brewing process – addressing the spirits, digging the beer-brewing trench, and so forth – these two must join forces. At this offering, as at all others I attended, the grandchildren brewed beer together. After nearly a month, the beer was ready and the offering proper could begin.

The morning of the offering

At around seven in the morning, men and women filled Omari's homestead. They totalled around sixty, women slightly outnumbering men. Some had come from the immediate area, though many had walked from villages up to eight miles away. Almost everyone wore black (-walʉ), the colour explicitly associated with rainclouds and thus considered auspicious for any rites dealing with ancestral spirits. White (-elŭ) is also an acceptable colour on such occasions. The colour red, on the other hand, is unequivocally inauspicious and is thus avoided on these occasions; it may potentially undermine the offering by attracting lightning, which is also said to be red (-kaŭku), hot (-pyu) and sharp or fierce (-taki). Most women, and some men including the grandson, wore on their heads fresh wreaths from the mŭmbĭlĭlĭ tree (Entada sp.), one among several species of 'cool trees' regularly used for dealing with the spirits.

Cutting the cattle door

As some women swept the homestead and surrounding area, others sat around the homestead talking quietly amongst themselves. Once the grandchildren, the chief and others had agreed on the precise location in the north-facing cattle fence where the new cattle door was to be opened, the grandson addressed the spirits and spat ancestral beer on the fence. Following his address, the granddaughter did the same. The grandchildren and others then began to open a doorway in the fence. They once again addressed the spirits, one after the other, while digging two holes on either side of the doorway into which the door's frame would eventually be placed.

The women stood, began singing and dancing their way through the new doorway to the outside of the homestead. Eventually, everyone returned to the courtyard and sat in distinct groups. Two diviners, the chief, a small group of male rainmaking assistants (ataata) and a few other elderly men sat in the northernmost part of the homestead in the cattle enclosure. The women sat in a group at the southern side of the courtyard near the kitchen. These seating arrangements were not entirely accidental, and follow a specific cultural logic that will be further explored below.[12]

The sheep sacrifice

The sacrificial sheep was then led through the courtyard and into the cattle enclosure where it was forced to the ground, just inside the new doorway. It was laid atop an east–west orientated pile of leafy branches with its head to the west, eyes to the north.[13] The grandchildren held down the sheep, smothering the animal until it had passed out. An Islamic man then approached and slit its throat.[14] The grandchildren began carefully carving up the sheep. A buffalo-leather shield and three wooden spears were placed on the ground near the new cattle door. All these items were of considerable age and were said to have been used in battle by the ancestors.

The grandson momentarily left the sheep to sprinkle some beer over the two new door posts and address the spirits. Between each of his two addresses, the women ululated. The granddaughter followed with her addresses. The grandson then spread some chyme from the sheep's stomach across the door's threshold. Following this, all of the chief's livestock were herded into the compound through the old door, and made to exit via the new door. As the animals passed through the new doorway, the grandson and granddaughter struck the animals with switches that had been dipped in the ancestral beer, while calling upon the spirits to observe what they were doing. The women ululated. Once all the animals had passed through the new doorway, and the spirits had presumably seen them do so, it was now time to start the ritual fire.

Starting the fire

The fire features centrally in all ancestral offerings and is deeply significant. If, at any offering I attended I had a momentary lapse of attention, people invariably made sure I noticed and noted down in my notebook the fact that the grandchildren were starting a fire, and that they were using firesticks to do it.

At this offering, as at all others, a grandson and granddaughter started the ritual fire jointly. The grandson twirled a long, slender firedrill (*kĩlĩndĩ*) into a hole in a smaller, stationary hearth (*kiziga*) which the granddaughter held.[15] The grandson addressed the spirits while so doing. The grandchildren then switched positions. The granddaughter spun the firedrill and addressed the spirits while the grandson held the hearth in place. The granddaughter and grandson went in turn twirling the firedrill while the other held the hearth. After several minutes, the fire started.

Reading the entrails

The grandchildren filled an oblong, wooden divining bowl (*ntua*) with various innards[16] and placed it, with an east–west orienta-

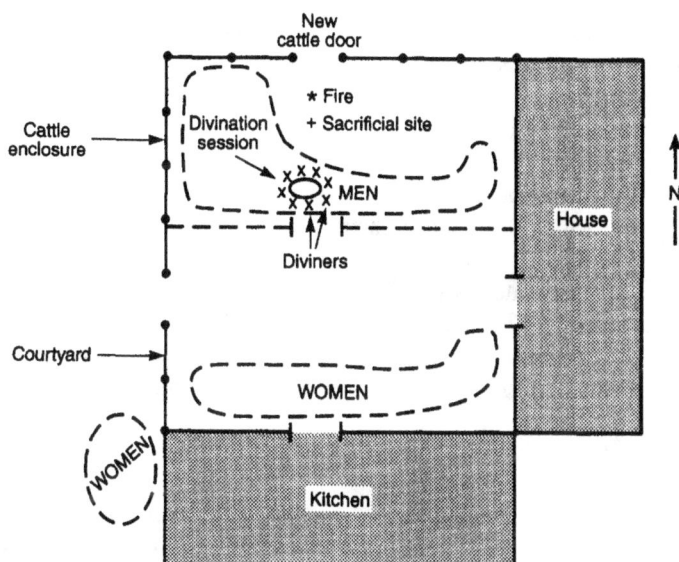

Figure 2.1 Spatial layout of Ihanzu ancestral offering

tion, in front of the two diviners. The men who sat nearby formed a small circle around the diviners in order to hear their soft-spoken pronouncements. The remainder – mainly women and novices – remained silent, listening intently from where they sat a distance on the southern side of the compound (Figure 2.1).

The diviners and men spoke in hushed tones amongst themselves for nearly an hour. When the reading had come to an end, one of the diviners summed up the results and broadcast them loudly so the women who sat at a distance could finally hear the outcome: the cattle doorway had been successfully opened, the spirits had accepted it and were content. They also prophesied that the rain would be substantial. The women ululated. It was now the grandchildren's task to carry out one of the more significant addresses of the offering: giving meat to the spirits.

Meat for the spirits (kūtagangīla)[17]

These particular addresses are the first in the offering in which something is given – in this case, meat – to the spirits. They are also the first-named addresses and are rarely omitted from people's descriptions of ancestral offerings. Like all addresses, these were delivered to the collectivity of royal spirits. Yet in this case individual male and female spirits, all royal clan notables from the past, were singled out by name. The grandchildren cut a long strip of meat from the sheep's upper chest (*nyama a kikua*), roasted it and cut it into small, bite-size pieces which they held in their hands. The grandson then stood, the crowd fell silent. He made a theatrical address to each of the four cardinal points tossing, before each address, a piece of meat in that direction.[18] Following each statement, the women ululated.

In the following transcription of these addresses I have marked males with a single asterisk (*) and females with two (**). The grandson began facing east:

1 *Ǔe Mǔnyankalǐ nǔpǔmie kǔ mǔtala wako nǔkǔlǔ n'ǔinzǔ kǔ mǔtala wako nǔnino, ǔsese apa itǐ kǔkete ipolyo.*
You, *Mǔnyankalǐ**, who come from your senior house and are going to your junior one, we here have an ancestral offering.

2 *Ǔse kǔipolya ipolyo kǔlǔgǔe mǔmpita.*
We are carrying out an ancestral offering to open a cattle door.

3 *Ing'ombe yǐtu ize tuga du mapaha.*
Let our cattle bear twins.

4 *N'ǔmǔzee ǔyǔ mǔnǔ, ngǐze wǐzǔkete ndwala ndwala, mǔmǔlekele kabisa!*
And this elder [the chief*] inside [the doorway to the house], if he has an illness, leave him alone!

5 *Mǐhi apa itǐ sehemu ǐyǐ apa itǐ ǐamamá mǔlekelwe mǐhi.*
And all those here, the grandmothers [i.e. women of the royal clan**], let them all be left alone.

6 *Mǔtuge nǐ amintǔtǐ.*
Let them bear twins.

7 *N'ǐmbula nǐnkǔlǔ. N'ǔse kǔloilwe kǔpone mailo nǐ dǔ.*
And [let there be] big rains. We want to get lots of sorghum and recover.

He then turned to the west, threw another morsel of meat, and continued:

8 *Uewe Mũnyankalĩ ũtwale ilũmbi.*
You, *Mũnyankalĩ**, take [with you on your journey] gratitude.

9 *Ũnene nkete ipolyo.*
I have an ancestral offering.

10 *Twala kũ ng'wanso endũgũmile mũ Nyanza.*
Take [the bad] there and toss it into Lake Victoria.

11 *Ũkũlekele lũkũlũ! Ũsese kũnũ ĩmbula ĩze, ĩze ĩlelo yĩyĩ.*
Leave us alone! For us here, let the rains begin, let them begin today.

12 *N'ĩana aze tuga ũkũtuga du.*
And allow the children to give birth.

13 *N'ũilei ilei shi kũloilwe lũkũlũ. Mũmatwale kũko nĩ mabĩ kũko ũmagũmile.*
And we really don't want quarrelsomeness. Take that evil and toss it out.

To the north he turned, threw some meat, and said the following:

14 *Napika kũ mbũga.*
I have arrived at the steppe, to the north.

15 *Napika kũng'wa Ikomba. Ũnene nkete ipolyo. Nakũlugũĩliya ũmũmpita waloma kũko lũkũlũ.*
I have arrived at Ikomba's.* I have an ancestral offering. I have opened a cattle door for you which faces there [north].

16 *Nĩ aKitentemi naũlimĩe kũ ng'wansu kũ mbũga ũleke lũkũlũ ĩnkani izi. Ũmùlango wako sũwũ.*
And Kitentemi,* [and] the one who was lost there on the steppe,* leave these words. This is your door.

Turning to the south and tossing his last piece of meat, the grandson finished his address:

17 *Kŭnŭ kŭ takamá, ŭnene nkete ipolyo.*
There in the south, I have an ancestral offering.

18 *aSumbĭ nĭ aNya Itŭtĭ.*
Sumbi** and Nya Ituti.**

19 *N'ŭyŭ naŭpandilwe ĭmbogo nŭkĭzadaya lelo, nŭalŭmbe du n'ŭng'wenso.*
And the one* who was run down by a buffalo, the one who was owed [an offering] today, let him be grateful.

20 *Nĭ aMpungati nĭ aNya Matalŭ ĭakombi nĭ aSagilŭ.*
And Mpungati* and Nya Matalu** and the old women** and Sagilu.

21 *N'ŭNkili alowe du.*
And Nkili,** rejoice!

22 *Nĭ aIkĭngu ĭa akombi nĭalŭmbe. Ŭnene nalugŭla ŭmŭmpita wao.*
And Ikingu* and the old women** be grateful. I have opened their cattle door.

23 *N'ŭnene ŭŭgwa ndowe. Kŭĭgwa ĭngĭlĭgĭlĭ. N'ŭe ŭze kŭa mŭkombi ĭngĭlĭgĭlĭ.*
And I am rejoicing. Ululate. And you, old woman, [he says jokingly, staring at a women who had apparently fallen asleep] ululate.

The granddaughter then stepped into the centre of the courtyard. Facing east she threw a piece of meat and began her address.

24 *Ŭnene kŭtambŭla nkehu da. (Mĭlŭnga ŭlĭ gwa kŭnŭ itĭ?) Ŭewe nŭpŭmie kŭ mŭtala nŭkŭlŭ, ŭsese kŭkete ipolyo. Aza kŭlŭgŭla mŭmpita.*
I will just say a few [words]. (What are you saying there?) You who come from [your] senior house,* we have an ancestral offering. We were opening a cattle door.

25 Ũewe Kali n'ũKitentemi n'ũyũ naũpandilwe ĩmbogo m'ihaka.
You Kali* and Kitentemi,* and that one who was run down
by a buffalo in the bush.*

26 Mũlowe mĩhi.
All, rejoice.

27 Nĩ aSagilũ ao mũlũmbe mĩhi. Nĩ aNya Matalũ ao mũlũmbe
mĩhi.
And Sagilu* and the rest, all be grateful. And Nya Matalu**
and the rest, [may] you all be grateful.

To the north she turned, tossed some meat and continued:

28 Nagoza kũnũ kũ mbũga naza mũtakile ĩa kola.
I am looking north towards the steppe, [towards] those who
were angered.

29 Kamũlũgũĩlya ũmũmpita wanyu.
We have opened your cattle door for you.

30 Ũnyenye Ikomba mĩhi mũlowe kũ ng'wanso.
All of you, Ikomba,* all of you there rejoice.

31 Ĩmbula ĩkũwe nĩnkũlũ n'ũilo ũze nũĩdũ. Kakatala kaga ĩnzala.
Let it pour rain and let there be heaps of sorghum. We are
tired of suffering from hunger.

Then to the west:

32 N'ũewe nũinzũ kũ mũtala nũnino, aya nĩmabĩ ĩhi endũgũmile mũ
lũzĩ. Atengwe lũpĩto nĩkĩza pũmia ũtikũ.
And you* who are going to [your] junior house, toss all the
evil into the place of water [Lake Victoria]. May those
[witches] who send aphids [to eat sorghum] be struck by lightning.

33 *Ũse kũloilwe ĩmbula ĩkũe ũng'waka ũwũ kũpũle kũlũnde n'ũkũ matembe.*
We want the rains to fall this year so we get lots of food to put on top of our houses [to dry in the sun].

34 *N'ũewe nũhongile kũnũ itĩ kũko.*
And you, who are going there.*

To the south the granddaughter ended her offering by tossing her final piece of meat and saying:

35 *Ngĩze anyatakamá nĩ, magũ, Anyĩlamba kũko n'ũnyenye mũlũmbe mĩhi.*
And the people in the south – I don't know – Iramba there, all of you be grateful.

Following these addresses, the grandson approached the chief who sat in the doorway of his house and fed him one of the pieces of meat. He then fed several other elderly clan members seated nearby. The granddaughter then did the same.

Addresses delivered on these occasions are composed on the spot, delivered at high speed and are never identical. Nevertheless, they always drawn on common themes. It is customary, first, to address *Mũnyankalĩ*, the name used for the sun in ritual contexts. Being neither God nor spirit, *Mũnyankalĩ* may be understood as 'a visible and tangible symbol of a supernatural world about which nothing can be known' (Adam 1963: 22).[19] In these addresses reference is always made to the fact that *Mũnyankalĩ* – who is unequivocally said to be male – is moving from one wife's house in the east to another wife's house in the west (Adam 1963: 11–12, 22; Kohl-Larsen 1943: 303–5). As he does so, the grandchildren urge him to make it known to the spirits that an offering is under way, and to remove whatever evil there might be (i.e. witchcraft) and to cool it in the waters of Lake Victoria, the (perhaps mythical) homeland of the Ihanzu people. All spatial references in these rites to the east–west axis, in fact, people explicitly link to *Mũnyankalĩ*'s regular celestial movements.

The communal feast

The grandchildren now congregated about the ritual fire and began roasting and handing out the sacrificial meat. As is common at all offerings, tending the fire and distributing the meat was done solely by the grandchildren. Moving stealthily over to the pile of raw meat, a jester snatched the liver and a flaming stick from the fire, and ran out of the compound to eat the meat alone 'in the bush' (*mihaka*).

Most ate where they sat. A few *ad hoc* groups of men and women formed to visit and feast on two royal graves: that of Mpungati (the male ritual leader between 1902 and 1927) and Nya Matalu (the female ritual leader between *c*. 1870 and 1947). Those who went to Mpungati's grave were given a front leg from the sacrificial animal; those who went to Nya Matalu's grave the animal's loin (*kiuno*). Though people I spoke with were undecided about the significance of the leg going to the male grave, they all agreed that the loin must go to the female once since it is this part that is associated with birth.

What went on at the two graves was identical. On one grave they set a gourd of beer and started a fire nearby using embers from the ritual fire the grandchildren had started earlier. They roasted the meal and ate it while sitting around the grave. Following this, all sat on and around the grave and drank the ancestral beer. Before leaving, they pinned some small pieces of the ancestral animal's hide on the grave, and spit the remainder of the beer over the grave and fire. When they returned to the chief's homestead, they 'returned the fire' they had lit by returning a stick from it to the original ritual fire. Once everyone had returned to the homestead, men and women danced and sang around the courtyard.

It was now about 1 o'clock. Everyone sat as before. Standing in the centre of the courtyard, the grandchildren made another series of addresses to the spirits, this time spraying beer from their mouths to the four cardinal points. They then placed two small strips of the sacrificial sheep's skin atop the newly created cattle doorway, while telling the spirits what they were doing. They then returned to the centre of the courtyard to begin the second essential address of any offering: beer for the spirits.

Beer for the spirits (*kŭlonga shalo*)

The grandson stood in the centre of the courtyard holding a ritual whisk (*nsing'wanda*); at his feet sat a divining bowl (again, placed east–west) into which he had poured some of the ancestral beer and water. Dipping the whisk into the bowl and splashing it to the east, he began a dramatic and theatrically intoned address to the spirits:

36 *Alĭ gwa lelo, ĭmbula lelo ĭze ĭlelo yĭyĭ.*
All right already. [Let there be] rain today, let it come today.

37 *Ŭnene nalŭnga apa itĭ kŭkete ipolyo. Ipolyo kipolya ŭza.*
I have said here we have an ancestral offering. We have carried out the offering well.

Then turning to the west, and after splashing the crowd with his whisk, he continued:

38 *N'ŭewe kŭnŭ nŭinzŭ, ŭsese kŭkete ipolyo iza du.*
And you there,* who is going there [west], we have a good ancestral offering.

39 *Ŭtwale ilŭmbi du kŭ ng'wanso. Ŭsese kŭkete ipolyo.*
Take [with you] gratitude there. We have an ancestral offering.

To the north the grandson then said this:

40 *N'ŭnyenye kŭ ng'wanso, Ikomba, kŭ mbŭga, ŭmŭlango wanyu wanona lelo. Sŭwŭ. N'ĭnkolo sĭyo hapa n'imputa sizo. Mŭhangĭle palŭng'wĭ!*
You all there, Ikomba,* to the north on the steppe: we have fixed your door today. This is it. And here is this sheep and these sheepskin bracelets; work together!

Then turning to the south:

41 *Nūnye kūnū kū takamá aNya Matalū nī aNya Itūtī: ilūmbi du
imputa yanyu sizi hapa.*
You all there to the south, Nya Matalu** and Nya Ituti:** be
grateful for your sheepskin bracelets which are here.

42 *N'īnkolo nīndwalu yīyī naīmūmūdaiye.*
And this black sheep which you were owed.

With this the grandson stepped aside. The granddaughter moved
to the centre of the courtyard and began:

43 *Ali n'ūkū ng'wanso mūpole mīhi nimūkolī apa itī. Ūse kalūmba.
Īmītugo īzelela īmapaha du. N'īmbula īkūe nīnkūlū.*
All right, all of you [spirits] who are here, cool off. We are
grateful. Just let the livestock bear twins. And allow the rains
to pour down.

She then turned to the west, splashed the *nsing'wanda* and continued:

44 *(N'īmbula nīkīza mīlūnga). N'ūko nūinzū kū ng'weli kū mūtala
nūnino mūlūmbe n'ūkū ng'wanso mīhi.*
(I will talk about rain). And there in the west where you* are
going to your junior house, all there be grateful.

45 *Ūse kūloilwe ūng'waka ūwū kūpūle ūilo nūīdū n'ūtikū mūlīmīlye.*
We want to reap a large sorghum harvest this year and [we
want] you to make the aphids go away.

And then to the north:

46 *N'ūnye Ikomba kū ng'wanso naza mūlīīe ūmūmpita wanyu. Ūse
īmbula īze n'igana.*

All of you there – Ikomba* – those who were yearning for your cattle door. For us, allow it to pour for a long time.[20]

47 *Īze kũa, īze segenselya ũtikũ ga. Ihĩ ītonte.*
Allow it to rain, allow it to rain slowly, gently, all night long [so that] the land becomes saturated.

The granddaughter's address was followed by two others: one by the chief's classificatory father, and one by a jester. Both these addresses followed the same general pattern as those above. Though plenty could be said about these addresses, the noteworthy point for the moment is that all address both male and female spirits and that these gendered spirits are told to 'work together' (e.g. line 40).

When the addresses were completed, it was nearly 2 p.m. The day's rites had now finished. People sat and continued to drink the ancestral beer until late that night which, I was told by some, would please the spirits greatly. The spirits had received their beer.

Addresses on the final day

The grandchildren slept on the chief's homestead, as did many others, and most arose just before sunrise. The granddaughter immediately set about cooking stiff porridge at the chief's hearth while the grandson roasted some meat remaining from the previous day's sacrifice. The diviners and some male clan elders collected themselves just outside the doorway of the house. They sat in a semi-circle facing the doorway where the chief himself was seated in the threshold.

The grandson and granddaughter divided the stiff porridge in half and put the two portions into two separate calabash bowls (*lũkũlũ*). Similarly, they divided the roasted meat between two bowls. The grandson took two of the calabashes – one filled with stiff sorghum, the other with roasted meat – out of the house and set them on the ground in the centre of the group of elders. The granddaughter followed with her two calabashes, setting them next to the grandson's. It was 6.30 in the morning and the sun was just coming up; the third and final series of significant addresses and offerings was about to begin.

The grandson picked up a piece of the recently roasted meat from his calabash along with a small piece of stiff porridge from his second calabash. Facing the rising sun in the east, he tossed the piece of meat in that direction, immediately followed by the piece of stiff porridge, and began his address to *Mūnyankalī*. He repeated this to the west. He then addressed the spirits in the south and north, each time tossing a piece of meat and stiff porridge in that direction. The granddaughter followed the grandson, throwing her meat and stiff porridge in each direction followed by her addresses. In structure and content these addresses were nearly identical to their earlier addresses transcribed above.

When the granddaughter finished her final address, the grandson walked over to the chief who was sitting in the doorway throughout, made a brief address to the spirits, and then fed him a piece of cooked meat and stiff porridge. A few other royal lineage members were fed too. The granddaughter then did the same. With the addresses finished, the small group of male elders that had been sitting near the doorway began eating their stiff porridge and meat.

Other men sitting further away were then served by the grand-children. And when they had finished, the women who sat in their own group received their portion: two bowls of stiff porridge (one from each grandchild) and two of meat relish.

Drinking inside the house

After all had eaten, the grandchildren brought out the ancestral beer and distributed it likewise – clan elders near the door, men and then women. It was at this point that the small group of elders near the door entered the house to drink beer just inside the door. Some elderly women also joined them. In the centre of the group sat two special long-necked calabashes (*mūmbū*) with white beads around their necks, both filled with ancestral beer.[21] One of the calabashes also wore a large white bead on a leather thong, the chief's insignia of office (*kīlungu*). People poured the beer from the ritual calabashes into calabash bowls and shared it.

Extinguishing the trench fire

At around half past eight, the women began singing and dancing. They slowly danced their way over to the trench fire, the one the grandchildren had used to brew the beer prior to the offering, and began to fill it. The grandson started the actual filling. Others then followed. The bones from the sacrificial animal were dropped into the trench as it was filled. The grandson stood at the west end of the trench and told the ancestors what they were doing: filling the trench after the offering. He sprayed beer from his mouth over the trench. The granddaughter followed. Women ululated.

When the trench was filled, some of the singing women sat in a row along the length of it, legs stretched out in front of them. They then began bouncing over the trench to pack down the earth. This officially marked the end of the offering.

GENDERED PERFORMERS, GENDERED PERFORMANCES

Ancestral requests

To return to the beginning, it will be recalled that prior to the offering, the royal spirits made their demands clear through an oracle: they asked for beer and a black sheep born at night. These are very common ancestral requests. In fact, I have never attended an offering without beer and an animal sacrifice and, to the best of my knowledge, it would be impossible to carry out an offering in Ihanzu without these things (Kohl-Larsen 1943: 305). What varies from one offering to the next is the quantity of beer and the type of animal.

As was suggested above, when the Ihanzu talk about the complementarity of the genders, they often imply that grain and its by-products are female-coded, in the same way that livestock and its by-products are male-coded. This suggests that, from the beginning, the spirits are making a request that they be given both female and male elements from the world of the living, in the form of beer and meat respectively. A ritual performance of gender is required to please the spirits and cure the ill cattle. That ritual participants are offering male and female in different forms is evident throughout in the content and structure of ancestral addresses.

Ancestral addresses, offerings and the spirits

Central to all ancestral addresses is the somewhat ill-defined figure, *Mŭnyankalĩ* – ill-defined, that is, since all we know about him is that he is male, and that the sun is his this-worldly manifestation. No one I spoke with could say more. But this apparent paucity of information is, in and of itself, telling, for what people find significant is this: first, that he is *male*; and second, that he, as the sun, crosses the sky each day from east to west, between the houses of his two wives. Clearly, addresses to *Mŭnyankalĩ*, like all east–west spatial references found in these rites, serve as spatial commentaries on an idealized gender order in which male and female work and live together harmoniously, each filling his or her half of the gender bargain. Male is active, female passive.

Mŭnyankalĩ moves from east (*kŭkilya*) to west (*kŭng'welĩ*) each day, a movement that also evokes cycles of life and death. The Ihanzu associate the east and morning with new life, birth, upwards, growth and renewal. This is where *Mŭnyankalĩ* is reborn each morning. Life-giving rain comes from the east; divination sessions, which usually occur in the morning, face east; the royal rainshrine is opened each year in the morning, when the sun is rising in the east. Ancestral sacrifices take place in the morning (see Pender-Cudlip 1974: 61–2).

The west, on the other hand, is inauspicious and commonly associated with death, downwards and decay. It is in this direction that *Mŭnyankalĩ* dies each evening. All Ihanzu graves have an east–west orientation and the head is invariably placed to the west. People sometimes suggest that this is so that the dead can return to the Island of Ukerewe in Lake Victoria, the long-claimed homeland of the Ihanzu people (Kohl-Larsen 1943: 194).[22] When the winds occasionally cause rains to fall from the west, men and women comment that these are bad rains (*mbula mbĩ*) that bring aphids, lightning and other destructive forces. And the rainshrine is closed each year in the evening, when the sun is setting. (The north–south axis provides secondary spatial references and is symbolically much less elaborate).

What is noteworthy about people's focus in ritual on east–west spatial references, and the way they understand *Mŭnyankalĩ's* movements along that axis, is that both genders are always present. There is never a time – in the daily cycle, in the individual life-cycle or in the larger cosmic movement between the living and the dead – when male and female are apart. Female and male are found at all times in the east and the west, in this world and the next. This gender ideal is purposively reflected in the offering's seating arrangements (Figure 2.1). (Seating arrangements in these rites are doubly determined in the sense that women always sit in and around the female kitchen and hearth, while men normally sit in the male cattle enclosure). It is this gendered cosmic congruency, where male and female are distinctive but always together, to which all addresses to *Mŭnyankalĭ* and his wives refer.

Also evident in the content of these addresses is the fact that both male and female spirits are appeased (Adam 1963: 21). Unlike in some areas of Africa where only men become ancestral spirits (Jacobson-Widding 1990), or where male and female spirits are seemingly dissolved into a genderless collectivity (Bloch 1987: 326–8), in Ihanzu both men's and women's spirits (*alŭngŭ*; sing, *mŭlŭngŭ*) remain differentiated as they move from this world into the next. Once there, gendered spirits are said to live out their deaths doing more or less what they did while alive: herding and hunting, farming and fishing, drinking and dancing, singing and socializing. Male and female spirits are generally said to co-operate in the underworld (*ŭlŭngŭ*). When they intervene in this world to afflict or heal the living, they invariably do so jointly. There is no apparent tendency in Ihanzu for maternal or paternal spirits to be any more troublesome, nor do male and female spirits trouble the living with different sorts of afflictions (cf. McKnight 1967). Rather, in Ihanzu, male and female spirits must be addressed together, as is clear from the transcriptions above, and they are commonly asked to work together (e.g. line 40) to heal the afflicted.

Beyond this, the sequence of addresses is itself suggestive. Granddaughter and grandson make all addresses jointly, but never simultaneously. The grandson must go first, the granddaughter follows, emphasizing once again the idealized gender ordering and their co-operation. Of all the addresses made, three take on particular significance: first, the address made by tossing meat to the cardinal points (pp. 55–60); second, the one made using the whisk and beer (pp. 62–4); and third, the address on the final morning during which meat and stiff porridge are tossed at the same time (pp. 64–5).

The first of these, *kŭtagangĭla*, is made by tossing roasted meat which, as we have already seen is masculine. If meat in general is male-coded because of its associations with men's subsistence activities, it is, in this context, further male-coded through roasting, a process that removes from the flesh the soft, watery, fatty and hence feminine bits, while simultaneously creating a hard, dry and lean male meat. The second notable address of the offering, *kŭlonga shalo*, is always made with beer and is therefore feminine. Once again, grain is female-coded and, whether offered as beer or stiff porridge, is doubly feminine for its soft and wet constitution. 'Natural' male (flesh) and female (grains) are transformed into 'cultural' male (meat) and female (beer or porridge). Thus, the sequence of these addresses mirrors the idealized relationship between the genders. The last significant address, made on the final day of the offering, is made by tossing a piece of meat and stiff porridge together. As before, male (meat) precedes female (porridge), this time not in separate addresses but within the same address. The overall sequence of addresses thus broadly conforms to the ideal state of gender relations: the first is male; the second is female; the third is male-female or dual-gendered, but with male still preceding female. Matters become more complicated when we consider the actual roles (and genders) of ritual participants.

Ritual participants

Grandchildren featured centrally throughout this offering, as they do in all such offerings. From beginning to end, from initiating the offering to the closing ceremonies, the grandchildren must jointly labour at all tasks. Without these grandchildren, men and women often told me, the offering would undoubtedly fail to please the spirits and, thus, fail to heal the afflicted animals. Perhaps even more telling were the remarks made when I enquired into the possibility of either two grandsons, or two granddaughters, conducting these rites. Quite simply, this was seen as a logical impossibility. The rites would fail. The ultimate success of ancestral offerings is dependent upon male and female working together. But it is not just differently gendered grandchildren that are at issue.

We have already seen how the various ancestral addresses are themselves gender coded. Yet, of particular interest is the fact that, although ideal gender relations are acted out in these addresses, it is *not* the case that the grandson makes 'male' addresses while the granddaughter makes 'female' ones. Cosmic gender categories, in other words, are not necessarily linked directly to men's and women's bodies. What we find instead is two opposite gendered grandchildren, co-operating and working together to offer to the spirits each gender separately. Thus, the first address, although made by a man and woman, is a masculine address. The second address, by the same token, is made by both genders, but is feminine. Nonetheless within each individual address, the grandson always precedes the granddaughter. Male and female, as ideal categories, are therefore combined in multiple and somewhat complicated ways, but always alluding to the same ideational system of gender complementarity. The grandchildren's other ritual activities confirm this.

One of their central tasks is to light the ritual fire, a feat they accomplish with the aid of a firedrill and hearth. The ritual fire and firesticks, both of which drew such attention in this offering and in others like it, are seen as transformative agents and are commonly used as metaphors for sexual intercourse. The ritual firesticks themselves, in fact, provide an apt metaphor for the powers of the complementary combination of masculine and feminine principles of a gendered Ihanzu universe.

The firedrill that is twirled round is active and determined and, for this reason, male; the short, stationary piece of wood with a hole in it, the hearth, is passive and thus female (cf. Århem 1985: 13; Jacobson-Widding 1990: 68).[23] An elderly Ihanzu man from Matongo village, in an unsolicited remark, put it this way:

The long fire stick (kilĩndĩ) and the short one (kiziga) are like a man and his wife. The one on top is male; the one underneath is female. Can one start a fire without the other? No. But if they work together, both of them, fire is born.

The point of interest, once again, is that gender is not only about bodies. Firedrills and hearths are also gendered and capable of effecting transformation – in this case, they produce fire – in much the same way that male and female in other realms unite as equals to bring about change. Furthermore, the gendered bodies of the grandchildren cannot be linked directly and unproblematically to gendered firesticks. It will be recalled that the grandson made the first address, holding and spinning the male firedrill as he did so. But he soon swapped genders with the granddaughter, allowing her to spin the 'male' firedrill while he held the female hearth firmly in place. Thus, two (embodied) genders perform two (disembodied) genders, the former not always corresponding with the latter. Men perform male and female; women perform female and male.

Now, an obvious question that still demands attention is, why grandchildren? What distinguishes the grandchild–grandparent relationship from other possible relationships and makes it relevant in the context of ancestral offerings? To answer this requires a cursory examination of this relationship.

In Ihanzu, the grandparent–grandchild relationship is characterised by easiness and mild teasing (*maheko*),[24] 'affection and equality' (Adam 1963: 23). Grandparents do not discipline their grandchildren but instead leave this to the children's parents. Grandmothers often look after their grandchildren when they are young. And children may spend extended periods of time living with their grandparents when parents leave Ihanzu to do migrant labour, for example. Children, also, are commonly named after their grandparents.

Grandparents and grandchildren often refer to each other as siblings (*aheu* or *ng'waitu*) and, as these labels imply, the relationship is marked by an equality that is never found, for instance, in parent–child relationships (cf. Turner 1955). Moreover, given that grandchildren and grandparents are seen as structurally equivalent, it logically follows that grandsons may woo their grandmothers and vice versa; just as granddaughters may court their grandfathers and vice versa. There is, in fact, a great deal of sexual joking between grandparents and grandchildren along these lines, usually to the effect that a grandson is scheming to steal 'his' rightful wife (i.e. his own grandmother) away from his grandfather (cf. Beidelman 1997: 63).

The grandparent–grandchild relationship thus presents itself as an ideal one for ancestral offerings in a way that other relationships simply cannot. For one, it is the most blatantly 'sexual' relationships, albeit in a joking manner. A husband–wife relationship might of course be an alternative choice, but this relationship is not always marked by the same notion of equality between partners as is evident in the grandparent–grandchild relationship. As ancestral offerings require, then, the grandparent–grandchildren relationship offers a model of gendered entities that can conjoin sexually as equals. There is still one more way, too, that this relationship is made appropriate for ancestral offerings.

It will be recalled that both grandchildren together initiated all ancestral activities during the offering. At the same time the 'grandparent' – in this instance, the chief – initiated nothing. He spent most of his time sitting in the doorway of his house. As is invariably the case, '[t]he chief himself played a passive role at this time, as throughout the other rites' (Adam 1963: 21) while the grandchildren took the leading role. In non-royal offerings the pattern is the same: grandchildren are active, those for whom the ritual is being conducted are passive.

This suggests that ritual participants are once again playing on gendered themes. First, the two differentially gendered grandchildren, given their active roles, become symbolically male. Simultaneously, the 'grandparent' remained passive throughout the offering, making him symbolically female. As with firesticks and other things gendered, male acts upon passive female. Grandparents and grandchildren may thus combine as differentially gendered equals, even though the gender of the ritual performers does not neatly coincide with the gender they are performing.

One of the last notable events of the entire ritual sequence is when senior women and men drink ancestral beer inside the house. People make much of this seemingly inconsequential and semi-private affair. The focus of attention is two special long-necked, beer-filled calabashes, one tended by the grandson, the other by the granddaughter. Such ritual calabashes are referred to as *mŭmbŭ*, the term also used, intriguingly but perhaps not surprisingly, for the womb (cf. Kaare, this volume). Thus the beer that flows from these gendered calabash-wombs is analogous to the waters that flow from a woman during childbirth (*mazĩ a mŭmbŭ*) – both evoke and evince, so it seems, the successful combination of the Ihanzu cultural categories 'male' and 'female'. That such 'births' take place inside the house, rather than out, is only proper. Consuming beer inside the house is thus the final display of the abilities of the living to join the genders in appropriate ways.

CONCLUDING REMARKS

In final analysis, what the spirits appear to be asking for in these ancestral offerings is a ritual demonstration – a performance, if you will – of the appropriate ordering of gender relations among the living. The living, in other words, are asked by the dead to 'do gender' through ritual. And ritual performers do just that: they act out and conjoin in a complementary fashion 'male' and 'female' through a complex series of rites. These rites are, above all else, a cosmic performance *of* gender. The content, referents and sequence of ancestral addresses, together with the gendered people who make those addresses, the ritual fire-starting implements and men's and women's participation in these rites, all admit to myriad possibilities of gendering, degendering and regendering in an apparent effort to combine, in appropriate ways, masculine and feminine elements of a thoroughly gendered cosmos. In this case we see that 'doing gender' is not in the main about men and women, nor is it about men's and women's bodies. Rather, the Ihanzu are positioning themselves, through ritual action, as the central actors in a cosmic drama on gender complementarity. By acting out the principle of gender complementarity in the world of the living, ritual participants hope to spur those in the world of the dead into action. Only when the (gendered) spirits see that the living can join the genders in the proper way will they rejoice and, by 'working together' themselves, heal the afflicted animals. Through the act of joining male and female, ritual participants aim to gain access to the divine powers of the universe, and in so doing, transform their world for the better.

NOTES

1 Any number of early works might be used to support this point. See, for example, Schapera (1940), Richards (1939; 1956), Turner (1957), and Radcliffe-Brown and Forde (1950). Some early ethnographies were produced jointly by husband and wife teams, the latter concentrating 'upon magic and religion, family life, and women's activities' while the former dedicated his efforts to 'law and political organization, history and man's activities' (Krige and Krige 1943: xiv; also 1954).

2 A much neglected but important source of information on these and related topics are the numerous articles in the journal, *African Women*; this journal began in 1954 and, in 1963, broadened its geographic scope to become *Women Today*.

3 The number of volumes produced on women in Africa, especially since the early 1970s, is immense. For some of the seminal texts see Paulme (1971), Hafkin and Bay (1976), Robertson and Berger (1986), Stichter and Parpart (1988) and Parpart and Staudt (1989). See also the special issue of the *African Studies Review*, 'Women in Africa', vol. 18 (1975). For a reasonable synopsis of some of the more important works on women and gender in sub-Saharan Africa written primarily in the 1970s and 1980s see Potash (1989).

4 To be sure, the issue of *how*, exactly, women were represented, especially in much of the early material, remains problematic and became a topic of much debate inside and outside of feminist circles from the 1970s (H.L. Moore 1988).

5 Butler's central problematic is gender while the topic is notably absent from the works of Bourdieu and de Certeau. The latters' contribution, which to some extent meshes neatly with performance theory, is their attention to everyday, embodied practices (cf. Giddens 1979). Butler's approach to 'gender performativity' has been widely discussed and heavily criticized. Yet even her most severe critics seem to acknowledge the importance of her critique (e.g. Assister 1996; Hood-Williams and Cealey 1998; Hughes and Witz 1997). For an excellent overview of the literature on performance theory and gender from an anthropological perspective, see Morris (1995).

6 The fieldwork on which this chapter is based was carried out in Ihanzu, north-central Tanzania, between 1993 and 1995. For financial support I am grateful to the US National Institute of Health, the London School of Economics and Political Science, the British Government's ORS Awards Scheme, the Malinowski Memorial Research Fund, the Irwin Fund and the Royal Anthropological Institute's Radcliffe-Brown Trust Fund.

7 Literally, *ipolyo* (plur, *mapolyo*) means 'a cooling'. There are two types of *mapolyo*: for illnesses (*ipolyo la ndwala*) and for rain (*ipolyo la mbula*). This chapter focuses on the former, though the two types are virtually identical in structure and symbolic content. *Mapolyo* have been carried out in Ihanzu, Iramba and Iambi for many years. When he was in Ihanzu in 1911, Erich Obst attended one such offering to cure his malaria. His exceedingly detailed observations are by all measures accurate and make clear that, as far as these rites go, things have changed very little since the turn of the century (Obst 1912: 115–17; also Kohl-Larsen 1943: 304–5; Adam 1963: 21–3).

8 This case study is based on an offering that took place on 26 November 1993, and events leading up to it. I have attended a total of nineteen similar offerings at homes and at sacred clan sites around Ihanzu and Iramba, most of them for personal afflictions. Furthermore, I recorded the details of many additional offerings and have had numerous discussions with men and women about the various rites and the symbolism in them.

9 During some offerings, more grandsons or more granddaughters participate, though this is not always the case. For royal *Anyampanda wa Kirumi* offerings like this one, it is normal that three grandchildren participate: a grandson and granddaughter who are themselves of this royal clan-section and, simultaneously, the grandchildren of it; and a grandson of the *Anyansuli wa Kingwele* clan-section who is also from this latter clan-section. The latter grandson represents the *Anyansuli* spirits, the former owners of the rain. The *Anyampanda* and *Anyansuli* are considered 'brother' (*aheu*) clans, and are said to have once been one and the same.

10 On this occasion he collected *mũlama* (*Combretum molle*), *mũmbĩlĩlĩ* (*Entada* sp.), *ipolyo* (*Rhoicissus tridentata*) and *mũhingiha* (*Boscia angustifalia*), all of which are commonly used for such royal offerings. The Ihanzu divide trees and shrubs into two general categories: cool and hot. The former are good for rain offerings, the latter are not.

The nearby Gogo similarly divide trees into two distinct categories that correspond fairly exactly to the Ihanzu divisions (Rigby 1966: 9). The Sandawe, like the Ihanzu, have a class of cool trees (Ten Raa 1969: 41) as do the Turu (Jellicoe 1978: 80) and Maasai (Spencer 1988: 205).

11 This sorghum is always white, never red. It is the colour, not the variety, that is ritually significant. Red is inauspicious and is likely to anger the spirits and/or bring on lightning strikes.

12 At all ancestral offerings I attended or enquired into, men and women sat in distinct gender-specific groups. Oral sources, as well as early written and photographic sources, make it clear that this has long been the case (cf. Obst 1912: 116, n2).

13 The branches were from *mŭlama* (*Combretum molle*), *mŭmbĭlĭlĭ* (*Entada* sp.) and *metembwetembwe* trees.

14 According to elderly informants and early sources, sacrificial animals used to be suffocated to death (Obst 1912: 116). Slitting their throats is a relatively recent ritual innovation which probably began either in the late 1930s under Chief Sagilu, the first Muslim Ihanzu chief, or under Chief Gunda in the 1940s who was also a Muslim. Many elders told me that they recalled attending offerings in their youths during which the sacrificial animals, once tied to a tree by one leg, simply died on their own accord, having been taken directly by the spirits, an old story indeed (Kohl-Larsen 1943: 168).

15 The former is made from the *mŭtala* tree, the latter from the *ipolyo* tree (*Rhoicissus tridentata*). Fires at ancestral offerings are always started with firesticks but in everyday life Tanzanian matches are the norm.

16 These included the sheep's liver (*itĭma*), lungs (*mapŭpŭ*), spleen (*ihela*), intestines (*mala*) and a large membrane that lies under the chest meat covering the front of the rib cage (*ilugali*).

17 This series of addresses is sometimes carried out prior to the divination session.

18 At some offerings I attended, though not at this one, an additional piece of meat was thrown directly down as well.

19 There are several terms for 'sun' and 'God'. In ancestral addresses the sun is always referred to as *Mŭnyankalĭ*, though informants and early sources report that the term *Lyoa* or *Dyiowa* was formerly used (Obst 1912: 115). Today, *Lyoa* is the word for 'sun' in everyday contexts. God, on the other hand, is referred to as *Itunda*, a term that elderly informants claim is of Iramba origin, its advent unmysteriously coinciding with the advent of Christianity in Ihanzu in the early 1930s (Pender-Cudlip c.1974: 3ff). *Itunda* is used interchangeably with the Swahili term for God, *Mungu*.

20 *Igana* literally means 'one-hundred' but *igana* is also a specific type of female rain, one which is slow and lasts a long time.

21 These particular calabashes are royal property, and many lineages own such calabashes which they display on the final day of ancestral offerings. *Mŭmbŭ*, the word for long-necked calabash, is also the word for 'womb'. The white beads worn by the calabash are deeply

significant for the people of Ihanzu, who were themselves long ago dubbed 'The Bead People' (*Perlenvolk*) (Obst 1923: 222) for the extraordinary number of such beads men and women wore on their bodies. These beads are today associated both with the ancestors who wore them and with girls' initiation rites where they are worn by many.

22 Hitchens, 'Mkalama Annual Report 1919/1920' (16 April 1920), p. 4, Tanzania National Archives, doc. 1733/1. An unsigned entry in the Mkalama District Book made around 1926 confirms this: 'Tradition states unanimously that the tribe formerly inhabited Ukerewe Island' (p. 18).

23 As Beidelman notes of another Tanzanian group: 'For Kaguru, kindling a fire clearly alludes to sexual intercourse. In making fire with firestick, Kaguru use an active stick of hardwood and a passive stick of soft and easily combustible wood. The passive stick, the one drilled, is the female' (1997: 205). In spite of the manifest symbolic similarities with the Ihanzu, it appears that the Kaguru construct fire-making as a domain which implies male domination (Beidelman 1997: 205).

24 These teasing relations (*maheko*) are categorically different from the more extreme joking relations (*isoi*) shared between members of particular clans (Sanders 1998).

REFERENCES

Adam, V. (1963) 'Rain making rites in Ihanzu', conference proceedings from the East African Institute of Social Research, Makerere College.

Århem, K. (1985) *The Symbolic World of the Maasai Homestead.* Working Papers in African Studies 10, African Studies Programme, University of Uppsala.

Assister, A. (1996) *Enlightened Women* (London: Routledge).

Barr, S.S.M. (1946) 'Mureri, the rain goddess', *NADA*, 23: 60–2.

Bazeley, W.S. (1940) 'Manyika headwomen', *NADA*, 17: 3–5.

Beidelman, T.O. (1964) 'Pig (*guluwe*): an essay on Ngulu sexual symbolism and ceremony', *Southwestern Journal of Anthropology*, 20: 359–92.

Beidelman, T.O. (1993) *Moral Imagination in Kaguru Modes of Thought* (Washington DC: Smithsonian Institution Press).

Beidelman, T.O. (1997) *The Cool Knife: Imagery of Gender, Sexuality, and Moral Education in Kaguru Initiation Ritual* (Washington DC: Smithsonian Institution Press).

Blacking, J. (1969a) 'Songs, dances, mimes and symbolism of Venda girls' initiation schools, part 1: Vhusha', *African Studies*, 28 (1): 3–35.

Blacking, J. (1969b) 'Songs, dances, mimes and symbolism of Venda girls' initiation schools, part 2: Milayo', *African Studies*, 28 (2): 67–118.

Blacking, J. (1969c) 'Songs, dances, mimes and symbolism of Venda girls' initiation schools, part 3: Domba', *African Studies*, 28 (3): 149–99.

Blacking, J. (1969d) 'Songs, dances, mimes and symbolism of Venda girls' initiation schools, part 4: the great *domba* song', *African Studies*, 28 (4): 215–66.

Bloch, M. (1987) 'Descent and sources of contradiction in representations of women and kinship' in J.F. Collier and S. Yanagisako (eds) *Gender and Kinship: Essays toward a Unified Analysis* (Stanford: Stanford University Press).

Bourdieu, P. (1977) *Outline of a Theory of Practice* (Cambridge: Cambridge University Press).

Bourdieu, P. (1990) *The Logic of Practice*, translated by R. Nice (Stanford: Stanford University Press).

Brain, J.L. (1978) 'Symbolic rebirth: the *mwali* rite among the Luguru of eastern Tanzania', *Africa*, 48: 176–88.

Broch-Due, V. (1993) 'Making meaning out of matter: perception of sex, gender and bodies among the Turkana', in V. Broch-Due, I. Rudie and T. Bleie (eds) *Carved Flesh/Cast Selves: Gendered Symbols and Social Practices* (Oxford: Berg).

Bujra, J.M. (1975) 'Women "entrepreneurs" of early Nairobi', *Canadian Journal of African Studies*, 9 (2): 213–34.

Butler, J. (1990) *Gender Trouble: Feminism and the Subversion of Identity* (London: Routledge).

Butler, J. (1993) *Bodies that Matter: on the Discursive Limits of 'Sex'* (London: Routledge).

Caplan, P. (1989) 'Perceptions of gender stratification', *Africa*, 59: 196–208.

Chege, J. (1993) 'The politics of gender and fertility regulation in Kenya: a case study of the Igembe', PhD thesis, Lancaster University.

Child, H.C. (1958) 'Family and tribal structure and status of women', *NADA*, 35: 65–70.

Cohen, R. (1977) 'Oedipus Rex and Regina: the Queen Mother in Africa', *Africa*, 47: 14–30.

Collier, J.F. and S.J. Yanagisako (1987) 'Introduction' in J.F. Collier and S.J. Yanagisako (eds) *Gender and Kinship: Essays Toward a Unified Analysis* (Stanford: Stanford University Press).

Crehan, K. (1997) *The Fractured Community: Landscapes of Power and Gender in Rural Zambia* (Berkeley: University of California).

Culwick, G.M. (1939) 'New ways for old in the treatment of adolescent African girls', *Africa*, 12: 425–32.

De Certeau, M. (1984) *The Practice of Everyday Life*, translated by S. Rendall (Berkeley: University of California Press).

Dobkin, M. (1968) 'Colonialism and the legal status of women in francophone Africa', *Cahiers d'Études Africaines*, 8 (3): 390–405.

Driberg, J.H. (1932) 'The status of women among the Nilotics and Nilo-Hamites', *Africa*, 5 (4): 404–21.

Drucker-Brown, S. (1993) 'Mamprusi witchcraft, subversion and changing gender relations', *Africa*, 63 (4): 531–49.

Durkheim, E. and M. Mauss (1963) *Primitive Classification*, translated by R. Needham (London: Cohen & West).

Emanatian, M. (1996) 'Everyday metaphors of lust and sex in Chagga', *Ethos*, 24: 195–236.

Feldman-Savelsberg, P. (1994) 'Plundered kitchens and empty wombs:

fear of infertility in the Cameroonian Grassfields', *Social Science and Medicine*, 39: 463–74.

Feldman-Savelsberg, P. (1995) 'Cooking inside: kinship and gender in Bangangte idioms of marriage and procreation', *American Ethnologist*, 22: 483–501.

Giddens, A. (1979) *Central Problems in Social Theory* (Cambridge: Cambridge University Press).

Glaser, C. (1992) 'The mark of Zorro: sexuality and gender relations in the Tsotsi subculture on the Witwatersrand', *African Studies*, 51 (1): 47–67.

Gluckman, M. (1935) 'Zulu women in heocultural ritual', *Bantu Studies* 9: 255–71.

Goody, J. and J. Buckley (1973) 'Inheritance and women's labour in Africa', *Africa*, 43: 108–21.

Greene, S.E. (1996) *Gender, Ethnicity, and Social Change on the Upper Slave Coast: A History of the Anlo-Ewe* (London: James Currey).

Hafkin, N.J. and E.G. Bay (eds) (1976) *Women in Africa: Studies in Social and Economic Change* (Stanford: Stanford University Press).

Håkansson, N.T. (1994) 'The detachability of women: gender and kinship in processes of socioeconomic change among the Gusii of Kenya', *American Ethnologist*, 21: 516–38.

Harrison, S. (1985) 'Ritual hierarchy and secular equality in a Sepik River village', *American Ethnologist*, 12: 413–26.

Herbert, E.W. (1993) *Iron, Gender, and Power: Rituals of Transformation in African Societies* (Bloomington: Indiana University Press).

Hill, J.D. (1984) 'Social equality and ritual hierarchy: the Arawakan Wakuénai of Venezuela', *American Ethnologist*, 11: 528–44.

Hodgson, D.L. and S. McCurdy (1996) 'Wayward wives, misfit mothers, disobedient daughters: wicked women and the reconfiguration of gender in Africa', *Canadian Journal of African Studies*, 30 (1): 1–9.

Holas, B. (1953) 'Décès d'une femme Guerzé (Cercle de Nzérékoré, Guinée Française)', *Africa*, 23 (2): 145–55.

Holy, L. (1985) 'Fire, meat, and children: the Berti myth, male dominance, and female power' in J. Overing (ed.) *Reason and Morality* (London: Tavistock).

Hood-Williams, J. and W. Cealey (1998) 'Trouble with gender', *Sociological Review*, 46 (1): 73–94.

Howell, P.P. (1953) 'Observations on the Shilluk of the Upper Nile, customary law: marriage and the violation of rights in women', *Africa*, 23 (2): 94–109.

Hughes, A. and A. Witz (1997) 'Feminism and the matter of bodies', *Body and Society*, 3 (1): 47–60.

Hunter, M. (1933) 'The effects of contact with Europeans on the status of Pondo women', *Africa*, 6 (3): 259–76.

Jacobson-Widding, A. (1990) 'The fertility of incest' in A. Jacobson-Widding and W. van Beek (eds) *The Creative Communion: African Folk Models of Fertility and the Regeneration of Life* (Uppsala: Acta Universitatis Upsaliensis).

Jaques, A.A. (1934) 'Genealogy of male and female chiefs of a Sotho tribe', *Bantu Studies*, 8 (4): 377–82.

Jeffreys, M.D.W. (1956) 'The Nyama society of the Ibibio women', *African Studies*, 15 (1): 15–28.

Jellicoe, M. (1978) *The Long Path: Social Change in Tanzania* (Nairobi: East African Publishing House).

Kaplan, F.E.S. (ed.) (1997) *Queens, Queen Mothers, Priestesses, and Power: Case Studies in African Gender* (New York: New York Academy of Sciences).

Kohl-Larsen, L. v. (1943) *Auf den Spuren des Vormenschen* (Stuttgart: Strecher und Schröder).

Kollehlon, K.T. (1984) 'Women's work role and fertility in Liberia', *Africa*, 54 (4): 31–45.

Kratz, C.A. (1990) 'Sexual solidarity and the secrets of sight and sound: shifting gender relations and their ceremonial constitution', *American Ethnologist*, 17 (3): 449–69.

Kratz, C.A. (1994) *Affecting Performance: Meaning, Movement, and Experience in Okiek Women's Initiation* (Washington DC: Smithsonian Institution Press).

Krige, E.J. and J.D. Krige (1943) *The Realm of a Rain-Queen: A Study of the Pattern of Lovedu Society* (London: Oxford University Press).

Krige, J.D. and E.J. Krige (1954) 'The Lovedu of the Transvaal' in D. Forde (ed.) *African Worlds: Studies in the Cosmological Ideas and Social Values of African Peoples* (Oxford: Oxford University Press).

Lewin, J. (1959) 'The legal status of African women', *Race Relations Journal*, 26 (4): 152–59.

Little, K.L. (1948) 'The changing position of women in the Sierra Leone Protectorate', *Africa* 18 (1): 1–17.

McKnight, J.D. (1967) 'Extra-descent group ancestor cults in African societies', *Africa*, 37: 1–21.

Mandeville, E. (1979) 'Poverty, work and the financing of single women in Kampala', *Africa*, 49: 42–52.

Manicom, L. (1992) 'Ruling relations: rethinking state and gender in South African history', *Journal of African History*, 33: 441–65.

Meigs, A. (1990) 'Multiple gender ideologies and statuses' in P.R. Sanday and R.G. Goodenough (eds) *Beyond the Second Sex: New Directions in the Anthropology of Gender* (Philadelphia: University of Pennsylvania Press).

Moore, H.L. (1988) *Feminism and Anthropology* (Cambridge, Polity).

Moore, S.F. (1976) 'The secret of the men: a fiction of Chagga initiation and its relation to the logic of Chagga symbolism', *Africa*, 46: 357–70.

Moore, S.F. and P. Puritt (1977) *The Chagga and Meru of Tanzania* (London: International African Institute).

Morris, R.C. (1995) 'All made up: performance theory and the new anthropology of sex and gender', *Annual Review of Anthropology*, 24: 567–92.

Murray, C. (1975) 'Sex, smoking and the shades: a Sotho symbolic idiom' in M.G. Whisson and M. West (eds) *Religion and Social Change in Southern Africa: Anthropological Essays in Honour of Monica Wilson* (Cape Town: David Philip).

Obst, E. (1912) 'Die Landschaften Issansu und Iramba (Deutsch-Osta-frika)', *Mitteilungen der Geographischen Gesellschaft in Hamburg*, 26: 108–32.

Obst, E. (1923) 'Das abflußlose Rumpfschollenland im nordöstlichen Deutsch-Ostafrika' (Teil II), *Mitteilungen der Geographischen Gesellschaft in Hamburg*, 35: 1–330.

Ortner, S. (1996) 'Gender hegemonies' in *Making Gender: The Politics and Erotics of Culture* (Boston: Beacon).

Parpart, J.L. and K.A. Staudt (eds) (1989) *Women and the State in Africa* (Boulder: Lynne Rineer).

Paulme, D. (ed.) (1971) *Women of Tropical Africa* (Berkeley: University of California Press).

Peletz, M.G. (1994) 'Neither reasonable nor responsible: contrasting representations of masculinity in a Malay society', *Cultural Anthropology*, 9 (2): 135–78.

Pender-Cudlip. P. (1974) 'The Iramba and their neighbours' in K. Ingham (ed.) *Foreign Relations of African States* (London: Butterworths).

Pender-Cudlip, P. (*c.*1974) 'God and the sun: some notes on Iramba religious history', unpublished manuscript held at the British Institute in Eastern Africa, Nairobi.

Perlman, M.L. (1966) 'The changing status and role of women in Toro (Western Uganda)', *Cahiers d'Études Africaines*, 6 (4): 564–91.

Perlman, M.L. (1969) 'Law and the status of women in Uganda: a systematic comparison between the Ganda and the Toro', *Tropical Man*, 2: 60–106.

Perrot, C.-H. (1979) 'Femmes et pouvoir politique dans l'ancienne société anyi-ndenye (Côte d'Ivoire)', *Cahiers d'Études Africaines*, 19 (1–4): 219–23.

Potash, B. (1989) 'Gender relations in sub-Saharan Africa' in S. Morgen (ed.) *Gender and Anthropology: Critical Reviews for Research and Teaching* (Washington DC: American Anthropological Association).

Radcliffe-Brown, A. R. and D. Forde (Eds) (1950) *African Systems of Kinship and Marriage* (London: Oxford University Press).

Rangeley, W.H.J. (1952) 'Two Nyasaland rain shrines: Makewana – the mother of all people', *Nyasaland Journal*, 5 (2): 31–50.

Richards, A. (1939) *Land, Labour and Diet in Northern Rhodesia* (London: Oxford University Press).

Richards, A. (1956) *Chisungu: A Girl's Initiation Ceremony among the Bemba of Zambia* (London: Routledge).

Rigby, P. (1966) 'Dual symbolic classification among the Gogo of central Tanzania', *Africa*, 36 (1): 1–17.

Rigby, P. (1968) 'Some Gogo rituals of "purification": an essay on social and moral categories' in E.R. Leach (ed.) *Dialectic in Practical Religion* (Cambridge: Cambridge University Press).

Ritzenthaler, R.E. (1960) 'Anlu: a women's uprising in the British Cameroons', *African Studies*, 19 (3): 151–6.

Robertson, C. and J. Berger (eds) (1986) *Women and Class in Africa* (New York: Africana).

Rosenthal, J. (1997) 'Foreign tongues and domestic bodies: gendered cultural regions and regionalized sacred flows' in M. Grosz-Ngaté and O.H. Kokole (eds) *Gendered Encounters: Challenging Cultural Boundaries and Social Hierarchies in Africa* (London: Routledge).

Saakse, J. (1952) 'The visit to Mujaji the Rain-Queen', *NADA*, 29: 83–6.

Sanders, T. (1997) 'Rainmaking, gender and power in Ihanzu, Tanzania, 1885–1995', PhD thesis, London School of Economics.

Sanders, T. (1998) 'Making children, making chiefs: gender, power and ritual legitimacy', *Africa*, 68 (2): 238–62.

Schapera, I. (1940) *Married Life in an African Tribe* (London: Faber & Faber).

Schwartz, A. (1979) 'Images de la femme Kru à travers une cérémonie de funérailles (Côte d'Ivoire)', *Cahiers d'Études Africaines*, 19 (1–4): 323–7.

Shope, J.J. (1994) 'Separate but equal: Durkheim's response to the woman question', *Sociological Inquiry*, 64: 23–6.

Silberbauer, G.B. (1963) 'Marriage and the girl's puberty ceremony of the G/wi Bushmen', *Africa*, 33: 12–24.

Spencer, P. (1988) *The Maasai of Matapato: A Study of Rituals of Rebellion* (Bloomington: Indiana University Press).

Stichter, S.B. and J.L. Parpart (eds) (1988) *Patriarchy and Class: African Women in the Home and the Workforce* (Boulder: Westview).

Strathern, M. (1981) 'Self-interest and the social good: some implications of Hagen gender imagery' in S. Ortner and H. Whitehead (eds) *Sexual Meanings: The Cultural Construction of Gender and Sexuality* (Cambridge: Cambridge University Press).

Strathern, M. (1988) *The Gender of the Gift: Problems with Women and Problems with Society in Melanesia* (Berkeley: University of California Press).

Strathern, M. (1993) 'Making incomplete' in V. Broch-Due, I. Rudie and T. Bleie (eds) *Carved Flesh/Cast Selves: Gendered Symbols and Social Practices* (Oxford: Berg).

Sunseri, T. (1997) 'Famine and wild pigs: gender struggles and the outbreak of the Majimaji war in Uzaramo (Tanzania)', *Journal of African History*, 38: 235–59.

Taylor, C. (1990) 'Condoms and cosmology: the "fractal" person and sexual risk in Rwanda', *Social Science and Medicine*, 31 (9): 1023–8.

Ten Raa, E. (1969) 'The moon as a symbol of life and fertility in Sandawe thought', *Africa*, 39: 24–53.

Turner, V.W. (1955) 'The spatial separation of adjacent genealogical generations in Ndembu village structure', *Africa*, 25: 121–37.

Turner, V.W. (1957) *Schism and Continuity in an African Society: A Study of Ndembu Village Life* (Manchester: Manchester University Press).

Van Allen, J. (1972) ' "Sitting on a man": colonialism and the lost political institutions of Igbo women', *Canadian Journal of African Studies*, 6 (2): 165–81.

Van Allen, J. (1976) ' "Aba riots" or "Igbo women's war"? Ideology, stratification and the invisibility of women' in N.J. Hafkin and E.G.

Bay (eds) *Women in Africa* (Stanford: Stanford University Press).

Vincent, J.-F. (1979) 'Place et pouvoir de la femme dans les montagnes Mofu (Nord-Cameroun)', *Cahiers d'Études Africaines*, 19 (1–4): 225–51.

Walker, C. (ed.) (1990) *Women and Gender in Southern Africa to 1945* (London: James Currey).

Wells, J.C. (1983) 'Why women rebel: a comparative study of South African women's resistance movements in Bloomfontein (1913) and Johannesburg (1958)', *Journal of Southern African Studies*, 10: 55–70.

Wentzel, D. (1944) 'The legal plight of the African woman', *Race Relations*, 11 (3–4): 66–9.

West, C. and D.H. Zimmerman (1987) 'Doing gender', *Gender and Society*, 1 (2): 125–51.

White, C.M.N. (1953) 'Conservatism and modern adaptation in Luvale female puberty ritual', *Africa*, 23: 15–24.

White, J.D. (1977) 'Amakusikasi: some notes on the queens and families of Mzilikazi and Lobengula', *NADA*, 11: 109–13.

CHAPTER 3

THE LION AT THE WATERHOLE

THE SECRETS OF LIFE AND DEATH IN CHEWA RITES DE PASSAGE

DEBORAH KASPIN

INTRODUCTION

When a Chewa girl undergoes puberty initiation, the most important lesson impressed upon her is the prohibition against sex
when she menstruates. The rule is conveyed in coded images as in
the following song:

> When your lover says, 'Where is my water?'
> You must say, 'When I went to the river to draw water,
> Lion cubs came and bit me.'
> When I ask you, 'What is biting you?'
> You say, 'What is biting me is menstruation.'

Women say that this song simply reminds the girl of the menstrual
prohibition, but it does several other things as well. First, it
provides her with a euphemistic way to tell her husband that she is
menstruating without actually saying 'menstruation' (*nkhole*), a
taboo word. The euphemism is the water pot that women keep
near their beds, so their husbands can bathe after sex. By
emptying and overturning the pot, a woman tells her husband that
sex is refused. Second, the song provides the girl with an image of
her body as a source and vehicle of power. The watering hole is
her belly whence sexual fluids and blood can flow. But if they flow
at the same time – if, that is, she has sex while she menstruates –
her lover will die. The image of predation conveys this warning
forcefully, for if a woman bleeds because a lion attacked her, the
man had better stay away lest he become its next victim.

This song is reminiscent of bodily representations throughout Africa which describe physiological processes through technological, economic and ecological metaphors: birth and death, gardening and cooking, hunting and warfare, rainfall and drought, all provide images of each other. The linkages appear not only in rites of passage (Richards 1995; Turner 1967, 1969), but also in rainmaking ritual (Kaspin 1990; 1996; Gelfand 1959; Sanders 1998; Schoffeleers 1992; Taylor 1993), curing practices (Devisch 1993; Taylor 1993; Turner 1968), theories of conception, place names, and other sites of productive practice. Following Durkheim (1965; also Durkheim and Mauss 1963), classic social anthropology explains these symbolisms by tracing them to a semantic source – social structure and its contradictions. Audrey Richards (1995) first drew Africanists' attention to girls' initiation as a site of the social creation of women, while Max Gluckman (1954) focused on rituals of rebellion as a means for restoring social cohesion. But Victor Turner (1968) most fully developed Durkheim's symbolic sociology by showing how elements of Ndembu social structure were represented in ecological and physiological symbols. Ndembu ritual used this lexicon of symbols to trace illness and infertility to breaches of social relations, and to correct their physical effects by encoding their social origin.

French structuralism inspired alternative approaches to body symbolisms which abandon the sociological template in order to grasp the implicit worldviews as systems *sui generis*. Marcel Griaule (1965) introduced us to the intellectually gifted Ogotemmeli who created a cosmology by tracing conceptual schemata from body to house to community to universe. Anita Jacobson-Widding (1979) sought a more general model by exploring the triadic logic of Bantu thought, using the colours red, black and white as an organizing rubric in ritual magic. Christopher Taylor (1993) found the sense of Rwandan calendrical ritual and curing practices in a cosmology of production based on the circulation and containment of life-generating fluids across several sites of productive practice. And Rene Devisch (1993) found a similar philosophy of life and rejuvenation among the Yaka for whom generative power is obtained from numerous sites of production and woven into the human body to achieve health and fertility.

The following analysis of Chewa life-cycle rites belongs to the second group, in so far as it seeks in ritual symbolisms, not the rules and ruptures of social structure, but a philosophy of life, death and renewal. This means treating each rite of passage not as a self-contained event, but as an element of a ritual *system*, an organic whole which generates its own universe of meaning. Minimally, the ritual system includes funerals and puberty initiations, the principal rites provided by the Nyau society. This is a secret association of men who disguise themselves as 'wild animals' (*zilombo*) and dance in village courtyards on these important ceremonial occasions. The question on which my analysis turns is a simple one: what is the relationship between the 'wild animals' of Nyau who perform in public, and the corpses and adolescents who are treated in private? The answer lies in the symbolic code which the public dances and private procedures share. Accordingly, men are predators, women are game, sexuality is predation, and the spilling of blood, whether in menstruation, childbirth or hunting, is the source of death and renewal (cf. Bloch 1992). Chewa rites of passage thus describe the transformation of the person through the metaphors of hunting and consumption, and suggest that life depends on the exchange of blood for blood, substance for substance, across human and animal realms. It is this symbolism of life and death that this chapter explores.

THE WORLD OF NYAU

Chewa life-cycle rites are carnivalistic occasions when people from a wide community assemble to eat, drink, and carouse, and to enjoy the often-hilarious dances in the village courtyard. While the assembly is engaged in this public spectacle, the ritual experts are in seclusion behind the scenes with boys, girls or new chiefs, engaged in the serious business of educating novices about their new life statuses. Although their paths cross infrequently, the participants in the public and private sides of the ceremony move in synchrony, their activities representing two parts of a single ritual format which underpins the ostensibly free-flowing character of the celebrations. At particular times, specific Nyau masks must appear in the village. And at particular times, the initiate must acquire certain objects, consume certain medicines, don certain decorations and come to the dance arena to be viewed by the public. These fixed elements reveal a subterranean symbolic field in which humans co-exist with animals, and the living with the dead.

This symbolic field is reflected in the spatial parameters that orient Nyau performance. They are the village, the graveyard and the bush. The village is the site of the dance arena (*bwalo*) where public dances are performed. It is owned by the village headman who invites Nyau to perform there. The graveyard is the site of the Nyau meeting place (*dambwe*) where members congregate, masks are made and stored, dances are rehearsed, and new members are initiated. And the bush is the site of several initiation sites where different kinds of game – Nyau and human – are captured.

These spatial referents are represented by the male officials of Nyau and by the female ritual experts. 'The man in the village' (*wakubwalo*) directs the dancers and drummers at the public meeting ground in the village. 'The man at the hiding place' (*wakudambwe*) directs the preparations of costumes and dances in the graveyard. The women ritual experts (*anamkhungwi*) conduct the private initiatory proceedings for girls and new chiefs. And all of them are directed by 'the man of the pathway' (*akunjira*) who is the principal in charge of Nyau. He co-ordinates the activities in each of the three locations, to ensure that the ceremony unfolds in proper sequence.

Nyau ritual also relies on certain organizational categories within its repertoire of masks. Here I refer not to particular masks, but to their general classifications. All Nyau masks are called 'wild animals' (*zilombo*), which are subdivided into two types, the wild animals of the day and the wild animals of the night. The daytime animals are primarily predators, scavengers and hunters. They include face masks and a body covering, but retain a human outline. Their costumes typically include animal skins and feathers, evidence of their predatory habits. In contrast the night-time masks are game animals. These are free-standing structures made of wicker and other vegetable products such as grass, maize husks, and sisal, and represent herbivores like the elephant, antelope and hare. Each is carried by one or more men who remain hidden within the basket-like structure.[1]

In each ritual, the private procedures performed in the grave-yard and bush are thematically linked to the public performances in the courtyard. These linkages reflect a series of exchanges transacted between Nyau and the spectators, and between the several worlds they represent. The graveyard and the courtyard are places of contact in the network of exchange, and the daytime and night-time animals – that is, the predators and game – represent respectively the agents and objects of exchange. This implies a corresponding division of the human world. While animals are made up of predators and prey, humans are made up of men who hunt and women whom men pursue. The exchange between human and animals worlds presupposes and reinforces the association of predators with men, and game with women.

The principles of complementarity between Nyau animals and human beings are played out throughout the ceremonies. For example, women dance and sing lascivious songs when the predatory Nyau dancers arrive in the village, while men remain subdued and silent. Later the women retreat when the game animals approach, while the men leap forward in pursuit of the animals. The special affinity of women for Nyau predators and men for Nyau game suggests an underlying attraction of opposites, and, correlatively, the identification of men with predators, and women with prey. These identifications are elaborated during the rites of passage, as the next section will detail. For now it is sufficient to note that masks are implicitly gendered by virtue of their physical shape: the predatory masks are recognizably male in outline, while the game masks are containers concealing men within their bodies like so many unborn children.

NYAU AND THE LIFE-CYCLE

Nyau dances are performed at funerals, puberty initiations and chiefs' installations. These rituals depict the person's transformation as a journey from one place to another, reminiscent of van Gennep's account of the territorial passage as the paradigmatic *rite de passage* (van Gennep 1972: 15–25). Each journey is not, however, complete in itself, for the several rites of passage represent several journeys which conjointly complete a circuit of exchange. Ultimately the passage from one phase of life to the next is an expression of the exchange of substance for substance, flesh for flesh, blood for blood, between human and animal realms.

Funeral rites

The funeral is the most straightforward depiction of the circuit of exchange. Funerals take place in two stages, the burial at death, and the commemoration several months later when the souls of the dead have completed their journey into the spirit world. The two rites together describe the transformation of the dead as an exchange of human for animal flesh between the village and

Nyau, with Nyau animals claiming the corpse at the burial and returning meat to the village at the commemoration.

During the burial rite, women remain in the village around the hut of the deceased to tend the body and offer comfort to the bereaved. They bathe the dead and wrap it in cloth; they keep a vigil over it at night to ward off vermin and witches; and they interject a light note by singing the songs and dances of pregnancy (*chisamba*). In the mean time the men go to the graveyard. There they prepare the coffin, dig the grave, and assemble the costumes of the Nyau creatures who will accompany them to the village. These include only the daytime masks, for only predators will come to the village when a body awaits burial.

When the men arrive in the village, the women's dances of pregnancy stop, and the Nyau dances of the dead begin. These are sexually provocative and often entertaining performances, during which some of the dancers enter the hut of the deceased to inspect the body. When the dances end, the men move into the hut to carry the body away. Women wail as the dead person is taken from them, and as they accompany the procession to the graveyard. But they stop at the mouth of the graveyard, while the men continue to the grave and inter the corpse.

During the burial rite only maize and leaves are eaten in the village, for this is the time when the wild animals receive their due, namely, the human carcass.[2] The debt is repaid months later during the commemoration rite which celebrates the arrival of the souls of the dead in the spirit world. Now the Nyau dancers return to the village, including both daytime and night-time masks. Among them is the Antelope, whose name, Kasiyamaliro, means 'the funeral is finished', and whose arrival heralds the fact that the journey of the deceased is finished. The Antelope is accompanied by the Elephant whose own epithet, Dzalanyama, means 'plenty of meat'. The appearance of these enormous game animals signifies that meat from the bush is returned in abundance. So while everyone ate maize and leaves when the predators of Nyau took the dead away, everyone now eats meat as the game animals of Nyau return.

Puberty initiations

Funerals are predicated on the premise that the village and Nyau are distinct worlds, brought together through death and consumption. At death, predators visit the village to collect the dead, and months later they return with game for their human hosts. The rites also place women and men at complementary locations within the circuit of exchange, and therefore in the processes of life and death. Women remain in the village and perform tasks reminiscent of their daily duties of childcare and food preparation, as they bathe and protect the body, and cook for the bereaved. Men, in turn, go to the graveyard where the tasks of digging the grave, preparing the coffin, and preparing the masks – the 'wild animals' – are reminiscent of their daily duties of trench-digging, mat-weaving and hunting. Gender complementarity is accentuated by their different dances, with women performing the dances of pregnancy, and men the dances of death. Evidently women are associated with life and the human world, men with death and the animal world.

Puberty rites also play on the relation between human and Nyau worlds, and on the exchange of human for animal meat. But here the embeddedness of gender in exchange becomes more important and more complex than the division of ritual labour suggests. During puberty initiation the presumption that the village and Nyau represent separate worlds is exposed as fiction: boys learn that Nyau's animals are really only men wearing costumes, and that the masks are jokes perpetrated by men against women and children. Reciprocally girls learn that the faces of men often lurk behind the faces of animals who would eat them. At the same time, boys and girls begin to learn a deeper truth, that the consumption of meat is an enactment of sexual consumption. Boys become predators who hunt and eat all kinds of meat, including and especially women. Girls become game, sought after by all predators, but especially by men. Their transformation into sexual beings thus makes each the complement of the other.

Within both initiation rites, menstruation provides the focal symbol through which boys and girls claim opposite roles as sexual people and as animals in a chain of consumption. As the song cited above suggests, menstruation means that the body has been savaged by a predator. Boys become men and predators by spilling animal blood, while girls become women and meat by spilling their own blood in menstruation. The worlds of Nyau creatures and sexual humans are thus transposed upon each other.

Boys' initiation

I look first at boys' initiation, since it is here that the Nyau society recruits new members and in so doing creates itself as a community of men who double as animals. To do so, each new member is reborn as a child of Nyau, and then transformed into a predator. On the day of initiation, the boys are taken out of the village and led to the graveyard. They are placed on the backs of their tutors, covered with cloth, and carried to the entrance of the graveyard. In this way, the men carry the boys as women carry their infants. At the mouth of the graveyard they encounter the Antelope mask, some eight to ten feet in height with a huge cavernous body. Each boy is thrown inside, beaten by a man hiding within, and then dragged out. The infantilized boy is thus encompassed by the female creature and expelled as a newborn child of Nyau.

If the first step of initiation is the analogue of birth, the second step is the analogue of menarche, for each boy must slaughter a chicken in a way that mimics sexual penetration and menstruation. He inserts a stake into the bird's vent and thrusts it toward its neck. The chicken bleeds to death internally, and when the stake is withdrawn the blood clings to it. The boy must lick the blood off the stake; pluck, clean and sear the chicken; and eat it half-cooked. Immolated in an act of penetration, the chicken is called 'menstruation' (*nkhole*), the consumption of which transforms the boy into a predatory animal. The stake with which the chicken is impaled is part of the same symbolism. The stake comes from a shrub (*chapyelo*) which grows in the graveyard and provides the materials for constructing the nocturnal Nyau animals. After the chicken is killed, the stake is burnt to charcoal, ground to powder, and eaten along with the chicken. The boy thus eats the substance of the female Nyau in order to become a male Nyau.

Girls' initiation

The sexual maturation of girls is the obverse of boys', for they must become game upon whom men will prey. The rite takes place shortly after menarche, and is conducted by older women at 'the tree of maidenhood' outside the village. In this vestigial bush the girl becomes an animal, first losing her human identity

THE LION AT THE WATERHOLE

to become a baby animal, and then becoming identified with edible side of Nyau.

For the first stage, she is stripped of her clothes, and painted with white spots. These are markings of the snake, *thunga*, revealed in her new epithet, 'snake child' (*mwana thunga*). In this guise she is carried into the village and presented to spectators at the Nyau dance arena. There she must lie on the ground and wriggle around, rubbing off the decorative spots in the process. The women brush off any spots that linger, so that the 'snake child' can shed her skin and rise nude and new.

The transformation of the girl into a snake coincides with the appearance of the Nyau Serpent (*chimkoko*) during the evening performances in the village. The Serpent is one of the largest of the nocturnal creatures, and is carried by at least four men. Although the Serpent and the initiate do not appear in the village together, they represent a thematic unity, for the Nyau serpent is the adult 'mother' who holds multitudes – that is, male dancers – within her body, while the girl is one of its newborn offspring.

The girl is now a creature of the bush, but she is in an ambiguous position. She is identified specifically with the python, which, unlike other snakes, is neither predator nor prey. It is not a poisonous snake like the cobra and puff adder, which are considered predators (*zilombo*). Nor is it one of the harmless snakes that some people eat as meat (*nyama*). The python is in a class of its own. As the python child, the girl has great reproductive power – she can shed her own skin and renew herself. But she neither draws blood nor bleeds herself, and therefore transcends the categories essential to the system of exchange between village and bush. Her transformation is thus incomplete.

The next day, the girl becomes a game animal who can be eaten. She is now given a costume of beautiful clothes, including a new dress, a new wrap cloth, scarves to decorate her arms, all to show that the child is gone and a beautiful woman has taken her place. But she is also given a peculiar hat. It is called 'the great hartebeest' (*chingondo*), a common game animal. A figurine sits on its crown, representing either the Elephant, the Hare or the Serpent, the most prestigious night-time masks. The figurine is painted white and decorated with red and black spots, representing the spots of blood from menstruation and from spearing. Once the girl puts the hat on her head, the women call her 'my meat' (*nyama yanga*), a prize they have captured in the bush.

The women will soon bring their catch to the village. But before they do so, the men must come to the village with evidence of their own success in hunting. This is the Elephant mask, worn by four men, and escorted to the village by masked hunters and unmasked men. Rather than killing the Elephant, the chief cuts a piece off its trunk, and releases the Elephant to return to the bush. The chief hands the piece of trunk to the women, who burn it into charcoal, grind it into powder and mix it into their own and the chief's food.

Once they receive their payment of men's 'meat', the women bring their own trophy to the village. They present the girl in her animal hat first at the chief's house, then at the houses of the village elders, and finally in the dance arena. No one may touch her while she wears her hat. But finally the women remove it, and the men and the Nyau dancers prepare to seize her. The predators of Nyau may snatch the girl and drag her around the meeting ground, until the women ransom her back. If she is already married, her husband will come forward, sometimes carrying a hunter's weapons, to claim his young wife. And if the girl has no husband, she simply returns to her hut, where she awaits the arrival of a 'hyena', a man who comes for a night of sexual congress, known as 'eating her maidenhood'. She is now ready to begin married life.

REPRODUCTION THROUGH EXCHANGE

When the secret words, costumes and characters of the Nyau rituals are systematically assembled, we discover a picture of parallel worlds whose separate existences depend upon the reciprocal acts of appropriation that bind them. The life-cycle rituals locate people within a system of exchange and depict the transformation of each person as a function of exchange. Boys become predators and girls become meat in the context of their puberty rites, with predation and bloodshed providing signs of sexual maturity. At death everyone is delivered to the graveyard as meat for the Nyau creatures who congregate there, and during the funeral commemorations the Nyau creatures send forth the game of the bush in return.

The core themes are encapsulated in a common myth motif describing a partnership between hunters and lions over the disposal of meat. In these stories man and lion confront each other as enemies, and one is captured by the other. (It varies as to who catches whom.) But instead of one devouring the other, the two strike a bargain, agreeing to pool their talents and share all game they capture. Thereafter, each animal they catch is divided between them, the lion claiming the viscera, and the hunter the flesh. But one day, inevitably, a woman walks into the trap, and because of the agreement, must be divided between them like any other game. The lion claims her viscera too, and the man must console himself with the woman's remains.

This mythic partnership between man and lion is echoed in numerous conventions reported in Chewa ethnographies. Lions are said to share their spoil with people, once they have gutted it, so if the remains of a lion's kill are found in the bush, the hunter claims it as a gift intended for him. But if a carcass is found with the viscera still intact, the hunter leaves it alone, on the assumption that the lion will return for it. This is consistent with the division of domestic meat into preferred and inferior cuts, for when a goat or ox is slaughtered, the choice innards are given to chiefs and strangers, less choice fatty flesh to the men of the household, and the inferior lean meat to the women and children.

The myth is also reminiscent of the initiation song at the beginning of this chapter in which a lion attack explains – or at least implies – menstrual flow. Similar linkages among sexual potencies and predation can also be found in the ethnographic literature. Schoffeleers (1968) reports that men store their hunting weapons near their beds so that prolonged exposure to sexual activity will enhance the weapons' ability to 'find' their animal target. He also reports that the blood of the animal spilled in the hunt is as dangerous to the hunter as is the menstrual blood of his wife: both must be spilled, but both can kill him.

But while the mythic image of human/beast reciprocities is evident in the ethnographic record, we must query its significance as the dominant trope of life-cycle ritual today. Certainly it does not reflect the economy of hunting in modern Malawi. The bush onto which Nyau projects its core concepts has virtually disappeared, the big game animals are gone and most of the large predators are gone too. There are still hyenas, serval cats, baboons and monkeys; snakes are still plentiful; and a variety of rodents are regularly hunted for meat. But the vast bush where brave men venture at great personal risk to stalk large game – this has disappeared. The fundamental model of renewal through cycles of exchange is implausible in the face of the physical landscape which is unable to renew itself.

Nor are Nyau symbolisms a mandate for men to assault women, nor for women to submit to circumcision and scarification. The only human blood that is spilled is that which the female body spills of its own accord. So, too, the enduring message of the lion/hunter myths is the identification of a woman's bodily rhythms with a paradigm of divided spoils: the lion periodically bites her stomach and makes her menstruate, but the rest of the time, the man, like any hyena, can 'eat' her.

This is where I locate the meaning of the rituals in the world of Chewa experience. The subterranean world of Nyau is enacted first in the body's own functions, and in the embeddedness of reproduction in bloodloss and of life in death. Menstruation is not simply the negation of sexual activity, but the precondition of productive sexuality, for, without menstrual flow, sexual congress yields nothing. The pregnancy which follows arrests the flow of blood for a while, but in childbirth the woman's body opens up again and the newborn emerges covered with its mother's blood. And yet, the spilling of blood can yield death as well as birth, for as every Chewa woman knows, she risks her own life to bring forth from her body a new one. In a very concrete and ordinary way, the spilling of women's blood and the risk of her death are the inescapable foundation of new life.

The fate of the Nyau costumes reflects the same interdependency between death and renewal. The masks and costumes of the daytime, predatory creatures are kept year after year, hidden in pots and in trees in the graveyard. But the large nocturnal creatures, the basket-like structures which contain many men, these are burnt to ashes at the end of each year and built anew the next. The destruction is said to be essential to their return, for the ashes are buried in the graveyard to provide food for the animals who wander through and produce more young. But this cycle of renewal has a deeper logic. The destruction of nocturnal masks coincides with the burning of garden rubble, grassland and brush at the end of the farm year. It is thus part of the panorama of seasonal cycles in which the annual destruction of vegetation ensures its renewal the following year. This includes the new garden crop, the fruits on the trees, the grasses to feed farm animals and game, and the raw materials from which new Nyau masks can be made. Sexuality, hunting and agriculture thus represent parallel arenas of production governed by similar paradigms of death and renewal. Accordingly, the feminine sites of production must be sacrificed in order to replenish the whole: women bleed, animals are slaughtered, and the land is burnt, so that cycles of production can continue in perpetuity. So, too, the productive processes of each domain are mapped onto the others. This yields a far more complicated fabric of cross-referencing metaphors than the fragment I have presented here. Not only is hunting analogous to sexual appropriation, but rainfall is analogous to hunting. This is reflected in the name of the rain-giving spirit, 'the Great Bow' (*chiuta*) and of the rainbow, 'the Bow of the Spirit' (*uta wa leza*) who sends showers of arrows in the form of rain to inseminate the land. So, too, ecology and physiology are isomorphic in important ways. Thus, the land is like a woman's body which receives the penetrating male essence and then yields fruit. This is conveyed in another initiation song which represents the woman's body as an anthill, sex in marriage as the cultivation of the anthill, and the children she bears as the potatoes she and her husband harvest at the end of each season (Kaspin 1996).

The cycles of fecundity, production and destruction are laid out in the seasonal cycles, and this, the most extensive arena of production encompasses the rest. The year divides into a six-month rainy season, and a six-month dry season, while the dry season divides in turn into a cold season and a hot season. The long period of rainfall is the time for agricultural production, while the short period of cold weather at the beginning of the dry season is the time of harvest and rest. This leaves the hot season, a two- to three-month period that marks the end of the farm year. During this time, brushfires are set to burn off grass and garden rubble. Animals fleeing from the burning brush are killed and eaten, and excursions are taken into the bush to hunt whatever game can be found. This, too, is when the big Nyau festivals are held, when girls are 'snared' by women and 'eaten' by men, when the game animals of Nyau come to the village, and when everyone feasts on meat. The flow of blood, fire and regenerative heat continues unabated until the rains return.

Then a new year of production gets under way, and the cycle of production begins again in all domains of life.

THE BODY OF EXPERIENCE: A CONCLUSION

An analysis of life-cycle ritual that seeks direct linkages between principles of social organization and ritual symbols may make sense to the ethnographer, but it may also miss the universe of meaning that the rituals conjure up for its participants. This is not to say that rituals do not convey the rules of conduct on which a community depends (cf. Beidelman 1964; 1997; Richards 1995; Turner 1967), only that decoding the rule does little to explain either the rule or its representation. Simply knowing that the song of the lion refers to the menstrual prohibition explains neither the prohibition nor its metaphorical disguise. This raises an anterior question: is the purpose of ritual to reveal social structure, or to render the panorama of experience intelligible?

The logic of Nyau ritual lies in a philosophy of generativity that is shaped by the exigencies of peasant life, and is articulated in parts and patches in numerous arenas of expressive action. This philosophy is body-centred. On this point I am in sympathy with Devisch (1993) who, in his analysis of Yaka fertility cults, treats the body as the semantic centre of a world rendered meaningful through ritual. Accordingly, ritual makes sense of the world of experiences as they are rooted in the body, and must find meaning in the homologies between the body and the realms of experience it knows. In the Chewa case, body symbolisms are profoundly shaped by the modes and mechanisms of material production that dominate this agrarian society. But as Emily Martin (1987; 1994) has shown, we can expect different formulations of the body in societies dominated by different modes of experience – by industrial production in an industrial society, and by information-transfer in the contemporary United States.

Chewa body symbolisms also suggest an underlying premise about the nature of human experience. They treat the body as an object acted upon by forces external to it. Here I am reminded of Godfrey Lienhart's ethnography of the Dinka religious imagination, in which people are not simply agents acting on their own behalf, but the recipients of actions performed on them by forces – visible and invisible – in the world around them. Lienhart explains this metaphysic by contrasting it with western notions of agency. While as westerners we understand that 'action' is committed by a person on the world, we do not understand its etymological reciprocal, 'passion', to refer to an action performed by the world on a passive subject. Rather the twin notions of passion as passivity and as emotion – that is, as suffering – that were inherited from earlier stages of western thought, exist today as an etymological possibility only. In contrast, the notion of the subject as passive object lies at the heart of a Dinka philosophy of human experience (Lienhart 1987).

Chewa life-cycle ritual similarly describes subjective experience as passions and actions, as a world acting upon a passive subject, and as the subject endeavouring to redirect those forces outward. Human beings enter and exit their lives as helpless creatures, as birth ushers them into the world, and death wrests them from it. Those who survive the hazards of childhood and reach adolescence must learn to deal with the forces that act on them. The pivotal event for girls is menarche, for this is a sign that the power of life and death that originates outside her body now flows through her. She must learn to use it judiciously, if she and the people around her are to thrive. Boys, in turn, learn about the powers that act on them through the ritual mimicry of menstruation, so that they will know how to unleash the regenerative benefits of life forces without succumbing to their lethal effects. Within this philosophy of passion and action, it matters little if the masks of Nyau are false fronts hiding human faces. They are potent, nevertheless, as the interface between a natural world vested with productive and dangerous powers, and the human world dependent upon those powers to regenerate itself. Otherwise there would be no reason to eat the ashes of Nyau masks as medicine, nor to offer them as food to the animals.

NOTES

1 This is consistent with the marked and unmarked meanings of the word *zilombo* in everyday usage. *Zilombo* can mean any wild animal of the bush, but in its more limited sense it is the antithesis of game, *nyama*, and refers specifically to the very dangerous, carnivorous beasts.
2 Anyone eating meat during a burial rite would be suspected of witchcraft.

REFERENCES

Beidelman, T.O. (1964) 'Pig (*guluwe*): an essay on Ngulu sexual symbolism and ceremony', *Southwestern Journal of Anthropology*, 20: 359–92.

Beidelman, T.O. (1997) *The Cool Knife: Imagery of Gender, Sexuality and Moral Education in Kaguru Initiation Ritual* (Washington DC: Smithsonian Institution Press).

Bloch, M. (1992) *Prey into Hunter: The Politics of Religious Experience* (Cambridge: Cambridge University Press).

Devisch, R. (1993) *Weaving the Threads of Life: The Khita Gyn-eco-logical Healing Cult among the Yaka* (Chicago: University of Chicago Press).

Durkheim, E. (1965) *The Elementary Forms of the Religious Life*, translated by Joseph Swain (New York: Macmillan).

Durkheim, E. and M. Mauss (1963) *Primitive Classification*, translated by Rodney Needham (Chicago: University of Chicago Press).

Gelfand, M. (1959) *Shona Ritual with Special Reference to the Chaminuka Cult* (Cape Town: Juta).

Gluckman, M. (1954) *Rituals of Rebellion in South-East Africa* (Manchester: Manchester University Press).

Griaule, M. (1965) *Conversations with Ogotemmeli: An Introduction to Dogon Religious Ideas* (Oxford: Oxford University Press).

Jacobson-Widding, A. (1979) *Red-White-Black as a Mode of Thought: A Study of Triadic Classification by Colours in the Ritual Symbolism and Cognitive Thought of the Peoples of the Lower Congo* (Uppsala: Almqvist & Wiksell).

Kaspin, D. (1990) 'Elephants and Ancestors: The Legacy of Kingship in Central Malawi', PhD dissertation, University of Chicago.

Kaspin, D. (1996) 'A Chewa cosmology of the body', *American Ethnologist*, 23 (3): 561–78.

Lienhart, G. (1987) *Divinity and Experience: The Religion of the Dinka* (Oxford: Clarendon).

Martin, E. (1987) *The Woman in the Body: A Cultural Analysis of Reproduction* (Boston: Beacon).

Martin, E. (1994) *Flexible Bodies: Tracking Immunity in American Culture from the Days of Polio to the Age of AIDS* (Boston: Beacon).

Richards, A. (1995) *Chisungu: A Girl's Initiation Ceremony among the Bemba of Zambia* (London: Routledge).

Sanders, T. (1998) 'Making children, making chiefs: gender, power and ritual legitimacy', *Africa*, 68 (2): 238–62.

Schoffeleers, M. (1968) 'Symbolic and social aspects of spirit worship among the Mang'anja', PhD thesis, Oxford University.

Schoffeleers, M. (1992) *River of Blood: The Genesis of a Martyr Cult in Southern Malawi c. AD. 1600* (Madison, WI: University of Wisconsin Press).

Taylor, C. (1993) *Milk, Honey and Money* (Washington DC: Smithsonian Institution Press).

Turner, V. (1967) *The Forest of Symbols: Aspects of Ndembu Ritual* (Ithaca: Cornell University Press).
Turner, V. (1968) *The Drums of Affliction: A Study of Religious Processes among the Ndembu of Zambia* (Oxford: Clarendon).
Turner, V. (1969) *The Ritual Process: Structure and Anti-Structure* (Ithaca: Cornell University Press).
Van Gennep, A. (1972) *The Rites of Passage*, translated by Monika Vizedom and Babrielle Caffee (Chicago: University of Chicago Press).

CHAPTER 4

FIRST GENDER, WRONG SEX

CAMILLA POWER AND IAN WATTS

INTRODUCTION

Symbolic reversal of sex roles or characteristics has been a persistent theme in the literature on African initiation (e.g. Barley 1983: 64–5, 81; 1986: 51; Gluckman 1949; Richards 1956: 20, 73–5, 98–9, 154; Turner 1967: 96, 223, 253–4). Gluckman ascribed a cathartic function to these 'rituals of rebellion' (1963: 126). Women and girls at initiation or other ceremonial occasions would act 'male' to let off steam as release from their normal subordination. Stereotypical ritual behaviour involved sexual licence and predatory aggression by girls against men, often coupled with transvestism (e.g. Gluckman 1949; Lamp 1988; Turnbull 1988: 174).

Yet Gluckman's explanation does not account for the corresponding recurrent 'feminization' of male initiates. This takes more or less explicit form: boys may be made to wear dress or ornaments of female relatives (e.g. Hollis 1905: 298; Raum 1940: 309), identified with names of female body parts (e.g. Stoll 1955: 159), or described as 'having their periods' (Calame-Griaule 1965: 158). Initiation ceremonies may focus on anthropomorphic imagery of specific androgynous creatures, or construct an implicit gendering through manipulation of symbolic and cosmological categories. Among the Dowayo 'the passage from boy to man involves moving from wet to dry' with uncircumcised boys occupying an intermediate position as male/females (Barley 1983: 81). Yet, to become 'dry' the Dowayo initiate must experience the extreme of wetness (femaleness), being circumcised in a riverside grove, kneeling in running water at the height of the rainy season.

In describing the liminal phase of *rites de passage*, Turner saw sacredness – the mystical 'powers of the weak' (Lewis 1963) – as inherent in inversion of normal social order, or anti-structure (Turner 1969: 93, 95). At his installation, a novice Ndembu chief must undergo ritual reviling, including symbolic feminisation associated with taboo and sterility, to demonstrate his shared endurance of the suffering of his people. Only once subject to the authority of the whole community could he represent the undifferentiated *communitas* (1969: 82ff.). The representation of unity – the key feature of liminality – always entails paradox, contradiction, logical antitheses (Turner 1967: 99). Sacred things are impossibilities, monsters, creatures that cannot exist in the 'real' world; neophytes have at the same time no sex, and both sexes. Out-of-this-world monstrosities, by their very characteristic of combining elements that never can be combined in the real world, startle neophytes into contemplation of symbols, cosmologies and moral systems (Turner 1967: 105).

In focusing on rituals of inversion among the Khoisan peoples of Southern Africa, we will revisit Turner's identity between sacred power, counter-dominance – that is, assertion of egalitarian relations – and counter-reality, a world of deliberate paradox. Gender among these hunter-gatherers and hunter-herders is constructed as an impossible unity, comprising attributes of both sexes. As the fundamental signal of both counter-dominance and counter-reality, gender ritual carries the entire community into the 'other' world.

IS SEX TO GENDER AS NATURE TO CULTURE?

Butler presents drag – performances of cross-dressing and cross-sex impersonation – as the arch-metaphor, the quintessential act of gender, which enacts and reveals gender's imitative function (1990: viii, 137; also Morris 1995: 580). This single, dazzling image takes us to the heart of what gender is that sex is not. Animals do not play 'pretend' with their sex. At a stroke, Butler captures the parodic relationship between gender and sex that has eluded feminist research for the past twenty years. But discussion of that relationship entails problematizing the origin of culture itself – as Ortner originally recognized when focusing on nature *versus* culture as a gendered dichotomy (1974). How does gender arise as the 'counter-reality' to sex?

Despite the power of her own metaphor, Butler, a follower of Foucault in postmodern tradition, rejects any notion of sex as an animal 'reality' which gender can counter. As a performative, gender constitutes its own identity, she argues; it does not refer to or express some underlying absolute truth or falsity of identity (1990: 25). She calls into question any formulation of gender as culture to sex as nature (1990: 7). Where gender is theorized as 'radically independent of sex', she claims it can break out of the constraints of binary structure, offering the possibility of a 'multiple interpretation of sex' (1990: 6). Yet if 'gender is performatively produced and compelled by the regulatory practices of gender coherence' (1990: 24), surely this constrains the emergence of a multiplicity of genders. Drag artistes themselves rely on the underlying binary structure of sex to perpetrate subversive acts of symbolic reversal. If anybody can be any number of genders imaginable, what is being subverted? If collective expectations are not aroused, what is being imitated? Drag performance may differ in its mode of transgression from hypermasculine gay and hyperfeminine lesbian sexual identities (see e.g. Bell *et al.* 1994). But all these performances rest on extreme precision of mimicry to signal their identities. They are constrained by all such performances that have gone before.

In her attack on the 'naturalness' of the masculine/feminine opposition, Butler assumes that a binary gender structure is implicitly hierarchical, and must constrain gender within compulsory heterosexuality (1990: 6). In this view, counter-dominance can only emerge with multiplicity – the very opposite of Turner's notion of *communitas*. Ortner had a similar presumption of binary structure as heterosexual hierarchy. She described ritual as a universal mechanism by which human societies signal the primacy of culture in regulating and ordering givens of nature (1974: 72). Culture, identified with ritual power in Ortner's model, mapped onto the masculine gender category, and thence reductively onto biological males. Here, culture or ritual power offers no space for counter-dominance – again, a contention opposite to Turner's.

But there is an alternative view. Suppose gender – and culture – *emerged in a performance of compulsory non-heterosexuality*. Retain the binary structure of sexuality, because we do in general retain male and female bodies. But suppose that gender, insofar as it is performance, is a function of *ritual, performative* power, not of biological sex. Gender oscillates through time as performance occurs or does not occur. Here gender is constrained by binary structure; it maps onto a nature/culture divide such as that described by Ortner. But it does not embody sexual hierarchy, since either sex may 'perform' the same gender at any given time. Gender has a mutable relationship to sex, mimicking own sex at one time, opposite sex at another.

Such a model is the corollary of a recent theory on the origins of symbolic culture, the 'sex-strike' hypothesis. Knight (1991; Knight *et al*. 1995; and see Knight 1997) posits a model of symbolic cultural origins based in a female strategy of periodically refusing sex to all males except those who returned 'home' with meat. The symbolic domain emerges through collective female defiance expressed in ritual performance. The predicted signature of sex-strike is systematic reversal of the 'normal' signals of animal courtship (Knight *et al*. 1995: 84). Where mate recognition in the animal world involves signalling 'right species/ right sex/right (i.e. fertile) time', sex-striking human females would deter male advances through ritual pantomime of *'wrong species/wrong sex/wrong (i.e. infertile) time'*. In the light of sex-strike theory, gender at origin is inseparable from ritual power, and from ontological ambiguity – humans metamorphose into non-humans, females into males. Gender signals both counter-dominance, mobilizing the 'powers of the weak', and counter-reality, forcing all participants and onlookers to engage with a symbolic, non-perceptual world.

Do gender performances embody counter-dominance and counter-reality, as Turner envisaged? And are such performances prerequisite for sacred or ritual power, in fact for the origins of symbolism? The three models of the relationship between sex and gender discussed here will be used in an investigation of Khoisan gender ritual, aiming to shed light on these questions (Ortner 1974; Butler 1990; Knight *et al*. 1995). Two of these models (Ortner 1974; Knight *et al*. 1995), though diametrically opposed, conceptualize gender and culture as emerging at a single point of origin, while Butler refutes the possibility of searching for origins of gender (1990: viii–ix). The main problem for Ortner's model, given its equation of culture with dominance hierarchy, is how it can generate or accommodate counter-reality. The other models both read gender as parody, hence intrinsically counter to reality, one in terms of 'drag' (Butler 1990), the other 'wrong sex' (Knight *et al*. 1995). But is counter-dominance promoted by licence to multiplicity or by extreme constraints on performance?

If gender is tightly constrained within a binary performative structure, with ritual power either 'on' or 'off' as sex-strike theory would argue, can we adequately account for a so-called 'third sex' or 'third gender' (cf. Herdt 1994)?

IDEOLOGICAL CONTINUITY AMONG THE KHOISAN

Despite considerable differences in their former subsistence pursuits, the Khoisan 'share a great number of common features of territorial organization, gender relations, kinship, ritual and cosmology' (Barnard 1992: 3). Khoisan linguistic and genetic diversity indicate great time-depth of shared cultural structure. Barnard (1992: 297) warns that the recent focus on the past 2,000 years of hunter-herder interaction (cf. Wilmsen 1989) has highlighted 'those aspects of culture which are most susceptible to outside influences – those related to production and trade'. These, he asserts, are the least 'structural' of cultural elements. Such an approach 'grants the Bushmen history, but it minimizes the uniqueness and resilience of their cultures' (1992: 298). To explain change, Barnard continues, 'we need to understand the basic structure of belief' (1992: 298).

Few have done more to elucidate this basic 'structure of belief' than Lewis-Williams, who has revolutionized rock art research through his decoding of Khoisan rock paintings in terms of trance experience. His fieldwork in the Kalahari with Biesele (Lewis-Williams and Biesele 1978) revealed significant correspondences between Ju/'hoan (!Kung)[1] initiation and the ritual practices of the extinct /Xam of the Cape Province. The /Xam ethnography gathered by W.H. Bleek and Lloyd (1911), in turn, compared closely to descriptions of certain Drakensberg rock paintings elicited by Orpen (1874) from a young Maluti Bushman. There are no reliable estimates of the age of Drakensberg paintings (Mazel 1993). However, Lewis-Williams found the art and the nineteenth century ethnography to be 'complementary expressions of a single belief system' (1981: 34). He demonstrated a coherence of structure and metaphor operating in menarcheal, first-kill and marriage ritual contexts, shamanic rainmaking and medicine dances. Ritual trance experience, in his view, was the prime ideological means – 'symbolic work' – for organizing relations of production and exchange, central to social harmony and healing (Lewis-Williams 1982). But, as Lewis-Williams himself originally showed (1981), and Solomon (1992; 1994; 1996a) and Parkington *et al.* (forthcoming) have recently re-emphasized, initiation is also represented in Khoisan art, and clearly overlaps in its structure with trance.

KHOISAN RITUAL CONSTRUCTION OF GENDER: FEMALE INITIATION

The most renowned of Khoisan initiation practices is the Eland Bull Dance, the climax of a girl's first menstruation ceremony. Prevalent in the Kalahari, this dance or its close equivalent probably belonged to southern groups as well. A painting at Fulton's Rock in the Drakensberg Mountains has been interpreted as representing the dance (Lewis-Williams 1981: 41ff.; Solomon 1996b: 89).

A Ju/'hoan initiate lies under a cloak inside a seclusion hut. The 'new maiden' is 'created' a woman when the women of the band dance pretending to be eland (Lewis-Williams 1981: 62). Properly costumed for the dance, the women remove their rear aprons, tying strings of ostrich eggshell beads to hang down between their bare buttocks 'simulating the tail of the Eland' (England 1995: 274; also Lewis-Williams 1981: 44). Heinz (1966: 123) reports similar costume for the !Xõ. Such exposure is considered highly erotic, but men are generally banished to a distance to protect themselves and their hunting weapons (England 1995: 266). In typical Ju/'hoan or Nharo practice (Barnard 1980: 117–18), an older man, or possibly two, in the grand-relative category to the maiden may join the dance wearing horns as 'bulls'.

England describes the peculiar movements of the Eland Dance as 'heavier and more deliberate than any other' (1995: 271). The women's steps thud down flat-footed on the sand, 'all of the dancer's flesh sags toward the ground ... her body ornaments follow the motion downward, adding a small but clear clicking sound effect to the movement'. Timed with the step and designed to imitate the sound of eland hooves is a sharp clinking of adze-blades. The entire effect, says England, 'conjures a picture of the grandly muscular, fleshy eland, trotting along unhurriedly on the *veld*' (1995: 271).

The stick headdress of a 'bull' may be more or less elaborate (England 1995: 275), the tilting and bobbing motion of the horns enhancing the effect. As a 'bull' joins the dance he sidles up to one of the cows, tilting his horns at her and sniffing her rear, until challenged by another 'bull'. Stepping fluidly, the Bulls 'weave smoothly in and out of the dance line while the women continue to dance determinedly forward' (1995: 276), tracking an ellipse or figure-of-eight around the hut. The whole clearly mimics rutting behaviour of eland, especially in the climax as noted by Lewis-Williams:

> the dancing women ... move their buttocks violently from side to side, causing the 'tails' of ostrich eggshell beads to lash to and fro. My informants seemed to consider this to be the climax of the dance. The whole dance, they claimed, is so beautiful that the girl in the menstrual hut weeps, overcome by the wonder of it (1981: 45).

Men are dispensable to the ceremony. Ju/'hoan women sometimes dance without men (Lewis-Williams 1981: 45). Among the !Xõ, Heinz reports that he did not see men participating (1966: 124). Among the Kua, the name used by Valiente-Noailles for G/wi and G//ana groups, it is women who perform as Eland Bulls (1993: 95–6). Shedding their European clothes, the women dance 'adorned with very beautiful ornaments, their breasts nude and their body [sic] engaged in sensuous movements' (Valiente-Noailles 1993: 95). Two of them carry straight, pointed branches. According to the Kua, this is 'to make the dance more interesting and prick the men if they come too close and laugh'. These branches are used to imitate the horns of the antelope, while tails are again held to the buttocks (1993: 96).

The entire pantomime of the Eland Song and Dance – a fantasy of animal sex – may be performed on every day of the girl's menstrual flow (Heinz 1966: 119; England 1995: 266). Among the Kua it happens each day, all day for the full month of the girl's seclusion (Valiente-Noailles 1993: 95).

MALE ASPECTS OF THE MAIDEN: LIMINALITY AND COUNTER-REALITY

The menarcheal maiden, during her seclusion and on her emergence, possesses male attributes and potencies (Power and Watts 1997: 542–6). She plays the role of a hunter, and her performance promotes future successful hunting; yet, she is equated with the bull Eland, the most desirable prey. She has the dangerous, unpredictable powers of the male Moon and the male Rain –

powers that can only be contained through proper respect of ritual observance. The Eland, the Moon and the Rain themselves appear as conceptual equivalents in Khoisan cosmology, powerful and gender-ambivalent.

Beliefs about the danger for hunters and their weapons if they come into contact, even by sight, with a menstrual girl are widespread (see England 1995: 266; Solomon 1992: 313; Schmidt 1986: 331, 345). Roles are reversed: the Nama and Dama believe that a hunter who is 'unclean' through contact with women will be attacked by dangerous animals (Schmidt 1986: 331; and see Biesele 1993: 93). Yet, precisely in the context of initiation, the maiden herself performs as a hunter. A Ju/'hoan metaphor for first menstruation is 'She has shot an eland' (Lewis-Williams 1981: 51). Among the !Xõ, on the final day of seclusion, a gemsbok-skin shield is hung at the back of the menstrual hut, and the maiden is helped by the mistress of ceremonies to shoot it with arrows. This, comments Heinz, 'the only time a girl touches weapons, is done to bring these luck' (1966: 122).

Evidence in Drakensberg paintings (Figure 4.1) suggests that the Maluti Bushmen worked a similar drama into female initiation. Solomon (1992; 1996a) has identified a series of gender-anomalous figures holding bows and arrows as representing initiate girls. Responding to Humphreys' assumption (1996) that the figures must be male because they have male equipment, Solomon points to the problem of levels of reality. Khoisan women in daily life were forbidden from touching men's hunting equipment. However, notes Solomon:

to carry this over into interpretation of the art is highly problematic, since it contains an implicit assumption about what art 'is' and does. It assumes that art faithfully mirrors everyday realities, rather than always mediating, representing and, indeed, *creating* reality (1996a: 33).

Artistic representation of ritual departures from reality are performative, not to be assessed in terms of correspondence to the 'real' world (cf. Rappaport 1979: 198).

Lewis-Williams and Dowson (1989: 173), in line with their shamanist theory of rock art, read the Willcox's Shelter image (Figure 4.1) as 'hallucinatory', deriving from the spirit world of trance experience. To counterpose 'trance' to 'initiation' in this

Figure 4.1 Double-sexed image, Willcox's Shelter, Drakensberg, Natal (from A. Solomon, '"Mythic women": a study in variability in San rock art and narrative' In T.A. Dowson and J.D. Lewis Williams (eds) *Contested Images: Diversity in Southern African Rock Art Research* (Artist: J. Wenman; originally published in Anne Solomon, '"Mythic women": a study in variability in San rock art and narrative', T.A. Dawson and J.D. Lewis-Williams (eds.), Contested images: diversity in South African rock art research (1994). Reproduced by permission of Anne Solomon and Witwatersrand University Press).

imagery is to miss the point about ritual action as performative. Khoisan representation of supernatural potency, it seems, conflates the world of trance with the body of the menarcheal maiden, appropriating the 'grammar' of counter-reality and liminality rooted in gender ritual (see also Huffman 1983: 52; Garlake 1995: 85ff.). A paradoxical unity of opposites (cf. Turner 1967: 99), the Willcox's Shelter figure displays a blood-red emblem of potency underneath the thighs. A hunter with bows and arrows, yet also an animal, she possesses *both* vulva and penis. The image signals ritual potency through the metaphor of the 'female' whose attributes are 'male' and animal.

The fatness and animality displayed in this image relate to liminal properties of the Eland, prime *animal de passage* of Khoisan initiation (Lewis-Williams 1981: 72). Like the Willcox's Shelter figure, the Eland unifies opposites, standing between 'male and female, availability and non-availability for marriage, this world and the spirit world' (Dowson, cited in Lewis-Williams 1990: 80). Alone among the antelopes hunted by the Ju/'hoan, the male eland is fatter than the female. !Kun/obe, an old Ju/'hoan woman, told Lewis-Williams:

The Eland Bull dance is danced because the eland is a good thing and has much fat. And the girl is also a good thing and she is all fat; therefore they are called the same thing (1981: 48).

This identity of the Ju/'hoan girl with the Eland Bull, marked by androgyny and fatness, is prescribed during seclusion through language use and taboo: her menstruation is 'eland sickness'; she must use special respect terms for eland; and she must not eat eland meat. On her emergence, the identity is ritually enacted: she is painted with an antelope mask and anointed with eland fat; as she comes out she must keep her eyes down, so that the eland will not see the stalking hunter (see Power and Watts 1997: 543 for refs.). Similar injunctions were placed on /Xam, !Xõ and Kua maidens. Merely by looking up, the /Xam girl could make the game 'wild' (Hewitt 1986: 285). This 'ancient analogy' between women and game was drawn by Nama and Dama hunters: women had to 'behave in the same way that the hunter wished the game to behave' (Schmidt 1986: 333).

The fat of the girl and the Bull embody the fat of the land. The Ju/'hoan girl receives the Eland Bull Dance, according to !Kun/

obe, 'so that she won't be thin ... she won't be very hungry ... all will go well with the land and the rain will fall' (Lewis-Williams 1981: 50). The Kua dance as eland 'because the Eland is the biggest antelope, and has a big croup, giving the idea of fertility and body development' (Valiente-Noailles 1993: 96). According to the Kua: 'it is a big animal, it has grown big and it increases the number of human beings'. In her dangerous condition of menstrual potency, if the initiate harmed her own body 'this could, in turn, harm others, the land, the plants, the animals, all that makes up the habitat and food of the Kua. It is for this reason that she cannot touch her body' (Valiente-Noailles 1993: 96). The girl is given special sticks for scratching herself during seclusion.

The desirable 'fatness' of the buttocks, associated with eland and emphatically signalled by women performers during the Eland Dance, carries connotations at the same time of eroticism and ritual respect and avoidance. Lewis-Williams (1981: 46–7) and Solomon (1992: 311–12) discuss examples in rock art of rear-end views of female eland in mating posture or female therianthropes – human females with large buttocks and eland heads. The /Xam respect word for eland is translated by Lewis-Williams as 'when it lashes its tail' (1981: 46). A probable equivalent of the respect word used by a Ju/'hoan girl during puberty ritual, it evokes the characteristic signal of the mating female eland, imitated by the women Eland dancers.

Eating or drinking fat is a Ju/'hoan euphemism for sex (Biesele 1993: 86). Men, as carnivores, hunt and 'eat' women, as herbivores (cf. McCall 1970). Fat, as a liquid solid, stands as a mediator – 'the cool result of a union of hot and cold' (Biesele 1993: 196). Consumption of fat, continues Biesele 'is metaphoric of the sexual mediation between semen (hot) and menstrual blood (cold)' (1993: 196). Understood in this metaphor is an opposition between sexual availability and non-availability. The good hunter fears eating or sleeping with his wife in case his arrow poison cools. After a successful hunt, however, he would greet his wife 'with special fervour. He would "praise the meat" ... he would see her buttocks and her legs and would be happy "because the meat had fat and was fat"' (1993: 197). It is hard to tell, comments Biesele, which meat – animal or woman – is being discussed: 'The metaphors tying women to the enchanted, hunted prey are so intricate as utterly to defy untangling' (1993: 197).

In the Eland Bull Dance, the symbols of blood and fat, hunting and sex work in dynamic interaction. The menarcheal maiden – as shown in the Willcox's Shelter image – is dangerous, potent, supremely unavailable; yet she is fat, a 'good thing', about to become available.

MAIDEN, MOON AND GAME

The Eland appears as an interchangeable symbol with the Moon in certain /Xam narratives (Hewitt 1986: 214ff.). Both were created by the gender-anomalous trickster /Kaggen from a shoe. In Nharo belief, the moon falls to the ground when it sets and 'turns into an eland' (Marshall 1986: 181). The moon's gender is mutable, turning, like the androgyny of the eland, on its fatness. The young, slender crescent moon is seen as male, a fat, full moon as female (Power and Watts 1997: 545; Solomon 1992: 302). This construction of gender reflects the widespread Khoisan ideal periodicity for hunting. Waxing moon is the phase that brings hunting luck; full moon is associated with satisfaction and repletion after a successful hunt (see Watts 1998 for references). A sexual tug-of-war underlies the lunar rhythm of the hunt depicted in this G/wi narrative:

> The moon is regarded as male and is believed to hunt once a month, when he kills a hartebeest, feeds his family on the meat, and makes of the hide a cloak for himself. His wife, who has no cloak, gets cold and gradually pulls the cloak from her husband until, at full moon, he has none of it. Then the moon feels cold himself and starts to pull it back until he has all of it again. No sooner has he got his cloak back than his children who, after all, have had no meat for a month, come and complain that they are hungry and eat up the hide...., so the moon has to go out hunting and get himself a new cloak' (Silberbauer 1965: 101).

For the Ju/'hoansi, coldness and fluidity connect women to the moon (Biesele 1993: 98, 196). In the cosmology of these Kalahari groups, the lunar cycle appears to frame a gendered oscillation between warmth and cold, sex and no sex, fat and no fat. For the /Xam of the northern Cape, the motif of the moon as jealous guardian of the game is recurrent:

Therefore, our mothers used to say to us about it, that we must not look at the moon when we had shot game; for, he would, if he did not swallow down the game's fat, he would not allow the game to die; for he would cool the mouth of the game's wound, that the game might recover, the game would not die ... he would allow the poison to become as water (Lloyd n.d.: VI, 5206)

A man catches, the moon does not like it, want it, the moon is angry if a man shoots, you must not steal it says. The moon owns those things, his possessions ... he made the things and refuses, the moon made them do not kill them for a time, do not kill them, he does not shoot, the moon is full, the moon is small, he shoots (Lloyd n.d.: V, 328–328 rev.)

The maiden's dangerous potency equated her with the male aspect of the new moon. Like the moon, she possessed the capricious power of cooling arrow poison, enabling the game to gallop away (Bleek and Lloyd 1911: 67, 77). The prohibition on hunters looking at the moon also refers to the terrible consequences for a man if the secluded girl should glance at him: he is turned into a tree or a stone (Hewitt 1986: 79). The identity of the girl with the waxing male moon is confirmed by scheduling of menarcheal rites among widespread Khoisan groups. The /Xam, the !Xũ and the Kua (G/wi and G//ana) all released a menarcheal girl from seclusion at the appearance of the new moon (Lloyd n.d.: VI, 4001–2; D.F. Bleek 1928: 122; Valiente-Noailles 1993: 94–7; and see Viegas Guerreiro 1968: 227).

MAIDEN AND THE RAIN'S BLOOD

The blood red dots, dashes and stripes on the white body of the Willcox's Shelter figure may refer to the ritually charged relationship between the maiden and the Rain (cf. Solomon 1992: 315). This too revolved around a gender paradox. The /Xam distinguished between the desired, gentle 'female' rain, which fell softly; and the destructive 'male' rain (D.F. Bleek 1933: 309). The danger lay in the maiden's capacity to summon and unleash this 'male' power. Violation of menarcheal observances roused the wrath of the being !Khwa, manifested as a whirlwind, black pebbles, lightning or Rain Bull. This caused the utmost social calamity. Culture itself unraveled – skin bags reverting to their 'raw' form as game animals – and the girl and her kin were transformed into frogs, the Rain's creatures (Hewitt 1986: 77–9). Female rain was never mentioned in puberty lore (Hewitt 1986: 284). The word !Khwa stood for water, and also connoted menstrual blood (Hewitt 1986: 284). /Xam informants emphasized that !Khwa was attracted by 'the odour of the girl' (Hewitt 1986: 285). The girl's contact with water was rigorously controlled during seclusion (1986: 279). Yet, on emergence, such contact was vitally necessary for *preserving* supplies. The maiden had to sprinkle the current water source with powdered haematite (Hewitt 1986: 281), otherwise !Khwa might cause the pool to dry. She painted the young men with haematite stripes 'like a zebra', to protect them from !Khwa's lightning. 'When she is a maiden, she has the rain's magic power' explained the /Xam informant Diä!kwain. She could snap her fingers to call the lightning and 'make the rain kill us' (D.F. Bleek 1933: 297).

In his analysis of Ju/'hoan music, England has discovered that the Rain Song and Eland songs, used in the Eland Dance, are composed in what he calls the Rain-Eland scale, comprising 'the oldest layer of Bushman tonal material' (1995: 264). The G/wi and !Xũ (Marshall 1986: 202) enact a direct symbolic association between the menarcheal girl and rain or lightning. Among the G/wi, Silberbauer saw the initiate, on emergence, taken on a run through a 'symbolic shower of rain' by the young women and girls (1981: 152). For some time after emergence from her month of seclusion, a Kua (G/wi and G//ana) girl must cover herself if it rains 'so that her body's smell cannot reach the rain, lest the lightning might kill people'. (Valiente-Noailles 1993: 97). Among the !Xũ, the male spirit, identified with the lightning *(//gãũa)*, led the initiate's dance. The girl was tatooed with marks in honour of *//gãũa* (D.F. Bleek 1928: 122–3).

The eland is readily identifiable as a rain animal. Schmidt argues that prior to the coming of pastoralism, the eland was the Rain Bull. The great antelope lay at the core of an ancient hunter-gatherer cultural complex which linked in a chain of symbols   'trickster/moon/lightning/rain/fertility/life/eland/horns' (Schmidt 1979: 219–20). In Ju/'hoan belief, people and certain large game animals possess a force called *n!ow* which influences the weather (Marshall 1957; Biesele 1993: 87ff.). Ju/'hoan hunters burnt eland horns to manipulate these forces. Biesele relates a tale of the trickster G!ara calling down the lightning with eland horns to lay low his antagonists, the lions (1993: 103ff.). In a / Xam narrative, the Rain Bull smells out a young menstruating mother and abducts her; she averts the dangers to herself and her kin by lulling !Khwa to sleep with the aromatic herb *buchu;* the old women return from gathering and appease the Rain with the smell of burning horns (Bleek and Lloyd 1911: 199). Another / Xam story collected by Lloyd tells of a beautiful maiden to whom the hunters give their best meat; when they return unexpectedly once, she is discovered to have horns on her head, and to be ugly (Schmidt 1989: 248). The hunters' aversion to the horned maiden connotes avoidance of menstrual fluid, and of looking at the moon, in case arrow poison cools. Possession of horns signals requirement of ritual respect. It is worth recalling the action of the Kua women who deploy their Eland horns 'to prick the men if they come too close'.

In Ju/'hoan thought, the most powerful and determinant effects of *n!ow* occur when:

> the *n!ow* of the hunter interacts with the *n!ow* of the antelope, the *n!ow* of the woman interacts with the *n!ow* of the child newly born ... when the blood of the antelope falls upon the ground as the antelope is killed, when the fluid of the womb falls upon the ground at the child's birth, the interaction of *n!ow*s takes place, and this brings a change in the weather (Thomas 1959: 162).

On the one hand we have the atmospheric effects of the shedding of women's birth blood and the blood of the great game animals; on the other, potentially disastrous atmospheric effects of a menstrual woman in too close conjunction with !Khwa.

The ingredients of Ju/'hoan rain medicine were placed inside an antelope (duiker) horn (Marshall 1986: 197). These comprised 'Rain's teeth' – lightning-fused sand which glittered like 'bits of splintered glass' – the red heartwood of *Acacia erioloba* and some moisture. The sun must not shine on this mixture (1986: 198). In her discussion of Bushman star lore, Marshall (1986: 196) argues that the Pleiades and their two horns (Canopus and Capella) are associated with rain. A Nama story of the |Khunuseti (Pleiades) and their hunter husband (Orion), titled *The Curse of the Women* (Hahn 1881: 74), has a close counterpart in Ju/'hoan lore

(Marshall 1986: 192). The women bid the husband to shoot 'those three zebras for us' (the stars of Orion's belt), but 'if thou dost not shoot, thou darest not come home'. The husband takes one arrow, and misses; because his wives cursed him, he cannot return but sits in the cold night, shivering and suffering, thirsty and hungry:

And the |Khunuseti said to the other men: 'Ye men, do you think that you can compare yourselves to us, and be our equals? There now, we defy our own husband to come home because he has not killed game.'

Comparable to this motif of shooting arrows at stars is a missionary's account, reported by Hahn, that Nama men might 'shoot their poisoned arrows at the lightning in order to arrest the destructive fluid' (1881: 51). Hahn also described how Nama initiate girls, emerging from seclusion, must 'run about in the first thunderstorm, but they must be quite naked, so that the rain which pours down washes the whole body'. This would ensure their fertility. He himself three times saw 'this running in the thunder-rain, when the roaring of the thunder was deafening and the whole sky appeared to be one continual flash of lightning' (1881: 87 n26). Of the ceremonial rain hymns collected by Hahn most remarkable is the *dance-song of the Lightning* (1881: 60). This is sung as a chorus by the members of a kraal one of whom 'was supposed to have been killed by the lightning', with a solo for the part of the lightning:

Chorus: Thou Thundercloud's daughter, daughter-in-law
   of the Fire.
Thou who hast killed my brother!
Therefore thou liest now so nicely in a hole!
Solo: (Yes), indeed, I have killed thy brother so well!
Chorus: (Well) therefore thou liest (now) in a hole.
Thou who has painted thy body red, like =Goro!
Thou who dost not drop the 'menses'.
Thou wife of the Copper-bodied man!"

Here, the Lightning – which has just killed a man – is described as an initiate in seclusion. She lies 'in a hole'; she does not drop her menstrual blood, relating to the familiar injunction on a menstrual girl not to let herself or her blood touch the earth; she paints herself red. Decoration with a ground red stone powder called *!naop* by the secluded girl and her visiting girl friends was Nama practice (Hoernlé 1985: 63, 65). Hahn notes the reports of Khoekhoe women painting themselves with red ochre in their 'worship' of the trickster god Heitsi-eibib, and in the recurrent festivities held for the new moon (1881: 37ff., 124).

Of the injunctions applied to a Khoisan initiate in seclusion the most general involved *keeping her out of the sun;* and not allowing her *to touch the earth.* Girls were wrapped in blankets or hide cloaks to keep the sun off, and had to wear special caps, sometimes for months afterwards (cf. Heinz 1966: 124 for the !Xõ; Valiente-Noailles 1993: 97 for the Kua; Fourie 1928, cited by Schapera 1930: 120, for the Hai//om). Failure to wear the cap could prevent coming of the rains. All contact with the outside world was mediated through close kinswomen, and if the girl had to move outside the space of her seclusion hut she was carried on the back of a kinswoman (cf. Marshall 1976: 278; England 1995: 266 for the Ju/'hoansi; Heinz 1966: 117–18 for the !Xõ; Hoernlé 1985: 63 for the Nama). The Nama lightning hymn quoted above refers to these ritual precautions. The initiate's hut formed a liminal space 'between heaven and earth'. A series of 'mythic women' in Zimbabwe rock art – fat female therianthropes with ceremonial sticks and large zig-zag or curving genital emissions stretching between heaven and earth – graphically depict this liminal state. Solomon (1994: 355–7) relates the imagery to Khoisan ideology of the weather-affecting forces of uterine fluids – birth and menstrual blood – while Garlake (1995: 87) construes the same images as metaphors of trance death and movement to the other world. Again, trance and gender ritual appear conflated. Lebzelter (1934: 53–4) records that a !Kung 'rain doctor' ascends to the sky by a thread and entreats 'the great captain' for rain by throwing him a red powder. This image of climbing threads to 'God's place' is used for trance generally (Katz 1982: 114).

The Nama rain ceremony (Hoernlé 1985: 75–6) involved the slaughter of pregnant cows or ewes by the banks of a stream, in time for the summer rains. The old men of the tribe 'who were good at prophesying would take the uteri, hold them over the fire and pierce them with sticks so that the uterine fluid would flow directly through the fire and down into the river'. Milk and fat would also be poured onto the fire to make great clouds of

smoke rise up to the sky. Compare this with the /Xam rainma-
ker's words, promising to 'cut a she-rain which has milk, I will
milk her, then she will rain softly on the ground ... I will cut her,
by cutting her I will let the rain's blood flow out, so that it runs
along the ground' (D.F. Bleek 1933: 309). Rain-making ritual
among the =Au//eisi involved sprinkling the ground with 'red
earth' (Kaufmann 1910: 158). The /Xam informant /Han≠kassō
spoke of celebrations for the new rains in these terms: 'they do
this when the rain falls, they come out, they run about. They are
all red' (Lloyd n.d.: VIII, 17, 7463).

The colour red signals 'supernatural potency'. The redness of
the rain can be understood as a deep structure of Khoisan cosmology, associated with the periodic bloodflow of women and of
the great antelopes. The seasonal periodicity of the flowing of the
rain's 'blood' was danced into step with the lunar periodicity of
the initiate's bloodflow in the Rain Song and the Eland Songs, to
the same ancient scale.

MALE INITIATION: PARALLELS WITH MENARCHEAL RITES

Among the /Xam, close parallels between menarcheal ritual and
the boy's eland-kill ceremony have been noted by both Hewitt
(1986) and Lewis-Williams (1981). Lewis-Williams has also
revealed striking correspondences between /Xam and Ju/'hoan
puberty and first-kill observances, as well as between the ceremonies for girls and those for boys within each culture (1981: 61; cf.
Lewis-Williams and Biesele 1978).

Like the maiden, the young hunter is symbolically identified
with the eland. Where the girl suffers 'eland sickness', the boy
limps slowly as the wounded prey; both boy and girl keep their
eyes down, so that the game will not look about; both boy and
girl are marked with specific 'eland' designs, and smeared with
eland fat in the course of initiation.

The young hunter is conceptually identified with the menstrual
girl *from the moment he has shot the poisoned arrow into the
antelope*. The /Xam explicitly likened the first-kill hunter to a
menarcheal girl (Lloyd n.d.: VI, 4386). Counterpart to the
super-destructive !Khwa, guardian of menarcheal observances, is
/Kaggen, a gender-ambivalent trickster (Hewitt 1986: 153–4).
Creator and protector of the game, /Kaggen tries to trick the
hunter out of his prey. During the critical waiting period before

the poison has taken effect and the hunter can start tracking the prey down, /Kaggen provokes the hunter to break the tenuous link between himself and the animal by sudden or vigorous movements which would revive the game and counteract the poison. The hunter's slow limping mimics the desired effect of the poison on the prey.

Like the maiden, the boy is in an antithetical relation to hunting weapons – he cannot touch the shaft of the arrow (Hewitt 1986: 126; Lewis-Williams 1981: 58ff.). In both cases there are strictures concerning bloodshed and the cooling of arrow poison; if /Kaggen comes in the form of a louse and bites the boy, the boy cannot kill the louse because 'its blood will be on his hands with which he grasped the arrow and when he shot the eland, the blood will enter the arrow and cool the poison' (Diä!kwain's account, in D.F. Bleek 1932: 233–40). Where the boy limps painfully back to camp, a girl who starts menstruating in the veld cannot walk back, but must be carried. She must not draw attention to her condition but sit and wait silently for other women or girls to approach. A young /Xam or Ju/'hoan hunter remains silent and peripheral until approached.

Like the menstruant, the first-kill hunter is secluded and tended as if 'ill' (Lewis-Williams 1981: 58). The same ritual injunctions are placed on both boy and girl – food avoidances and rationing, keeping away from cooking fire, keeping out of the sun, not moving or not touching the earth. The /Xam took precautions over the dangerous 'scent' of both boy and girl.

Elements of ritual performance are structurally similar in Ju/'hoan female and male ceremonies. An 'Eland Medicine Dance' is held beside the freshly killed eland while the men are still in the veld. Performed 'in praise of the fat' with no women present, this may be seen as the male counterpart of the Eland Bull Dance (Lewis-Williams 1981: 60).

Heinz's close account of !Xõ collective male initiation reveals point-by-point similarity in the treatment of initiate boys and the menarcheal girl (1966: 125ff.). The boys must not talk to each other, and must look at the ground. They have the same gemsbok mask painted on their faces as the maiden, and are sent a hat – just as the girl – to be worn until the rain breaks and to protect them from the sun (1966: 128). They too shoot at a gemsbok shield, to bring luck to the weapons (1966: 131). Other similarities in the boys' and the girls' rites include ritual tatooing;

'opening the eyes' of the candidate at the end of the ceremony; and the imposition of elaborate food taboos, which are lifted in a series of rituals subsequent to initiation. The dance parallel to the Eland Bull Dance is called *tsoma,* and may be danced in front of women on the men's return. Numerous sources on collective male initiation camps suggest that they lasted a month, beginning and ending with the waxing moon (e.g. Vedder 1938: 83–4; D.F. Bleek n.d.: 186, 300 rev., 314 rev., 417, 466 rev.; and see Watts 1998).

Among the Cape Khoekhoe, typical procedure included smearing the initiate with fat and soot, or ochre; urination on the boy by the elders (sometimes for three days in succession); washing the boy with animal blood and hanging fat or animal parts around his neck. Old sources on the Nama (cited in Schapera 1930: 279ff.) indicate lengthy seclusion, during which the boy subsists on cow's milk, followed by ritual scarring and tatooing. Ritual precautions surrounding contact with cold water were similar for both Nama boys and girls. Initiation practice among the Korana, recorded by Engelbrecht (1936: 157ff.), is noteworthy. The candidate endured a month of seclusion, and was explicitly 'feminized'. He was stripped and dressed in a 'small girl's hind-kaross'; brass rings were put on his arms, as women wore them; red ochre and fat were rubbed all over his body. He could eat meat, but only from the ends of sharp sticks, not from his hands.

Lewis-Williams comments on the symbolic androgyny of the eland in relation to Ju/'hoan initiates:

> The neophytes are, *like the eland,* considered to be sexually ambivalent: the girl is spoken of as if she were a hunter who had shot an eland, while the boy is secluded and cared for as if he were menstruating – both are neither male nor female during the liminal period of the rites (1981: 72).

But it is just as valid to say that maiden and hunter take on the potency of *both male and female,* a potency symbolized by the eland representing a *unified* gender. Just as the Willcox's Shelter figure emphatically displays its double sex, initiates prior to emergence *gain* attributes of the opposite sex, rather than losing potency of their own. In his classic essay on liminality, Turner (1967: 98) reads both androgyny and sexlessness as characteristic of the initiate, the combination expressing the contradiction of anti-structure. Such an anomalous state has been conceptualized as an intermediate 'third sex' or 'gender' category (Herdt 1994).

CONCLUSION

Nature, culture and counter-dominance

Solomon ascribes to a 'third gender category' (1992: 303) two of the most elaborated symbols and metaphors of Khoisan cosmology: the bull Eland and the trickster, both figures central to initiation. To these can be added the Moon. If an attempt is made to force these entities into a masculine/feminine gender hierarchy, in line with Ortner's model, their characteristics scatter between the two poles (see Solomon 1992: 299; Power and Watts 1997: 552–3). In other words, they embody contradiction within such a classification. Can we be satisfied with allowing contradiction and classification to co-exist (cf. Rapport 1997), or is Ortner's framework fundamentally flawed as a map of Khoisan gender conceptualisation?

In respect of a nature/culture dichotomy, the eland and the trickster reveal liminal, transformational properties. Narratives concerning eland depict a principle of oscillation between cultural artefact and natural raw state, as in the /Xam story of the eland's creation from an old leather shoe; or the danger, in case of breaches of menarcheal observance, of skin bags once more becoming game animals. During the Eland Dance, women perform as animals – mating animals – ostensibly mapping female to nature. Yet their performance establishes a ring of respect around the girl, marking the boundaries of sexual availability and taboo. Tricksters likewise act to enforce respect rules. These are taboos governing flesh consumption, whether of game animals, in the case of /Kaggen, or of menarcheal girls. //Gaũwa, the presiding deity of Nharo initiation (and trance), hovers around the menstrual hut in the role of jealous male guardian (Guenther 1989: 116–17).

Ortner's model locates women as intermediaries between nature and culture (1974: 83ff.). The liminal space of the menstrual hut can certainly be viewed as a confluence of nature and culture. The slightest failure in the performance surrounding the 'raw', 'wild' maiden would lead to the complete disintegration of culture (see Hewitt 1986: 79–80; Lewis-Williams 1981: 52). But she is charged with the power of a violent *male* force of nature. Hence, female to male as nature to culture is confounded.

Recurrently, the maiden signals her 'masculine' identity, by this means asserting the primacy of culture. The equation of culture and 'masculine' dominance appears in conformity with Ortner's hierarchy. But can the maiden be considered 'dominant'? Her very mode of 'dominance' – she snaps her fingers to call down the lightning and kill a man – exemplifies a defiant countering of reality. The maiden is best described as 'counter-dominant', expressed by the fundamental motif of *denial of the male gaze*. The worst possible breach of the menarcheal ritual observance would be if a man caught sight of the maiden in her hut. At a glance, she could turn him into a tree or stone.

Ortner's model faces its greatest difficulty in accounting for the counter-dominance and counter-reality featuring in male initiation. The young hunter is identified with the wounded prey – just as the girl is – and is treated as a menstruant in seclusion. Far from being glorified as a 'dominant' male, he is forbidden even to kill a louse. He is placed in an identical liminal situation to the girl, between nature and culture, while possessing less dire potency. The worst result of failure to perform male gender ritual might be loss of a hunter's productive powers – not calamitous threat to the entire group.

Logically, Ortner's model predicts that gender performance at initiation should emphasize difference: masculine 'cultural' empowerment *versus* feminine 'natural' weakness. Why, then, should males assert themselves culturally by signalling 'female'? Khoisan gender ideology revels in such confusion of roles. The processes of production and reproduction are mystically intertwined. To menstruate is to shoot a poisoned arrow; to give birth is to kill a large game animal. Solomon (1992: 304) argues that the fat male eland provides a metaphor by which males can appropriate desirable female qualities, constructing themselves as nurturers. Male figures in rock art with fat, female/eland-like buttocks (Solomon 1992: 312), taken together with the androgynous 'pregnant' males of Zimbabwe art (Garlake 1995: 85) support her contention. Parkington *et al.* (forthcoming) interpret a group of cloaked male figures, merged to form the outline of an eland torso, as a representation of solidarity engendered in secret contexts of collective male initiation. While Ortner's gender hierarchy model might allow ritually/culturally potent women to signal 'male', it is unclear why men should be compelled to display female 'natural' potencies. Instead of mapping onto reductive gender categories of masculine/feminine, Khoisan ritual potency is consistently expressed as counter-reality and counter-dominance.

Communitas: unity or multiplicity of experience?

Khoisan gender ritual can be conceptualized as constructing a *single* 'gender of power' in which both sexes equally participate (Power and Watts 1997). All initiates are treated in formally similar ways, each sex receiving attributes of the other sex. The experience of initiates, irrespective of biological sex, is unified through a series of constraints on their body and eye movements, position in space, consumption of foods, contact with water, exposure to the outside world, whether and how they talk. All this militates against 'multiplicity' in experience or performance.

Rather than permit proliferation of distinctions and categories, Khoisan gender ritual turns apparent opposites into conceptual equivalents. The maiden plays as hunter, the hunter as the hunted; images of female initiates stand for trance death. We see 'unification of disparate significata' in Turner's terms: natural and physiological phenomena blend in polysemic clusters, as water/blood/poison/illness or eland/dance/people/fat (cf. Barnard 1992: 94). The dialectical framework for these syntheses is the lunar cycle (Power and Watts 1997: 554). The gender-mutable moon, in its waxing, offers the fundamental metaphor for transformation from death to rebirth, cold to hot, wetness and blood to fire and fat. The major ritual preoccupation of the Khoisan, evident in both initiation and trance dance, lies in effecting these transformations. Ideological codings associated with the potency of a menstruant may be positive or negative, potentially multiple and negotiable. What stands beyond negotiation, allowing no licence to multiplicity, is the essentially similar ritual treatment of those who possess potency. To turn the dire blood potency of the male rain into soft, fruitful, female rain that produces fat of the land requires meticulous observance of menstrual ritual through the stages of seclusion and emergence. This is the performative force of initiation, compelling coherence.

For Turner, *communitas* is engendered through the 'stripping and levelling' characteristic of liminality (1967: 98, 100; 1969: 92–4). Initiates endure unified experience of deprivation as all social, sexual or status differentials are eliminated. This release from normal structures of multiple and fragmented social relations into a stark, simplified unity opens up space for contemplation of the sacred (1967: 102–5). Neophytes may play with sacred articles of simple but impossible configuration, like masks which combine features of male and female, animal and human, or human and landscape. 'Liminality is the realm of primitive hypothesis,' Turner writes, 'where there is a certain freedom to juggle with the factors of existence' (1967: 107). Here, unity of experience when deprived of normal structure generates counter-reality. This idea can be traced back to Durkheim's classic passage on ritual as the generator of collective representations (1915: 230–1). Only through precise homogeneity of movements can individual minds come into contact and communicate with each other, forming the group consciousness and enabling symbolization. Here, uniform ritual experience breaks down normal structures of individual cognition to promote a collective representation which has no necessary correspondence with individual perceptual representation.

Butler reads unity of gender experience as inevitably rooted in oppression:

> Gender can denote a *unity* of experience, of sex, gender, and desire, only when sex can be understood in some sense to necessitate gender .... and desire – where desire is heterosexual and therefore differentiates itself through an oppositional relation to that other gender it desires. The internal coherence or unity of either gender, man or woman, thereby requires both a stable and oppositional heterosexuality (1990: 22).

If commonality of gender is rooted in heterosexual polarity – women are one gender only in opposition to men as the other, more powerful gender – how can this structure of dominance be subverted? Butler's dilemma is that she yearns for multiplicity of gender experience to break down the binary heterosexual hierarchy, but acknowledges, paradoxically, that gender cannot in fact be 'a set of free-floating attributes' (1990: 6, 24). She is fully aware of the constraints on gender as performative, 'compelled by the regulatory practices of gender coherence'.

While Butler focuses on institutionalized reiterative process, in this chapter we have described the Khoisan Eland Bull Dance as a discrete ritual act constructing gender in defiance of sex. Commenting on Butler's formulation, Morris notes: 'the theory of gender performativity would probably eschew ethnographies in which a discrete ritual act or series of acts is seen as the source of sexual and gendered identity' (1995: 576). Theorists of *performativity*, in the sense of reiterative social process, as against spectacular *performance*, would see grand Durkheimian ritual as the 'antithesis of creativity' (Morris 1995: 576). If ritual is reiteration, asks Morris 'whence comes the new or non-normative act?' (Morris 1995: 576). In their bid to escape from hierarchical structures of social reproduction, performativity theorists reject ány notion of founding or originating acts.

Does collective ritual performance inevitably crush human creativity in the name of oppressive social hierarchy? Morris counterposes Turner's thesis on liminality and anti-structure as an alternative possibility of creativity to Durkheim's tradition of undifferentiated collectivity. We emphasize the common ground between the two paradigms. For both Turner and Durkheim, highly constrained, unifying ritual experience of 'sacredness' permits access to counter-reality and enables abstract contemplation (Turner 1967: 105; Durkheim 1915: 228, 230–1, 235, 237). If ritual entails *communitas*, why locate its roots in oppression? We could equally conceptualize ritual constraints as imposed by a transgressive or rebellious 'counter-culture', periodically asserted and fundamentally at odds with norms of everyday life. It may even be that culture itself must be periodically renewed in the same manner as it was first established, through collective defiance. That would make each subsequent staging of 'high' ritual into a celebratory re-enactment of culture's mythic moment of origins (cf. Rappaport 1979: 174).

In Gellner's (1992) reading of Durkheim, ritual is the prime mechanism for compulsively constraining concepts, without which there exists no possibility of communicable abstract thought. Rappaport (1979: 194) describes ritual as the 'meta-performative' which makes all other performatives possible – the ground of all symbolic generativity including language. Bourdieu remonstrates with Austin, the founder of speech-act theory, for supposing that the force of performatives lies in the words themselves: 'The power of words is nothing other than the *delegated power* of the spokesperson' (1991: 107). Ritual symbolism exerts power not autonomously, 'but only in so far as it *represents* ... the delegation' (1991: 115). Bourdieu states his position in classically Durkheimian terms:

> The performative magic of ritual functions fully only as long as the religious official who is responsible for carrying it out in the name of the group acts as a kind of *medium* between the group and itself: it is the group which, through its intermediary, exercises on itself the magical efficacy contained in the performative utterance. (1991: 116)

The novice (chief or initiate) described by Turner who silently and submissively accepts the authority of the total community, becoming representative of that community, is such an intermediary 'between the group and itself'. The Khoisan maiden, silent and submissive to her community, embodies that community, acquiring the performative force and magical efficacy of the lightning that strikes down any transgressor.

Ritual performative force is lost as licence to multiplicity is gained. Rather than discard gender ritual as a 'founding act' in favour of reiterative process, we may adopt a stance akin to Rappaport (1979: 174) on ritual as 'the basic social act'. Initiation acts as the meta-performative which makes all gender performatives possible.

Khoisan gender ritual, as a founding act, conforms closely to Butler's metaphor: gender *is* drag. Each sex plays pretend as the opposite sex when becoming ritually potent. Gender operates inside a binary framework, oscillating between ritual potency and relaxation of ritually imposed taboos. But, *contra* Butler and Ortner, this cannot be construed as heterosexual dominance hierarchy. Each sex accesses the 'gender of power' (Power and Watts 1997: 555–6) at the appropriate time through *unified* ritual experience, and relinquishes that gender as ritual power wanes. To be ritually potent is to display 'wrong sex'.

Gender and symbolic culture

In Butler's view, the subversive or doubly parodic force of drag lies, not in mimicking some 'natural' or 'original' state, but in parodying 'the very notion of an original' (1990: 138). The whole

thrust of Butler's work implies the domination of cultural constructs over any possibility of 'naturalness'. The Khoisan rites,
like all initiation rites, can be interpreted as culture asserting
itself over 'nature'. In line with Butler's theory, we agree fully
that gender as performed by the Khoisan does not refer to any
natural or original *sex*. However, we argue that it does in some
sense re-enact an *original gender* – first gender.

Only through extreme precision of performative constraints –
homogenization and synchrony of movements, experience and
sensation – can a whole community be compelled to engage with
concepts outside perceptible reality, such as those entailed in
Khoisan gender construction. The entire symbolic domain rests
on the constraints imposed by representation of counter-reality.
Gender as the fundamental such representation is hence symbolism's 'founding act'. It provides the template for all other such
ritual representations, including for the Khoisan trance death and
rainmaking rites.

Turner's realm of *communitas* – unified, ritual, anti-structural
experience – gives rise to sacred space and play with counter-
reality. Classifications are confounded by the signals that break
down normal social order – signals that counteract dominance,
asserting egalitarian relations. The unclassifiable neophyte,
outside normal structure, can juggle with 'out-of-this-world'
abstractions. Rapport contests the opposition between contradiction and social order, calling for:

> an appreciation of the simultaneity of classification *and* contra-
> diction. Social order is predicated not upon the absence of con-
> tradiction but upon its co-presence: *the cognitive co-presence of
> the contradictory, of both/and, together with the classificatory
> order of either/or* (1997: 657–8).

Such a view fits the dialectical fluidity of Khoisan classification
systems. On the one hand, we side with Turner in linking contradiction to counter-dominance, emerging in unified ritual experience. On the other, we join Rapport in asking for
'anthropological recognition that it is in cognitive contradiction
that socio-cultural order is rooted' (1997: 658). But we remain
resolutely Durkheimian: collective representation of contradiction,
ritually performed, constitutes socio-cultural order. This implies
that ritual display of counter-dominance – signalled by contradic-

tion of reality, deliberate play with paradox – creates cultural order.

In the Khoisan case, the crisis of cultural order is played out in the Eland Bull dance. The potential dominance of male hunters is countered by the glance of a girl and by the pantomime dance of her womenfolk who signal 'we are the wrong sex, and the wrong species'. Counter-reality arises directly from the signals needed to resist male dominance. In line with expectations of sex-strike theory (Power and Watts 1997: 555–7), assertion of culture's primacy over nature is constrained precisely by the normative periodicity of hunting and the lunar cycle, and by taboos placed on the flesh of bleeding women and bleeding game. To be ritually powerful is to play at 'wrong sex', is to be wounded and periodically bleed. First gender mobilizes the 'powers of the weak', countering dominance with signals that generate a shared domain of counter-reality. This act appears both necessary and sufficient to establish the symbolic domain.

NOTES

Thanks are due to Anne Solomon for permission to use illustrative material, and for discussion of aspects of her research. The African Studies Library, University of Cape Town, and the Rock Art Research Unit, Witwatersrand University, have made available unpublished manuscripts.
1 Where older texts employ the term '!Kung', current ethnography favours use of Ju/'hoan (pl. Ju/'hoansi), which is the people's own name for themselves (see Biesele 1993: 203).

REFERENCES

Barley, N. (1983) *Symbolic Structures: An Exploration of the Culture of the Dowayos* (Cambridge: Cambridge University Press).
Barley, N. (1986) *The Innocent Anthropologist: Notes from a Mud Hut* (London: Harmondsworth).
Barnard, A. (1980) 'Sex roles among the Nharo Bushmen of Botswana', *Africa*, 50: 115–24.
Barnard, A. (1992) *Hunters and Herders of Southern Africa: a Comparative Ethnography of the Khoisan Peoples* (Cambridge: Cambridge University Press).
Bell, D., J. Binnie, J. Cream, and G. Valentine (1994) 'All hyped up and no place to go', *Gender, Place and Culture*, 1: 31–47.
Biesele, M. (1993) *Women Like Meat: The Folklore and Foraging Ideology of the Kalahari Ju/'hoan* (Johannesburg: Witwatersrand University Press).

Bleek, D.F. (n.d.) Unpublished Angolan notebooks, African Studies Library, University of Cape Town.

Bleek, D.F. (1928) 'Bushmen of central Angola', *Bantu Studies*, 3: 105–25.

Bleek, D.F. (1932) 'Customs and beliefs of the /Xam Bushmen. Part II: the lion. Part III: game animals; Part IV: omens, wind-making, clouds', *Bantu Studies*, 6: 47–63, 233–49, 321–42.

Bleek, D.F. (1933) 'Beliefs and customs of the /Xam Bushmen, Part V: the rain; Part VI: rainmaking', *Bantu Studies*, 7: 297–312, 375–92.

Bleek, W.H.I. and L.C. Lloyd (1911) *Specimens of Bushman Folklore* (London: Allen and Unwin).

Bourdieu, P. (1991) *Language and Symbolic Power*, (ed.) J. B. Thompson (Cambridge: Polity).

Butler, J.P. (1990) *Gender Trouble: Feminism and the Subversion of Identity* (New York: Routledge).

Calame-Griaule, G. (1965) *Ethnologie et Langage: la Parole chez les Dogon* (Paris: Gallimard).

Durkheim, E. (1915) [1912]. *The Elementary Forms of the Religious Life: A Study in Religious Sociology* (London: Allen and Unwin).

Engelbrecht, J.A. (1936) *The Korana: An Account of their Customs and their History, with Texts* (Cape Town: Maskew Miller).

England, N.M. (1995) *Music among the Zu/'wã-si and Related Peoples of Namibia, Angola and Botswana* (London: Garland).

Fourie, L. (1928) 'The Bushmen of south west Africa' in C.H.L. Hahn, H. Vedder and L. Fourie (eds) *The Native Tribes of South West Africa* (Cape Town: Cape Times).

Garlake, P. (1995) *The Hunter's Vision: The Prehistoric Art of Zimbabwe* (London: British Museum).

Gellner, E. (1992) *Reason and Culture: The Historic Role of Rationality and Rationalism* (Oxford: Blackwell).

Gluckman, M. (1949) 'The role of the sexes in Wiko circumcision ceremonies' in M. Fortes (ed.) *Social Structure* (Oxford: Oxford University Press).

Gluckman, M. (1963) *Order and Rebellion in Tribal Africa* (London: Cohen & West).

Guenther, M.G. (1989) *Bushmen Folktales: Oral Traditions of the Nharo of Botswana and the /Xam of the Eastern Cape* (Stuttgart: Franz Steiner Verlag Wiesbaden).

Hahn, T. (1881) *Tsuni-//goam: The Supreme Being of the Khoi-khoi* (London: Trübner).

Heinz, H.J. (1966) 'The social organization of the !kõ Bushmen', MA thesis, University of South Africa.

Herdt, G.H. (ed.) (1994) *Third Sex, Third Gender: Beyond Sexual Dimorphism in Culture and History* (New York: Zone).

Hewitt, R.L. (1986) *Structure, Meaning and Ritual in the Narratives of the Southern San* (Hamburg: Helmut Buske Verlag (Quellen zur Khoisan-Forschung 2)).

Hoernlé, A.W. (1985) [1918] *The Social Organization of the Nama and Other Essays*, (ed.) P. Carstens (Johannesburg: Witwatersrand University Press).

Hollis, A.C. (1905) *Masai, their Language and Folklore* (Oxford: Clarendon).

Huffman, T. (1983) 'The trance hypothesis and the rock art of Zimbabwe', *South African Archaeological Society Goodwin Series*, 4: 49–53.

Humphreys, A.J.B. (1996) '"Mother goddesses" and "mythic women": an alternative view', *South African Archaeological Bulletin*, 51: 32.

Katz, R.S. (1982) *Boiling Energy: Community Healing among the Kalahari Kung* (Cambridge, MA: Harvard University Press).

Kaufmann, H. (1910) 'Die Auin. Ein Beitrag zur Buschmannforschung', *Mitteilungen aus den deutschen Schutzgebeiten*, 23: 135–60.

Knight, C.D. (1991) *Blood Relations: Menstruation and the Origins of Culture* (New Haven: Yale University Press).

Knight, C.D. (1997) 'The wives of the sun and moon', *Journal of the Royal Anthropological Institute*, 3: 133–53.

Knight, C.D., C. Power and I. Watts. (1995) 'The human symbolic revolution: a Darwinian account', *Cambridge Archaeological Journal*, 5 (1): 75–114.

Lamp, F. (1988) 'Heavenly bodies: menses, moon and rituals of license among the Temne of Sierra Leone' in T. Buckley and A. Gottlieb (eds) *Blood Magic: The Anthropology of Menstruation* (Berkeley: University of California Press).

Lebzelter, V. (1934) *Eingeborenenkulturen in Südwest- und Südafrika* (Leipzig: Karl W. Hiersemann).

Lewis, I.M. (1963) 'Dualism in Somali notions of power', *Journal of the Royal Anthropological Institute*, 93: 109–16.

Lewis-Williams, J.D. (1981) *Believing and Seeing: Symbolic Meanings in Southern San Rock Paintings* (London: Academic Press).

Lewis-Williams, J.D. (1982) 'The social and economic context of southern San rock art', *Current Anthropology*, 23: 429–49.

Lewis-Williams, J.D. (1990) *Discovering Southern African Rock Art* (Cape Town: David Philip).

Lewis-Williams, J.D. and M. Biesele. (1978) 'Eland hunting rituals among the northern and southern San groups: striking similarities', *Africa*, 48: 117–34.

Lewis-Williams, J.D. and T.A. Dowson. (1989) *Images of Power: Understanding Bushmen Rock Art* (Johannesburg: Southern).

Lloyd, L. (n.d.) Unpublished notebooks, Bleek and Lloyd Collection, Jagger Library, University of Cape Town.

McCall, D.F. (1970) 'Wolf courts girl: the equivalence of hunting and mating in Bushman thought' *Ohio University Occasional Papers in International Studies*, Africa Series No. 7.

Marshall, L. (1957) 'N!ow', *Africa*, 27: 232–40.

Marshall, L. (1976) *The !Kung of Nyae Nyae* (Cambridge, MA: Harvard University Press).

Marshall, L. (1986) 'Some Bushman star lore' in R. Vossen and K. Keuthmann (eds) *Contemporary Studies on the Khoisan*, 2 (Hamburg: Helmut Buske Verlag (Quellen zur Khoisan- Forschung 4)).

Mazel, A. (1993) 'Rock art and Natal Drakensberg hunter-gatherer history: a reply to Dowson', *Antiquity*, 67: 889–92.

Morris, R.C. (1995) 'All made up: performance theory and the new anthropology of sex and gender', *Annual Review of Anthropology*, 24: 567–92.

Orpen, J.M. (1874) 'A glimpse into the mythology of the Maluti Bushmen', *Cape Monthly Magazine*, 9 (49): 1–13.

Ortner, S.B. (1974) 'Is female to male as nature is to culture?' in M.Z. Rosaldo and L. Lamphere (eds) *Woman, culture and society* (Stanford: Stanford University Press).

Parkington, J., A. Manhire and R. Yates (forthcoming) 'Reading San images' in J. Deacon and T.A. Dowson (eds) *Voices from the Past: /Xam Bushmen and the Bleek and Lloyd Collection* (Johannesburg: Witwatersrand University Press).

Power, C. and I. Watts. (1997) 'The woman with the zebra's penis: gender, mutability and performance', *Journal of the Royal Anthropological Institute* 3, 537–60.

Rappaport, R.A. (1979) 'The obvious aspects of ritual' in *Ecology, Meaning and Religion* (Berkeley: North Atlantic).

Rapport, N. (1997) 'The "contrarieties" of Israel: an essay on the cognitive importance and the creative promise of both/and', *Journal of the Royal Anthropological Institute*, 3: 653–72.

Raum, O.F. (1940) *Chagga Childhood: A Description of Indigenous Education in an East African Tribe* (London: Oxford University Press).

Richards, A.I. (1956) *Chisungu: A Girl's Initiation Ceremony among the Bemba of Northern Rhodesia* (London: Faber & Faber).

Schapera, I. (1930) *The Khoisan Peoples of South Africa: Bushmen and Hottentots* (London: George Routledge).

Schmidt, S. (1979) 'The rain bull of the South African Bushmen', *African Studies*, 38: 201–24.

Schmidt, S. (1986) 'The relations of Nama and Dama women to hunting', *Sprache und Geschichte in Afrika*, 7 (1): 329–49.

Schmidt, S. (1989) *Katalog zur Khoisan-Volkserzählungen des sudlichen Afrikas*, vol 1 (Hamburg: Helmut Buske Verlag (Quellen zur Khoisan-Forschung 6.1 and 6.2)).

Silberbauer, G.B. (1965) *Report to the Government of Bechuanaland on the Bushman Survey* (Gaberones [Gaborone]: Bechuanaland Government).

Silberbauer, G.B. (1981) *Hunter and Habitat in the Central Kalahari Desert* (Cambridge: Cambridge University Press).

Solomon, A. (1992) 'Gender, representation and power in San ethnography and rock art', *Journal of Anthropological Archaeology*, 11: 291–329.

Solomon, A. (1994) ' "Mythic women": a study in variability in San rock art and narrative' in T.A. Dowson and J.D. Lewis-Williams (eds) *Contested Images: Diversity in Southern African Rock Art Research* (Johannesburg: Witwatersrand University Press).

Solomon, A. (1996a) ' "Mythic women": a response to Humphreys', *South African Archaeological Bulletin*, 51: 33–35.

Solomon, A. (1996b) 'Rock art in southern Africa', *Scientific American*, (November): 86–93.

Stoll, R.P.A. (1955) *La Tonétique des Langues Bantu et Semi-Bantu du Cameroun* (Paris: Institut Français d'Afrique Noire).

Thomas, E.M. (1959) *The Harmless People* (London: Secker & Warburg).

Turnbull, C.M. (1988) [1961] *The Forest People* (London: Paladin).

Turner, V.W. (1967) *The Forest of Symbols: Aspects of Ndembu Ritual* (Ithaca: Cornell University Press).

Turner, V. (1969) *The Ritual Process: Structure and Anti-Structure* (Harmondsworth: Penguin).

Valiente-Noailles, C. (1993) *The Kua: Life and Soul of the Central Kalahari Bushman* (Rotterdam and Brookfield: A.A. Balkema).

Vedder, H. (1938) [1934] *South West Africa in Early Times*, (ed.) C.G. Hall (London: Oxford University Press).

Viegas Guerreiro, M. (1968) *Bochimanes !khũ de Angola: estudo ethnográfico* (Lisbon: Instituto de Investigação Científica de Angola, Hunta de Investigações do Ultramar).

Watts, I. (1998) 'The origin of symbolic culture: the Middle Stone Age of southern Africa and Khoisan ethnography', PhD thesis, University of London.

Wilmsen, E. N. (1989) *Land Filled with Flies: A Political Economy of the Kalahari* (Chicago: Chicago University Press).

CHAPTER 5

SAISEE TORORElTA

AN ANALYSIS OF COMPLEMENTARITY IN AKIE GENDER IDEOLOGY

BWIRE KAARE

The Akie are a hunter-gatherer community in northern Tanzania. They form part of a larger group of peoples known in the anthropological literature as the Dorobo. The term 'Dorobo' derives from the Maasai word *Il-Torobo*, which means people of the forest, or poor people without cattle who live what Maasai consider to be the abominable beast-like lifestyle of hunting and gathering. The Akie, like other Dorobo groups, have had a long history of association with Maasai pastoralists and, until recently, the Dorobo were seen as an appendage of Maasai culture (see, for example, Van Zwanenberg 1976; Kenny 1981). However the Akie explain their relationship with their Maasai neighbours in terms of their own distinctive history and cosmological notions.

The Akie number around 5,000. Until approximately two decades ago they led a predominantly hunting and gathering way of life while at the same time maintaining close relations with their pastoral neighbours. They live in small groups whose size varies continually depending on hunting and honey-gathering movements and the seasons. Settlement is to a large extent dictated, though not entirely determined, by kin relations. People of common ancestry will in most cases live on their own clan land (*ilmot*). Settlement on clan land is vital since it is here that clan spirits live and clan rituals must be performed. The Akie are divided into eight patriclans. Clans are important for the Akie because they form the basis for the participation in collective land rights, essential for the recognition of honey rights. Every clan member has the right to exploit honey on his own clan land as well as on his mother's clan land. The Akie represent this by saying that they belong to two 'gates' (*ingihomii*). In addition to honey rights, the two gates or ties of kinship allegiance define relationships with the ancestors. The emphasis on ties both to one's patriclan and to one's mother's patriclan is connected with the fact that different clans and families must come together to effect ritual transformations that transcend the boundaries of the separate social categories to which they belong. The Akie believe that such ritual transformations are essential for creating order and continuity.

As will be suggested below, the union in ritual and kinship of two different elements, in which one element is complemented by the other, generates new access to both property and symbolic capital. Bringing two things together creates new practices and transforms the preceding reality to allow for, as the Akie express it, the perpetuation of meaningful life. On marriage, a husband gains access to his wife's patriclan land and its honey resources. Children have rights both in their father's and mother's property and other social and cultural rights, like rights to clan land and mother's and father's clan spirits. The ancestors of father and mother are recognized and believed to affect people's lives. Aggregation, here represented in the bringing together of a husband's people with his wife's people (or, of father's people with mother's people) is, I suggest, at the heart of Akie notions of life and social continuity.

THE DISCOURSES OF MYTH AND RITUAL PRACTICE

The Akie, like people everywhere, have theories about the world and their place in it: cosmological models of how the world is, and of how the world ought to be. The Akie cosmology is gendered; this is evident both ideologically and in practice. The central notion is that for meaningful practices to materialize there must always be a unity of complementary parts which, in turn, potentially generates new, transformed practices. For the Akie, cosmology is not an abstract set of symbolic relations, but a social arena where efforts and strategies are expended and employed in relation to specific cultural and other resources in an endeavour to gain access to them. However, the potential for social transformation is bound up with the imperatives of social continuity. Akie everyday and ritual practices are, in a very real sense, history-making practices, intended to make history repeat itself and thus to perpetuate the *status quo*. This process of cultural and social reproduction is responsible for the apparent coherence and consistency of social and ideational structures. The social structures which are designed internally in terms of power relations stand in a relation of domination, subordination or equivalence to each other by virtue of the access they provide to goods or capital in four categories: economic capital, social capital, cultural capital, and symbolic capital (Bourdieu 1991: 229–31). Individuals, as well as groups, engage with these social structures as agents whose strategies are concerned with the preservation or improvement of their positions with respect to different forms of capital.

The above model, I suggest, is helpful in understanding the Akie women's ritual known as *Saisee Tororeita*. This ritual is similar to other rituals found in East and Southern Africa known as rituals of rebellion (Gluckman 1963) or rituals of reversal (Rigby 1968). This particular Akie ritual is best understood by relating it to other Akie rituals and myths which emphasize the emergence of ordered structure through the combination of complementary elements. I thus contrast various rituals which are performed by men with the *Saisee Tororeita* ritual, which is the only one performed by Akie women. I show that this Akie women's ritual can best be understood as a re-enactment of the primordial unification as a necessary condition for the existence and perpetuation of the structure and existing social relations (see, for example, Jacobson-Widding and van Beek 1990).

For this reason I suggest that the various Akie rituals, myths and historical discourses must be understood in conjunction with Akie ideas about humanity and cosmology. Akie notions of humanity suggest that their existence as a unique community of hunter-gatherers resulted from a series of dramatic social and cosmological transformations. Akie rituals condense the Akie mythical past and history by employing a set of symbols that feature centrally in Akie notions of being. Akie ideas about being are viewed as a process which involves the unity of two complementary parts. These parts must fuse to transform the previous order. In this sense, rituals, like mythical and historical discourses, are memories which represent the Akie contemporary world. The Akie thus inhabit the present, understood both as a

THOSE WHO PLAY WITH FIRE

set of discursive practices and as a body of operative ideas and truths responding to the socio-economic and cultural needs of the Akie, and interacting with them.

Most Akie stories share a general pattern, namely, that the present Akie way of life and social organization are the result of what happened in the primordial period referred to as *ikaakeny* (literally, the past). The past is perceived as a non-dialectical and non-transformative period that the Akie themselves transformed through the combination of complementary opposites. This primordial period appears in Akie mythology to demonstrate the importance of gender differences and their continued unity both as a source and shaper of history. The primordial past – conceived of in terms of unity joined by a cord or strap – preceded the separation of a world conjoined and the emergence of differences which characterize contemporary Akie social and economic relations (cf. Århem 1991; Kipury 1983). The separation of the 'above' from the 'below' was a transformation which gave rise to social relations defined by gender, including the transformation of hunting and gathering from a gender-neutral to a gendered activity. For the Akie, the emergence of gender relations is the result of the attenuation of primordial social relations and their replacement by relations created by the Akie themselves. It could also be argued that Akie myths are metaphors for the various symbols seen by the Akie as central to notions of Akie identity. These symbols of identity, made apparent as themes in Akie mythology, seek to explain the genesis of the various forms of social relations which followed the transformation from the primordial period. Akie narratives emphasize the fact that transformation is only possible when substance is shared (or mixed) and when relations complement each other. The underlying logic of these myths and stories seems to suggest the inevitability of the mutual structuring of social relations, especially gender relations. It is ritual that provides the practice and legitimacy for these myths and stories because, among other things,

the credibility of a discourse is what first makes believers act in accord with it. To make people believe is to make them act ... Because the law is already applied with and on bodies, 'incarnated' in physical practices, it can accredit itself and make people believe that it speaks in the name of the 'real' (de Certeau 1984: 148).

According to Akie mythology, their history is divided into the past (*ikaakeny*) and the present (*horyo*). History is presented as a primordial past where cosmology had a singular gender and was undifferentiated. During this time, the heavens and the earth were joined by a strap (*talaita*). The Akie cosmos was wet and cold in this primordial period before the emergence of structure (cf. Jacobson-Widding and van Beek 1990). The past, which the Akie divide into three historical epochs, constitutes the period of their formation as a unique hunting and gathering community. These epochs are presented in folk narratives, myths and other stories to explain how the Akie have become the hunter-gatherers they are today.

In this chapter, I attempt to describe and make sense of an Akie women's ritual which is said to be, and indeed appears to be, the 'opposite' (or more appropriately, complementary) of men's rituals. In my presentation I suggest that in *Saisee Tororeita* women (re)enact a wide range of meanings which relate to people's conceptions about a way of life seen as complementary and essential to the continuity of the social whole. This particular ritual as well as others, myths and stories of origin, deploys the specific procreative powers and products necessary for the physical and cosmological reproduction of Akie society. In *Magic, Science and Religion and Other Essays*, Malinowski noted that 'an intimate connection exists between the word, mythos, the sacred tales of a tribe, on the one hand, and their ritual acts, their moral deeds, their social organization, and even their practical activities, on the other' (1954: 96). In this chapter I draw a connection between this women's ritual and other rituals, myths and stories to show how they may, in conjunction, reveal an Akie understanding of their identity as manifested in various aspects of their life. In order to elaborate, I briefly discuss Akie stories of origin and myths to suggest that, while Akie conceptions of gender emphasize the differences between sexes, the genders are seen as complementary and both are viewed as essential to the continuity of society as a whole.

Jacobson-Widding and van Beek (1990) have developed a model which explains how symbiotic relations between two or more human beings can transcend hierarchical or otherwise distinguishing boundaries between men and women and other social categories. These representations are common among Nilotic groups in Eastern Africa. On the cosmological and symbolic levels, this model is based on a set of binary contrasts between the male and the female that are critical for the production of life as the Akie perceive it and also figure as the essential factor in determining any future direction for the development of social forms. According to this model, the idea of a fusion between heaven and earth (Århem 1991) is connected with the creative process. In fact, this fusion is the original creation itself symbolized by the connection between heaven and earth. This connection represents the primordial and undifferentiated unity preceding the original creation. In most pastoral and agro-pastoral societies of Eastern and Southern Africa the idea of fusion is symbolized in terms of male/female, heaven/earth, above/below, hot/cold and so forth. And, as will be pointed out below, the merging of two or more elements tends to erase the hierarchical distinction between men and women and between social or conceptual categories classified as 'high' or 'low', superior or inferior. By the same token, to transcend duality and hierarchy by merging what appear to be opposites is at the centre of Akie notions of transformation. As Kratz (1994) has convincingly argued with reference to the Okiek of Kenya (who share close cultural similarities with the Akie) ceremonies which emphasize complementarity create a contradictory set of hierarchical intragender relations based on age and defined by a contradiction between complementarity in both production and reproduction (1994: 44) This is similar to the Akie case where the fusion of female and male elements is a symbolic prerequisite for the regeneration of all kinds of life in Akie practice, and where Akie ideas about being revolve around the unity of complementary parts as a necessary precondition for the transformation and reproduction of the existing order.

SAISEE TORORElTA

Saisee Tororeita is a type of ritual which, according to some African ethnographers, might be described either as a ritual of rebellion (Gluckman 1963; Spencer 1988) or as a ritual of reversal (Rigby 1968). According to Gluckman (1963: 118), the ritualized role reversals of the Zulu first-fruits ceremony (*umkhosi wokweshama*) and of the ritual of *Nomkhulbulwana* give otherwise subordinate women an opportunity to express, in reversed form, an alternative view of the social order. In this way, society at large maintains social solidarity and functional equilibrium (1963: 118). Peter Rigby argues that Gogo women of Tanzania take on male roles following calamities such as drought, women's barrenness, crop failure, and cattle disease to mitigate the situation by manipulating gender roles (Rigby 1968: 172–3). Women mimic men's demeanour and perform male tasks in order to bring about a reversal of the unwanted state of affairs. Paul Spencer (1988) suggests that women's protests among the Maasai have a brief reality of their own which readjusts the balance between the sexes, and is seen to bring a diffuse blessing that ensures the birth of future generations.

Contrary to the above approaches, Beidelman (1966) provides an analysis of the Swazi *Incwala* ritual based on indigenous cosmological notions. Indeed, as Beidelman argues, before one can write about various themes in rituals, one must understand the cosmology of the people involved so that one has some idea of what they themselves believe that they are doing with such rituals (1966: 374). It is on this basis that Beidelman criticizes Gluckman's approach to the interpretation of the Zulu rituals: Gluckman 'does not seem to have made such initial analysis with the symbolic acts he considers and ... this led him to some misplaced emphases and misinterpretations, in that he sometimes found conflict, aggression, and rebellion as dominant themes where this does not seem to be so' (1966: 374–5).

Beidelman's point is useful for rethinking women's rituals in Africa. More recent studies have shown that gender categories relate to broader understandings of people's cosmologies and notions of being (Herbert 1993). Gender categories, therefore, can be seen as part of the broader understanding of history and the perpetuation of meaningfully constituted life. In this context then, rituals, mythical and historical discourses, do not merely re-enact immediate experience, they also reconfigure themselves as signs of continuous becoming, by bringing the past into relation with the present. Rituals, and the mythical and historical past present themselves as wholes, as explanatory systems. The reason societies receive them as formulations of the past and as possible doctrines for the future is that they are processes which legitimize the present, simultaneously modifying their contexts, transforming or adapting references, and constantly reinventing the origin they are supposed to account for (Mudimbe 1991: 98).

Saisee Tororeita is an Akie women's ritual performed preferably each rainy season on the appearance of the first flowers with which bees make honey. Married women, preferably those with children, determine a suitable time to perform the ritual. Before performing this ritual women are supposed to determine the possibility of *amracheche Tororeita* – that is, the possibility of God descending. Akie agree that it is only women who can do this because God listens to women. The two important factors in determining the right time, as well as the possibility of God descending, are judgement and keen observation of events leading up to the ritual itself. Akie informants told me that this ritual is held only when there is a persistent threat to Akie well-being. This may be an enduring bad hunting season, women miscarrying regularly, or a wide range of unfortunate events which the community may have experienced during the season or over a number of seasons. Some informants suggested that the ritual is performed only when it is certain that God is angry with the Akie's behaviour.

God may be angered for a number of reasons, both social and natural. For example, the failure of men's *tyemasi* rituals to yield the expected results over a period of time may prompt women to perform *Saisee Tororeita*. *Tyemasi*, as will be explained below, is both a spirit and a set of rituals related to the powers of Akie ancestors (*asiiswante* (sing.); *asiiswe* (plur.)). Most day-to-day misfortunes are dealt with in *tyemasi* rituals by appealing to the ancestors. The ancestors have both benevolent and malevolent powers. They can reward or punish anyone who violates community norms, such as the principle of meat sharing. Those guilty of breach of etiquette are severely and sometimes immediately punished by the ancestors.[1]

Once it is clear to the married women that the time is right for the ritual, they summon the men to go into the forest and collect honey. The decision is not normally made by individual women. Rather, the idea for holding the ritual is conceived by a few women who might have discussed it on a number of occasions. The idea is then presented to other women. It is only when the decision has been made collectively by the women that men are requested to collect honey. While men are busy collecting honey, women start building the ritual village (*manyata*). The construction normally takes a day or two. They build the village by making a circular fence with two gates (*ingihomii*), one facing north, and another facing south. Small thatched huts are built inside the fence, all facing a central hearth. The huts are then joined together by a ritually significant strap which the Akie refer to as *talaita*.[2] *Talaita* is the same term as that used for the central pillar of the house, as well as for the strap which once joined the heaven above *(intoror)* to the earth below *(ng'wany)* prior to their separation.

Whereas men brew beer on all other ritual occasions (and more specifically, men who have undergone the Akie ritual male adulthood, *kalandaisye*), beer on this ritual occasion is brewed only by married women. Women brew beer in two large calabashes. Women's brewing of alcohol is a re-enactment of the mythical, primordial past *(ikaakeny)* when Akie beer *(kuumi)* is said to have been introduced to the community by a woman who was trying to poison her ailing husband to relieve him of his pain. Instead of dying, however, the man was healed. He then invited other men to enjoy the drink. Men later learnt how to make beer and ever since have deprived women of beer brewing. Brewing beer for this ritual can therefore be seen as a re-enactment of the original state when women first introduced it to the Akie community. Beer is brewed by mixing honey *(kumiante)* and *ratinyante* *(aloe secundeflora)*. In the story about how the Akie first obtained alcohol, the emphasis on the coming together of different, but complementary and mutually dependent elements is apparent. What ultimately transforms practices is perceived as a kind of mutual communication of differences, and this communication must precede any transformation of the *status quo*.

When brewing beer, women select one hut where they all assemble to prepare the yeast. The most important event at this stage is fetching water. The women do this collectively while singing women's songs associated with the *tyemasi* rituals. These songs are thematically varied: there are songs about fertility, the ancestors and men, and some are the same as those sung after giving birth. Beer-filled calabashes are left near the fire to ferment for at least two days. When the beer is ready, preparations for the ritual commence. The ritual begins just after sunset when the women enter their houses to steal their husbands' bows. When they emerge, they force the men into the huts in the ritual village by threatening them with the fact that God is descending. The threat is made by repeating *amracheche Tororeita* (i.e. God is descending) and singing over and over again a number of songs associated specifically with this ritual. *Saisee* songs are normally abusive to men, and depict them as timid, and their genitals as ineffective. They portray everyday Akie perceptions of masculinity as being subdued by femininity.

When all the men are in the huts, women take the beer from the hearth and dance in procession to the ritual village, which is normally located to the east of the main settlement. On the way, the women hold the bows in their right hands while singing. It is only on this occasion that all women, including pregnant women, are allowed to touch bows; under normal circumstances it is taboo for pregnant women to touch bows.[3]

Women enter the ritual site through the south gate (*ingihomii*). Both the south and north share the same name, *kophiko*. At the south gate, they place one of the two alcohol-filled calabashes. They then proceed clockwise to the northern gate while singing, with their bows in their left hands, beating the bows on the strap (*talaita*) and on the huts as they go. They then put the second calabash at the northern gate and close the gate. They repeat the process by proceeding to the southern gate and closing it with a similar strap. From this point on, the women sing one song for almost the entire night. While singing, they dance in clockwise circles four times each way, beating the bows on the strap and on the huts while, at the same time, hurling insults at men. This goes on until dawn. It is difficult for me to give a precise account of this part of the ritual since men are not allowed to come out of their huts while the women are praying to God outside. Akie say that during the singing, *Tororeita* descends to drink the beer in the two calabashes. Just as women are forbidden from seeing the spirit *tyemasi*, so are men forbidden from seeing *Tororeita*.

The dancing and singing goes on until the sighting of the morning star at dawn the following day. Once the star is sighted, women sing the morning star song (*matalaibenge*) to symbolize the beginning of a new day when the sun rises in the east. The east is known in Akie *as lang'unate;* the direction is also referred to as *meti* (up), the same term used for the head. Whereas the west (*raraitaita*) is an inauspicious direction, the east (*lang'unate*) is an auspicious one associated with the beginning of life. All major men's rituals (such as circumcision and initiation to manhood) take place just before sunrise. *Saisee Tororeita*, however, ends at this time. Before completing the ritual, the women make a final clockwise dance to the southern gate where

they are the first to witness whether God has descended to drink
the beer and sever the strap. Following this, by singing the
morning star song, the women signal to the men that the strap
closing the southern gate has been cut. Then the men come out
of the huts to meet the women at the central hearth. All then
proceed to the calabash at the southern gate to witness whether
God has descended to drink the beer, and then move anticlock-
wise to the northern gate to ascertain the same. From the
northern gate women take the now (ideally) empty calabash, and
proceed to the southern gate where they take the second
calabash, leaving the ritual village through the southern gate.

GOD ABOVE AND GOD BELOW: GENDERING THE DIVINE

The *Saisee Tororeita* ritual is associated with the powers of the
God above. My Akie informants told me that *Tororeita* has benevolent powers only. It is because of this that the Akie consider
him to be part of, yet superior to, the ancestors (*asiiswe*) who
have malevolent and benevolent powers. Akie ancestry is traced
through a father and a mother. In Akie cosmology, the world
below is feminine – the world of ancestors where both male and
female ancestors live. The underworld may be seen as a metaphor
for the womb or container where ancestors of both genders live
in unity. This may be seen as complementing the world above,
Tororeita, which is identified with the male gender. The two
genders in Akie cosmology are perceived as mutually dependent.
For Akie, all meaningful transformations occur through the symbiotic, mutually dependent combination of male and female
powers and products necessary for the physical and cosmological
reproduction of their society.

Akie say *Tororeita nga intoror bhabha; Tororeita nga ng'wany
amo* ('the God above is father; and the God beneath is mother').
This phrase captures a very broad and complex Akie understanding and construction of the cosmos which, to a large extent,
informs their ideas about their place in the world. The phrase is a
general description of the monumental change which occurred in
Akie history, and completely transformed their social relations,
recasting them in their contemporary form. To analyse the Akie
women's ritual, *Saisee Tororeita*, I will first describe the Akie
story about this common saying and then relate it to their
broader understanding of identity and social organization.

Broadly, the Akie life-cycle and history can be divided into three: (1) pre-birth construed in terms of symbols, metaphors and metonymies which stress the unity of substance, (2) birth and life involving the attenuation of previous ways of life, giving way to the emergence of new ways of life, which are nonetheless predetermined to a certain extent by the preceding way of life, and (3) death and its ramifications for the living. These three stages in the Akie life-cycle are seen as related to factors in the cosmic world, and to other Akie concepts of cosmic order, procreation, the regeneration of life, social organization. I will now attempt to show that the Akie women's ritual *Saisee Tororeita* is about re-enacting the logic of the cosmic order.

In the Akie origin myth, people emphasize the fact that primordial unity preceded the original creation. In this instance, as Jacobson-Widding and van Beek (1990) argue, the primordial order is linked with the idea of a non-structured unity. And it is only after the transformation of this period that structure and social relations emerge. I draw a link between *Saisee Tororeita* and the primordial unity of heaven and earth. The Akie say that in primordial times the heaven above (*-intoror*) and the earth below (*-ng'wany*) were joined together by a strap. The word for this strap, as noted above, is the same word for the ritual strap used in *Saisee Tororeita*. The primordial Akie are said to have been small and stout; and they allegedly slept in bees' nests. In other words, the primordial Akie were like children. Even so, these Akie (referred to as *eitumuna*) were hunter-gatherers. Hunting during this period was done by men and women. The Akie could kill animals with their gaze. However, God was dissatisfied with the stature of the ancient Akie, and decided to refashion them in his own image by mixing the dirt of their sweat (*simta*) in a *makata* gourd (an object which the Akie use for carrying and preserving honey). The newly fashioned Akie were tall and elegant, but had problems related to their newly acquired stature: they could not walk upright, and banged their heads when they tried, since heaven was very near. The advantage of this newly acquired stature, however, was that they could converse easily and directly with God. They could also put their individual problems to him by simply going up to the above. Yet during this period it rained constantly, something the Akie say hindered early men and women from hunting effectively. Tired of the situation, and being fully aware of how easily other smaller creatures lived, an Akie man decided to sever the strap, bringing about the separation of the heaven from the earth. The rain stopped. Since that day, rain only falls in particular seasons, causing plants to sprout and new life to begin. This separation led to the split between heaven and earth and each part subsequently acquired exclusive but mutually dependent features. *Intoror* – the place Akie speak of as belonging to the God above, who is father – has since this time been made up of water. When the split occurred, both God and the substance associated with him (water) went upwards. The myth also refers to the other God, the God below, as mother. These narratives provide a scenario in which the God above – father – is composed of or associated with water, while the God below – mother – is made up of hot substances and inhabits the world of the ancestors. The living Akie inhabit a space between these two gendered Gods. The efficacy of their ritual practices depends very much on the joining of these masculine and feminine parts of their cosmic universe. Some things, in other words, have to be shared or mixed for a transformation to occur.

The nature of this primordial separation is crucial to the understanding of a wide range of Akie cultural ideologies or schema that provide insights into concepts of personhood, kinship and gender. It was only after the separation of the above from the below that the various symbols which define the differences between these various aspects of their life came into existence. Yet most of these symbols express the importance of ritual action for the continuation of life. The symbols, metaphors and metonymies have to come together to regenerate life. It is this essential aspect, which when related to the broader categorization of the Akie gendered cosmos, helps to explain why women perform *Saisee Tororeita*.

In other Eastern and Southern African societies, ideas about hot and cold are commonly employed in a wide range of practical and symbolic transformations. According to De Heusch (1975), these ideas, which are part of a set of contraries on which people's philosophical understanding is based, portray the larger cosmological rhythm upon which life depends. These contradictory elements, which appear in myths and other belief systems in Eastern and Southern Africa, exist in a dialectical relation with each other and yet their action allows for processes of mediation to occur (De Heusch 1975: 362). Herbert (1993) argues that various transformative processes in Africa can meaningfully be understood by exploring the role gender plays and its relation to various African people's understandings of life. Indeed, as Morris argues, symbolic representations in which fusion is marked in terms of opposed principles – male/female, heaven/earth, above/below, hot/cold – can be understood as social processes which seek to express transformations that transcend those hegemonic forms which emphasize male dominance (Morris 1995: 43).

The existence of a set of active contraries in Akie thought is evident in a series of associations made in Akie myth and ritual practice. In the origin myth heaven is made of water, but the underworld is hot like a woman's womb. The Akie say: *orkorar asiiswe maa ng'enarita ng'wany*; that ancestors live in a hot place below where they make fire. The Akie also speak of a woman's womb as *arita maae*, as hot. Others suggested that the water in a calabash in which initiates bathe before circumcision is hot and can cause severe pains to the initiate. The Akie immerse several objects in this water, including the needle (*kaate*) used for mending women's skin clothing and honey-carrying bags, the traditional axe (*engetarya*), and the leaves of a certain tree called *emberepapa* (*Asparagus aethiopicus*) which, according to another Akie myth, sprouted from the tomb of the first Akie to die. The combination of these items, the Akie say, cools the water in the calabash and reduces the initiate's pain during circumcision. The calabash, like the world below and a woman's womb, is thought to contain hot substances. Indeed, there is a close symbolic association between these three containers – the woman's womb, the calabash and the world below. All are associated with heat. But more important, they are all places where transformations occur by uniting things which complement each other. The womb delivers both genders; the ritual calabash has objects immersed in it which define both female and male activities; and, in the world below, the ancestors live in a world where gender differences are blended.

THE ORIGIN OF HUNTING AND GATHERING

Severing the strap not only separated God the Father above from God the Mother below; it also led to the loss of the knowledge of how to secure one's livelihood in the primordial era. Myths which deal with the period after the severance of the strap emphasize the emergence of structures which define contemporary Akie practices. The Akie describe the post-primordial era as being, in part, God-given, but also as being modified by subsequent human actions. In other words, what has come to be the contemporary Akie way of life is the result of the merging of two understandings which again generated new practices.

The new Akie had to learn new ways to make a living. An Akie man and his Maasai counterpart approached God with a request to be taught new ways of life. God gave the Akie and the Maasai each a calabash (*makata*), and instructed them not to open them until they had reached their respective homes. The Maasai man took the calabash all the way home, opened it, and out came domesticated animals. In contrast, the Akie man, impatient with the whistling sound coming from the calabash, opened it in the bush on the way home. Out of the calabash came wild animals, and ever since, Akie people have relied on these animals for their livelihood. Unaware of what to do with the animals, the Akie man returned to God, who then gave him a bow and arrow and instructed him to live by killing the animals. Hence the generation of pastoralism for the Maasai, and hunting and gathering for the Akie.

Initially, God made life easy for the Akie hunters by allowing a wounded animal to make a whistling sound so hunters could easily track it. But this sound, which was known to all Akie, also alerted others to the wounded animal, thus making it impossible for a lone hunter to eat meat without sharing. The first Akie hunter to kill an animal could not endure the sound as he did not wish to share the animal with others. He struck the place from which the sound came. Miraculously, the animal came back to life and from then on animals wounded by hunter's arrows did not die. The Akie man then approached God with this new dilemma. God taught the Akie new ways of tracking wounded animals – following vultures or following the animals' tracks. Both methods made it possible for hunters to find meat without telling others and thus freed them from being compelled to share. But, as in other Akie stories, this was an inversion of the current ideal which emphasizes the sharing of meat. The story is told to explain why meat sharing is now carried out according to gender and age.

Another narrative about the post-primordial period explains the essence of death among the Akie. According to this narrative,

death came about because an envious, childless woman was
spiteful towards her co-wife's children. One of her co-wife's
children had fallen ill and was on the verge of dying. The woman
wanted to know what happens on death. The God above is said
to have told the woman the secret: 'Beings die and come back,
but the moon dies and goes for ever'. Then God instructed the
woman to tell this to her fellow Akie. But the woman instead
reversed this and told the community that: 'The moon dies and
comes back, but beings die and go for ever'. The child then died
and did not return. The woman returned to tell God. In
response, God told her that she had violated his will. God then
instructed her to go back and keep watch over the child's tomb
and to ensure that nobody cut anything that sprouted from it.
After some days, a green leaf sprouted from the tomb. The
woman herself cut it and ever since, beings die for ever.

The mystery of death remained unresolved until one day when
a child who had gone with his mother to collect berries went
missing. As it is narrated in this story, a group of women set out
to gather fruits in the bush. One woman left her boy in the shade
of a tree as she, with other women, collected berries at a distance.
On completing the task, she went back to retrieve the child, but
the child was gone. After about eight months, the young boy
reappeared in the form of a spirit. He revealed himself to an Akie
man. The boy told the old man that he had been taken by the
dead Akie elders (*asiiswe*) whose representative he had now
become – i.e. *tyemasi*. The *tyemasi* spirit, although male, has a
tripartite composition, in the sense that the Akie speak of the
spirit as a synthesized being made up of *tyemasi* (the spirit), his
wife and his child. The spirit manifests itself to the Akie in the
form of three sounds, each representing one character or element
of its composition. The *tyemasi* spirit has been appropriated by
men who are the only category of Akie people allowed to see it.
And it is only men who have undergone a ritual known as *kalandaisye* who are eligible to see the spirit. The spirit mediates
between the living Akie and the dead. The dead Akie are said to
inhabit the world below, where the feminine God resides – *tororeita nga ng'wany- amo*. The world beneath produces all the fauna
found in the Akie world and the Akie ancestors determine the
well-being of the living. All communication between the living
and the dead is mediated by the *tyemasi* spirit through men. All
rituals for blessing, healing, and so on are under men's control

because it is they who have access to *tyemasi*. In this way men have access to feminine powers because *tyemasi* gives them access to the feminine powers of the God below – mother.

RITUALS AND THEIR RELATIONS

In addition to the *Saisee Tororeita* ritual, the Akie perform other rituals – the circumcision ritual for both boys and girls (*latime*); and a rite to manhood (*kalandaisye*) exclusively for male youths. In both rituals, ancestral offerings *(kanaitaisye)* feature centrally. Ancestral offerings are also performed in a set of other rituals known collectively as the *tyemasi* rituals. These rituals are associated with the powers of the ancestors. The *tyemasi* spirit features in all cults and rites associated with the Akie concept of *ng'wany*, the underworld. The reason men are associated with these rites and cults is because they complement the gender of the divinity, as well as in some ways expressing aspects of men's power over women. However, what Akie myths emphasize is the reciprocal correspondence between the genders. While the powers of the God below are mediated by men through the spirit *tyemasi* which is associated with the ancestors below, the spatial relationship between the living and the ancestors is complemented by the living's relationship to the God above. This is evident in the Akie saying, 'our God put us below' (*Tororeita aeni nga ngw'any*). However, the God above is male and singular, while the God beneath is feminine and yet contains features of both genders. This is because *Ng'wany*, or below, is conceptualized as a womb and wombs contain both genders. In this sense, wombs are analogous to other containers in rituals, such as the calabash. In rituals, the objects which are immersed in containers symbolize the activities of both Akie genders. This notion appears in all Akie symbolic activities and metaphors which represent the relationship of the genders; in almost all instances, men appear to form a complementary part of the whole. All Akie cults and rites celebrate the respective powers of male and female, their mutual dependency, and the exchange between them of the gendered powers and products necessary to the physical and cosmological reproduction of society.

Men perform all rituals pertaining to the forces of the world below, just as women perform the *Saisee Tororeita* ritual associated with the God above. Just as the powers beneath are feminine, those above are masculine. It is to the masculine powers of the cosmos that the ritual *Saisee Tororeita* appeals. The obvious difference between *Saisee Tororeita* and other rituals is that the former does not involve an ancestral offering; ancestral spirits are not involved. In this ritual, rather, participants appeal directly to God. Women do this by (re)enacting their origin myth. Not all Akie can relate this ritual to their myth of origin in any straightforward way. When I asked women why they tied a strap around the huts, some said that they were doing something their ancestors had done in the past. In all the cases where I enquired about the association between this ritual and their myth of origin, only one person told me that the ritual was the re-enactment of the situation as it was before the separation of the heaven from the earth. However, all informants held to the view that the women's aim is to communicate directly with God. Thus, Akie explanations are congruent with my suggestion that the aim of *Saisee Tororeita* is to recreate, symbolically, the original state of the universe in which God and people were one.

Instead of looking at the differences between *Saisee Tororeita* and other rituals, it is helpful to look at the basic features of these rituals and how they relate to the Akie ideas about their coming into being. In most Akie stories, a heavy emphasis is placed on the symbolism of their identity and their emergence as a community, including those factors which distinguish them from their neighbours. *Saisee Tororeita* is a ritual which seeks, in Akie terms, to bring the powers of God back to earth, because the ritual is intended to re-establish the link between the God of above and the God of below, an attempt to re-establish the primordial cosmic order.

To transcend both the social and natural limitations related to these differences conceived in terms of gender, Akie engage in rituals which aim to bring together different but complementary parts to ensure the continuity of meaningful life. In doing this Akie engage in practices which may or may not transform the *status quo*, while at the same time providing meanings for various micro and macro level events. *Saisee Tororeita*, therefore, is a ritual which not only seeks symbolically to re-enact the past; it also reflects on their contemporary condition as it relates to the past. In this respect, the Akie reflect collectively, through ritual action, on their place in the universe, as well as construct models of how the world is, and of how it ought to be.

NOTES

1 One such incident occurred during my research when, after repeatedly being asked for beer, I decided to buy several Akie men some local grain alcohol (making Akie honey beer is time-consuming). Alcohol was purchased in the nearby village and was consumed for several hours during the day. While drinking, some men began singing songs and dancing *tyemasi* dances that should only be performed at night. That evening an elderly man came to my tent requesting still more money to buy more alcohol, this time for *Tyemasi*. When I asked why, he said that an elderly woman had been afflicted by the *Tyemasi* spirit because the *asiiswe* were angry that *tyemasi* songs and dances were performed in broad daylight; this had allegedly denied the ancestors their alcohol, as they cannot participate during daylight hours.
2 This strap is made from by the bark of a *siteeta* tree.
3 Akie believe that if a pregnant woman touches a bow or an arrow, she renders the poison ineffective. An animal shot with a poisoned arrow will not die and if it were to die the killer would not be able to follow its tracks. Worse still, if the animal died and the killer managed to track it and get meat from the animal, his wife would miscarry.

REFERENCES

Århem, K. (1991) 'The symbolic world of the Maasai homestead' in A. Jacobson-Widding (ed.) *Body and Space: Symbolic Models of Unity and Division in African Cosmology and Experience* (Uppsala: Acta Universitatis Upsaliensis).
Beidelman, T.O. (1966) 'Swazi royal ritual', *Africa*, 36: 373–405.
Bourdieu, P. (1991) *Language and Symbolic Power* (Cambridge: Polity).
De Certeau, M. (1984) *The Practice of Everyday Life* (Berkeley: University of California Press).
De Heusch, L. (1975) 'What shall we do with the drunken king?' *Africa*, 45 (4): 363–72.
Gluckman, M. (1963) *Order and Rebellion in Tribal Africa* (London: Cohen & West).
Herbert, E. (1993) *Iron, Gender, and Power: Rituals of Transformation in African Societies* (Bloomington: Indiana University Press).
Jacobson-Widding, A. and W. van Beek (1990) 'Chaos, order and communion in African models of fertility: introduction' in A. Jacobson-Widding and W. van Beek (eds) *The Creative Communion: African Folk Models of Fertility and the Regeneration of Life* (Uppsala: Acta Universitatis Upsaliensis).
Kenny, M.G. (1981) 'Mirror in the forest: the Dorobo hunter-gatherers as an image of the other', *Africa*, 51 (1): 477–95.
Kipury, N. (1983) *Oral Literature of the Maasai* (Nairobi: Heinemann).
Kratz, C.A. (1994) *Affecting Performance: Meaning, Movement, and Experience in Okiek Women's Initiation* (Washington DC: Smithsonian Institution Press).

Kuper, A. (1982) *Wives for Cattle: Bridewealth and Marriage in Southern Africa* (London: Routledge & Kegan Paul).

Malinowski, B. (1954) *Magic, Science and Religion and Other Essays* (New York: Doubleday).

Morris, B. (1995) 'Hunting and the gnostic vision', *Society of Malawi Journal*, 48 (2): 26–46.

Mudimbe, V.Y. (1991) *Parables and Fables: Exegesis, Textuality, and Politics in Central Africa* (Madison: University of Wisconsin Press).

Rigby, P. (1968) 'Some Gogo rituals of "purification": an essay on social and moral categories' in E.R. Leach (ed.) *Dialectic in Practical Religion* (Cambridge: Cambridge University Press).

Spencer, P. (1988) *The Maasai of Matapato: A Study of Rituals of Rebellion* (Bloomington: Indiana University Press).

Van Zwanenberg, R. (1976) 'Dorobo hunting and gathering: a way of life or a mode of production', *African Economic History*, 2: 12–21.

CHAPTER 6

CREATION AND THE MULTIPLE FEMALE BODY

TURKANA PERSPECTIVES ON GENDER AND COSMOS

VIGDIS BROCH-DUE

Once upon a time, Sky, *Akuij*, was full of rain and lay low over Earth, *Akwap*. The land was so wet that animals could hardly move; their hooves got stuck and sore. One day when men were hunting, women took their long-handled hoes used for gathering and cultivation and pushed the sky high up. When the men returned they were angry and afraid of the women's deeds. To let the water through, the men tried to pierce holes in the sky with their spears, but they failed. The land dried up in the sun, enabling animals to move faster along paths on the hardened earth's surface. *Akuij* presented people with livestock, and they turned from hunting to herding.

This creation story and many others like it did *not* appear in Philip Gulliver's well-known book on the pastoral Turkana, *The Family Herds*, first published in 1955. Nor would Gulliver's account, dominated as it is by a western discourse of domesticity, have easily accomodated a feminine divine figure and creative force such as the deity *Akuij*. This western discourse has woven itself from particular structures of values and reality claims characterized by a gendered split between the private and public domains (see Ortner 1974; Rosaldo and Lamphere 1974; Rogers 1975; Rapp 1979; Rosaldo 1980; Strathern 1980). From this point of view, God simply cannot be female. Rather, the familiar western story is dominated by patriarchal power relations and patrilineal kinship structures – whether we are dealing with firms, forts or *The Family Herds* of Jie and Turkana. Gulliver's title is slightly ambiguous since the main feature of his work is not family life but friendship between elderly men. Entrapped in this masculine mould, women remain muted throughout much of the text.

This particular Turkana account is similar to those of many other Nilotic peoples. Indeed, despite the social and symbolic diversity evident in the regional ethnography, anthropologists have appropriated East African pastoralists as examples of how the so-called agnatic principle, once formulated by Evans-Pritchard, supposedly permeates all aspects of daily and ritual existence. 'The pastoral' and 'the patriarchal' have become intertwining tropes, endlessly reproducing and representing each other. Yet, on closer inspection, ethnographic texts reveal that among different peoples, and in different contexts, 'the pastoral' is constituted by extremely different signs and social practices. In this chapter, my aim is to make a start at restoring the feminine within the pastoral, particularly the feminine forces of creation.

As a discursive formation, images of 'the pastoral' have been moulded by a long history of conflicting conceptualizations, metaphors and theoretical models. The persistent ideas about patriliny and patriarchy first started to fill the pages during the 1940s and 1950s. This was precisely the period after the Second World War during which the doctrine of domesticity had become the standard for social theory and policy in western societies. In social theory, as in social life, modernity and sexual difference formed part of the same conceptual package – an historical package that coincided with the advent of new modes of writing that were informed by modernist scientific schemas and, in anthropology, were associated with the Malinowskian School. But prior to the entrenchment of this academic professionalism there were other 'men-on-the-spot' (alas, very few women) – missionaries, explorers, scholars and the like – who collected information on these cultures and who aimed to disseminate it to a wider public. Many had varied (and sometimes dubious) stories to tell about cultural images and gender relations among pastoralists in these parts of Africa.

Some of the exotic and very eclectic evidence presented in earlier travelogues was critically evaluated – a surprisingly long ago – in an essay by J. H. Driberg entitled, *The Status of Women among the Nilotics and Nilo-Hamitics* (1932). Trained in the 1920s, Driberg exhibits all the hallmarks of the new-style ethnographers, filling a professional role that would later evolve into that of the academic anthropologist (see Clifford 1988). In a neutral and balanced tone, he advanced a unified interpretative argument about 'the status of women', by comparing women's and men's relative places and positions within and across societies. He took both sides to task in the debate about whether women's status was inferior since both arguments relied on 'uncritical generalizations'.

> It is doubtful, indeed, whether among the Africans the question of high or low status ever arises as a distinction between men and women. It is a different status, that is all.... Nevertheless since views on the subject are so divergent, and since these generalizations are apt to have political and social repercussions, it is desirable that we should come to some conclusion which is based ... on the evidence offered by different aspects of cultural activity (1932: 405).

Of particular interest is Driberg's emphasis on observational biases, particularly the ways that our own cultural imagery and taken-for-granted assumptions from home cloud our interpretations elsewhere. The following statement, dealing with the general claim of women's economic subordination, is a case in point:

> The fact is that it is *really we who have got the wrong perspective*. We assume that the work or occupation (whatever it is) is menial, just because it is assigned to women, whereas this consideration does not enter into the minds of Africans at all (1932: 405, my italics).

This could be read as a prescient cultural critique not only of the male anthropologists of the 1950s, but also of feminist scholars of the 1970s whose model of 'woman' was universalizing, and for whom, in consequence, pastoral gender relations were yet another reiteration of the worldwide configuration of male dominance. Llewelyn-Davies (1978) apparently holds this view about Maasai women; she suggests that these women, like pastoral women everywhere, perceive themselves and are perceived as 'property', their relative worth being measured against cattle on the marriage market by men, through the medium of cattle.

Indeed, Driberg's statement echoes the concerns of contemporary feminist anthropologists who have at last dispensed with the convenient and colonizing 'we' inherent in the neat category 'woman'. Instead we have a composite canvas in which gender constructs weave themselves from complex and conflicting beliefs and practices that can vary both contextually and biographically (Moore 1994; Broch-Due and Rudie 1993; Bianco 1991). From this perspective, Driberg's account is particularly illuminating, evincing the enormous range of differences within and between Nilotic life-worlds, in relation to women's and men's work patterns and property, as well as to their respective political and religious positions. One feature resonates strongly in all the settings he describes: the profound significance of *feminine symbols* in the construction of both supernatural and social phenomena in pastoral societies.

In another seminal and encyclopaedic publication, *The Cattle Complex in East Africa*, Melville Herskovits (1926) identified similar positive representations of the religious and social roles of pastoral women. Indeed one of this work's central organizing devices (which scholars have neglected entirely) is the profound regional variations in gender relations found in the societies he describes. We learn, for example, that among the Awiwa, 'women as well as men may own stock' (Herskovits 1926: 268). And supporting the importance of matrifiliation, he wrote that the 'mother is a "hill" which, standing alone, starts a new line among the Zulu houses. A man's status is determined entirely by the place from which the cattle given for his mother came' (1926: 271).

What is particularly significant for the purpose of this chapter is not only Herskovits's focus on gender relations among pastoral peoples, but also his style of reporting. In his account, he constructed a subject position for women of a very active kind. The following statement about the ways that constructions of kinship, and claims in cattle, can work to the advantage of pastoral women – in this instance, among the Turkana and the Tugen – is a case in point:

After a probationary period, the marriage is sealed by a final ceremony, the presentation of two female goats to the mother of the bride. At this time the woman has her only opportunity to get property, her husband drives his cattle past her door and when what she considers 'a fair marriage portion' has been driven past, she calls, 'Enough!' (Herskovits 1926: 365).

Notable here is the interpretative and active role the new wife plays in the marriage. It is she who decides whether reciprocity has been done, rights fulfilled or responsibilities met.

Like all anthropological accounts, both Driberg's and Herskovits's narratives clearly betray the historical contexts in which they were produced. I draw attention to these texts because they were written during the brief period between two world wars when Western science and society paid more positive attention to a female presence and feminist issues than would be the case during the decades immediately to follow. Aside from this relatively relaxed ideological climate concerning gender issues, an important factor behind the varied and vivid representation of 'exotic' women was the research method applied. Empirical and inductive approaches focused attention on ethnographic detail and description. The analytical ambition was very much limited to demonstrating the distribution and diffusion of cultural traits – 'The Cattle Complex,' for instance – aiming, at best, towards middle-range theories, but still far from building master narratives. Women's near disappearance from anthropological accounts coincided with the later construction of grand, globalizing theories like structural-functionalism, structuralism and Marxism in the period from the 1940s to the 1960s.

The surge of feminism in social theory in the 1970s aimed to recover women's experiences across time and space. Yet such efforts were more successful with reference to modern capitalist societies than they were in settings and situations structured by different cultural logics and livelihoods (see Moore 1988). Despite laudable efforts to theorize gender cross-culturally, the project largely failed, mainly because the gendered eurocentric ground rules that permeated the master models feminist scholars wanted to reform, were themselves never sufficiently scrutinized and criticized. Laden with such implicit assumptions, the 'anthropology of women' remained committed to the fundamental dualisms of modern, western philosophy – nature/culture; body/mind; private/public – where the feminine is 'always already' placed on the negative, passive and powerless side of this gendered equation (Gatens 1991). Equipped with a binary formula, the discovery of the 'female other' was from the outset destined to be a rather disappointing one. The inevitable outcome was yet another example of the seemingly endless marginalization of women under patriarchy. The sad case of Maasai women was only one among several that featured in *Woman United, Woman Divided*, one of the more influential volumes in this genre (Caplan and Burja 1978).

Benefiting from this pioneering work in feminist anthropology, and from those written earlier, more mature feminist scholarship of the 1990s is more firmly grounded in forms of comparison that integrate gender dynamics with other social and symbolic dimensions. While this kind of theorizing flourishes in most areas of anthropology, it has so far filtered into only a few major works on East African pastoralism (see Kettel 1986; Talle 1987; Kipury 1989; Broch-Due 1990a; 1993; Bianco 1991; Hodgson 1995; Hutchinson 1992; 1996). These more recent accounts provide fresh perspectives on gender and gendering devices. However, the mainstream follows well-established paths. This exemplifies a persistent epistemological problem in the ethnography of pastoral societies – a problem stemming from a mix of male bias and the obsession with unilineal descent models (Broch-Due 1990a). The combined effect of these biases has been the framing of an artificially narrow field of study and the deployment of modes of description which bear only a thin resemblance both to local constructs and observed patterns on the ground.

ENGENDERING NARRATIVES

The decidedly masculine inflections that have dominated accounts of Nilotic pastoralists since the Second World War have recently been subject to a fresh round of deconstruction and reconfiguration.

In a recent survey of the literature, Burton concludes that in their epic images of creation, Nilotic cosmologies are brimming with feminine symbols (1991: 81). He ends his essay by making a play on the (in)famous statement by Evans-Pritchard who, in his desire to keep the agnatic principle intact without dispensing with contradictory empirical evidence, claimed that it persisted 'because the tracing of decent through women is so prominent and matrilocality so prevalent'. To this Burton replies as follows: 'Based on the present review, one might posit in response that the feminine symbols appear so dormant precisely because the masculine presence was so imposed' (1991: 96).

This statement brings us back to the creation story that opened the chapter which, in narrative and plot, clearly runs counter to the ideas of excessive maleness that have biased representations of the Turkana. In my own work I have tried to demonstrate that Turkana women are structurally and socially positioned quite favourably in terms of property and power relations. While female settlers have lost out in Turkana, their pastoral sisters are still coming out as winners more often than pastoral women in neighbouring societies. Numerous historical, cultural and economic forces and social processes shape these patterns, but these are beyond the scope of this chapter (see Broch-Due 1987; 1990a; 1990b; 1993; also Wienpahl 1984).

Yet, bringing back women into the pastoral arena we construct in our accounts is not really a matter of just filling in the gaps left by the absent feminine to get 'the whole picture'. This is because gender constructs are reflective and relational and manifest themselves across an entire range of discursive and practical fields. The cultural construction of femininity is integrally linked to the cultural construction of masculinity, creating gender models that may differ from the dichotomous design dominant in the West. Turkana clearly hold more dynamic ideas about gender; they play with femininities and masculinities, both metaphorically and in practice, a fact evident in their perceptions of personhood and physicality, of landscape and livestock. As Driberg noted long ago, they simply have another *perspective* on gender and gendering devices.

The point of this chapter is to venture beyond the standard, stereotypical and often stale 'sex role' debate. In order to avoid the endless and exhausting production of conflicting discoveries about the position of 'woman' – be it Butler against Evans-Pritchard, or Broch-Due against Gulliver – I would suggest rather that we explore local perspectives on gendering. The question is, How can we better grasp these local notions? The answer, I suggest, is through local narratives and narrations.

This is because cultural narratives, like the one about the divinity *Akuij*, constitute an extremely valuable and valid source of information for local peoples and anthropologists alike. They are stories people tell themselves about themselves. Through such narrative form, a range of non-explicit dispositions and orientations to the world are shaped and made comprehensible. Narration is in itself an interpretative act, translating 'knowing into telling' (White 1987: 1). Everyday experiences become framed, formed and filtered through structures of meaning that follow specific narrative conventions. These structures of meaning are

THOSE WHO PLAY WITH FIRE

shaped by *metaphors* that are capable of coupling text and context.

This is precisely because metaphors work to link systematically the figurative, creative and conceptual, on the one hand, to the everyday, basic and empirical on the other. In our studies of narratives, we must be alert to the whole operational scope of metaphor and metonymy, seeing them not only as tropes twisted into thought, talk and texts, but also as practical and perceptual *techniques* employed in everyday actions and experiments involving active engagement with the environment (Broch-Due 1993). The metaphors we live by, as Lakoff and Johnson (1980) remind us, exist not only in some abstract, theoretical, conceptual realm but also in the existential realm of being and becoming in the world; indeed, their usefulness lies precisely in their ability to bridge these two realms.

Metaphors thus not only enlarge local actors' understandings of the world they construct, but also provide them with the discursive resources necessary to discover and negotiate their subject positions within it. Crucially, metaphors also offer those foreign to this world a point of entry into it. As outsiders we may not make complete sense of local thought patterns, but a story from another culture is probably the easiest entry point available into those thought patterns. A story travels with ease from one language to another while other discursive realms travel with greater difficulty. And yet since narratives form an integral part of the wider cultural discourse, their structures and symbolizing devices can aid us to move into less easily accessible discursive domains. These may be poetic, philosophical or, as Foucault reminded us, practical as well (Foucault 1972: 49).

For our purposes, creation stories like the story of *Akuij* are significant cultural scripts since they depict the ways people conceive the form and sources of creative power (see Sanday 1981). Creation stories are also gendered scenarios of subject positions. They provide a unique path into local constructions of femininity and masculinity, as well as the relationships set up between the tropes 'man' and 'woman'. This is because the central actors in such stories serve as metaphors for important gender identities and gendered forms of agency. Below, I will explore Turkana notions of female agency through the ways it is expressed in narrative form, and beyond that, in ritual and everyday practices.

THE PROBLEM OF THE FEMININE DIVINE

In Nilotic pastoral cosmologies, the local concept for High God commonly carries a feminine gender prefix. In other words, the 'Supreme He' is seemingly a 'Supreme She'. This is a puzzling and paradoxical fact, destabilizing the ideas of the pastoralist as the prototypical warrior and patriarch. Neither does it make much sense in light of the Cartesian body-mind split, or in the light of the notion that 'woman' and 'spirituality' are mutually contradictory, at least when we are speaking about the sacred and not the demonic (Auerbach 1982). Clearly, this divine feminine prefix is a problem for standard accounts of the Nilotic worldview. Although its occurrence is, more often than not, relegated or removed entirely from the main ethnographic corpus, it seems to lurk in the recesses of scholars' minds who sometimes feel obliged to attend to this apparent anomaly in footnotes. With few exceptions, such efforts generally attempt to render the phenomenon completely insignificant. This surprising feminine spirituality is reconstructed and represented as a curiosity which is of no concern for serious scholars of East African pastoralism.

Anthropology, as a comparative enterprise, has of course encountered many peoples, from Asia to South America, whose cosmology is constructed around a 'Mother Goddess' figure (e.g. Reichel-Dolmatoff 1971; Geertz and Geertz 1975; Sanday 1981; Wiener 1995). We find such societies in Africa too, for example, the Ashanti (Rattray 1927) and the Mbuti whose habitat and maternal heaven is the Ituri Forest (Turnbull 1961). But these societies are classified as hunters and gatherers or cultivators, not herders. And our scholarly conventions tend to channel our thought and discoveries along particular paths from which one can stray only with difficulty. The persistence of the agnatic principle as the organizing device of East African ethnography is one such a path. This is not to say that in certain cases and contexts agnation is unimportant or non-existent, but simply that there are other constructs of kinship that merit attention.

The point is that the agnatic principle resonates so deeply within western cultures that it becomes a part-for-whole trope, distorting fundamentally our perception of Nilotic cultures. The dominance of the masculine signifier is clearly shared by standard interpretations of divinity and agency in contemporary Christianity. This was not always the case, a fact that attention to older imagery and interpretation reveals. In Medieval times, worshippers represented Christ in paintings and poetry in more ambiguous and androgynous terms, wrapping him in maternal shapes with nurturing breasts (Ash 1990). Yet 'the past is a different country', as the saying goes. With modernity, this alternative vision has vanished entirely and Christianity has been reconfigured as a cultural script for male power. Sanday explains it as follows:

> In Western society, as individual males and females, we understand the meaning of the divine command in the Garden of Eden – 'yet your desire shall be for your husband, and he shall rule over you' – and we are affected by the attitude toward women expressed in the events that led to the fall of Adam and Eve. We also understand that when our founding fathers declared 'that all men are created equal; that they are endowed by their creator with certain unalienable rights,' they had men and not women in mind (1981: 15).

One of the points I want to make is that once we begin to think in unilineal masculine images, feminine divinity becomes 'matter out of place', in Mary Douglas's (1966) terms. The typical dismissals of a divine femininity are very telling because they are framed in the above terms. Objections range from those based on linguistic grounds ('a gender prefix is a arbitrarily feature of grammar' (Gulliver 1953)), to those based on religiosity ('how can a monotheistic God be a woman?'). More modern responses accept that the divine may be constructed as feminine, but deflate the feminine power either by invoking conventional characteristics carried by the feminine so it 'reflects the immanent nature of the concept' (Benson 1974: 76), or simply by suggesting that this spiritual force is really not feminine but 'genderless' (Århem 1991: 78).

I shall argue that divine femininity is neither a grammatical accident, nor an implication of ideas of immanence. On the contrary, the feminine divine is central to the ways that the construction of cosmology weaves itself from bodily imagery that is clearly and concretely gendered. The scene conjured up in the creation story cited at the outset is the birth of landscape and livestock, through which religious constructions are, through narrative, made concrete. We have something very similar to the story of the Mother Goddess.

Turkana share with other Nilotic pastoralists – like the Nuer (Evans-Pritchard 1940), the Dinka (Lienhardt 1961), the Murle (Lewis 1972) and the Maasai (Olsson 1989) – the notion that Sky and Earth were once contiguous and connected by a strap or rope. The Turkana speak of this rope as an umbilical cord tied to newborn humans and animals, who once lived in the humid belly of Sky (see also Kaare, this volume). In the same way that a foetus floating in the wet womb will eventually come out and continue to grow outside, so it was with these mythical beings.

Through a series of such creations, Turkana were converted from hunters and gatherers to cultivators and finally into herders. The Maasai, too, seem to have positive notions attached to this act of rebirth, since following the division they acquired cattle, let down from the sky by means of a rope woven from the bark of the *Oreteti* tree (Olsson 1989: 241). The Turkana represent women's views of the primordial closeness of Sky and Earth in terms of an irksome state of restricting dependence, while men's response is represented as having been more ambivalent. However much men were against the women's action of pushing the sky away, the outcome of the women's act was clearly positive, resulting in a return gift: the cherished livestock.

This is not so with the Dinka. Although the Dinka hold women responsible for the transformation, they interpret female action negatively because it was they who severed the dangling rope that had previously ensured humans' easy access to divinity. According to Dinka myth, the couple created under the tamarind tree, the male Garang and the female Abuk, had to take great care when they were planting and pounding because they were only allowed to produce small amounts of food. One day the 'greedy' Abuk decided to plant more grain than was permitted. When raising her long-handled hoe, she inadvertently struck Divinity who, being offended, withdrew and sent a small bird to sever the rope. Ever since, say Dinka, the country has been spoilt and humans have had to toil for food and are plagued with hunger (Lienhardt 1961: 34). Unlike the Turkana who imagine the separation as an overdue birth and deny that the foetal-like humans ever climbed up the divine cord, the Dinka seem to portray it more like a premature delivery, bringing about death and misfortune rather than cattle-keeping and wealth. Yet doubts also linger in the Dinka vision because the original closeness also confined and constricted humans. Their dilemma is that when joined with Divinity they wanted freedom, but by breaking free they remained dependant, having to contend with suffering and death. Lienhardt gave Dinka thought an obvious Christian flavour by focusing on notions of the Original Sin that resulted in their expulsion from their 'Garden of Eden', and their continued life of back-breaking labour that resulted (Lienhardt 1961: 35ff).

What kind of agency do these representations portray? Interestingly, the Turkana story is quite explicit about the fact that it required female agency to set the cosmogonic birth in motion. Women pushed the sky up and created a space for reborn people, plants and animals, to continue in drier environs outside the *Akai* (skeleton) of *Akuij*, but without severing the celestial version of the mother–child bond. Indeed these primordial peoples were lured out of their foetus-like existence by the rain's excessive and menacing wetness that threatened to destroy their nurturing environment. Clearly we have a cosmological projection of similar problems in human pregnancy, drawing creatively on the fact that the amniotic fluid filling the sac can be spoiled and the placenta can become unable to feed the foetus if the delivery is prolonged. And just as the newborn baby can satisfy its hunger by a new kind of nurture – mother's milk – the mythical people were rewarded with another source of food, namely, milk and meat from livestock.

What I want to draw particular attention to is the ways in which the story equates growth and creation in several domains simultaneously – landscape, people and livestock. Despite the obvious play on reality and reversals of events that take place in the text, these narrative elements are also extra-textual points of reference which point to a reality in which ecological relations profoundly influence everyday life. The climatic flavour of this creation story brings to the fore the ways in which the whole tempo of the Turkana world is governed by the turn of the seasons; the cycle between dry and wet, scarcity and plenty, singular and plural. The seasonal cycles are connected to the family herd's patterns of feeding, mating, calving and producing milk. Crucially, the overlapping growth cycles in livestock and landscape are channelled into the biological cycles of humans through the nurturing powers of herds. To ensure a successful outcome, human procreation, pregnancy and the beginning of a new life must be synchronized with animal breeding. As the myth appropriates for its own effect, the calving season, and most human births as well, occur at the outset of the wet season. The reason given by informants for this seasonal peak in delivery patterns, consciously planned and co-ordinated, is because fresh fodder and plenty of food are necessary for creating the milk-flows that connect the feeding relationship of cow–calf to the human one of mother–child (Broch-Due 1990b; 1993).

The positive side of the ways in which Turkana employ these ecological relations as the model for all forms of relatedness is the celebration of reproduction and growth. The inordinate importance of everything 'female' in the pastoral production process is both mundane and profound. The female sex – whether human or animal – is highly valued precisely because of the womb's capacity to produce equally valued outcomes, children and calves: the matter of wealth in this world! In other words, prosperity hinges on processes of fertility. For this is a society that depends for its survival over time on the successful coupling of livestock, labour and grazing land. Since the pastoral livelihood strategy is formed around the production of milk, rather than meat, female animals are far more numerous in Turkana than male ones, most of which are dispensed with at a young age. The number of people depending for their food on these nurturing milk-flows must be balanced against the number of fertile dams in the herd – and the needs of children and calves for the milk from the same udders must be synchronized. The amount of milk produced by the cows at any one time is also a measure of the quality of grass and availability of water.

The darker side of this intimate dependency on natural rhythms and the flux in resources suggested in the story is the very real potential for loss and death if the weather fails to produce the fine-tuned balance between wetness and dryness. In an effort to contain these ruinous forces of livelihood and land-scape, themselves capable of hindering growth inside women's and cows' bellies, Turkana are intensely concerned with promot-ing growth and fertility in all domains – people, livestock and nature. Most profoundly, procreation *is* production.

THE BODY SPIRITUAL, THE BODY SOCIAL AND THE BODY OF NATURE

What is very clear from Nilotic cosmic images of the body is that they are not merely abstract or formal ones but rather visceral images that pulsate with female physicality and processes. The cosmos is conceived of as containing the whole world within it, an image modelled on the mature, maternal body.

At first glance it seems that we are confronted here with the all too familiar Western equation between 'nature' and 'woman'. In this familiar equation, the trope 'woman' is constructed as a passive object embodying an empty container into which cultural value is poured and sociality extracted. The infinite malleability of 'woman' in western philosophy has imbued the female body with the capacity to stand for things other than herself – above all, Nature (Gatens 1991; Benjamin 1993). The obvious but none the less important point is that the qualities of the source domain in this metaphorization process – the feminine, passive, submissive and mute – are moved to the target domain imparting these characteristics to 'nature' which becomes infused with negative imagery. What I want to emphasize here is that this negative characterization of the feminine is due to metaphors reproducing taken-for-granted meanings, and not to any in-built and unchanging essential negativity inherent in the link between the two tropes, 'woman' and 'nature'. Again, metaphors are located within historically specific horizons of understanding and meaning – indeed, they both signify and constitute that cultural configuration (Fernandez 1982).

In marked contrast to these modern Western representations of the relation between 'woman' and 'nature' mediated through the body, the source domain of the Nilotic metaphorization process is a feminine physicality brimming with energetic activity and creative agency. And these traits are transported to the target domain so that nature becomes infused not with mute passivity but with spirituality and power. Recall how the pastoral peoples mentioned above posit their relationships to the feminine Divinity in stories beginning with the supposed joining, and then separation, of Earth and Sky – the advent of the world as it is. This image of the divine enveloping everything within herself, bringing forth the earth and sky and all that lives and moves as creatures from her belly, clearly equates fertility and transformation on all levels: celestial, natural and human. This provides peoples like the Turkana with a sense of divinity inherent in nature, not transcendent from it as in contemporary interpretations of Christianity. This Nilotic notion of a living nature, spiritual and solid at the same time, is conceptually contained and constantly re-created in feminine flesh.

In order to appreciate the way these constructions cluster around the material body, we have to deconstruct the predominance of abstract metaphorical European thought and create a central space for the concrete metonymic. Nilotic constructions of the cosmos draw immediate attention to visceral bodily images in which the mental and the material, meaning and matter, are interwoven. The body of feminine Divine figures simultaneously as a solid surface – a landscape – and the scene for social inscription. The plot, actors and acts in these creation scenarios weave together the experiencing and particular body (practice and performance) with the representing and abstract body (the symbolic and semantic). Most profoundly, within the divine bodyscape of *Akuij*, earth and sky 'touch upon' one another. This metaphoric statement, in its image of touching and continuity between apparently disparate realms, ties into itself the movement of metonymy and collects Turkana tropes and ideas about spirituality around a very concrete body.

This prototypical feminine body pulsating with agency and purpose is also a knowing body. One of the keys to Turkana conceptions of knowledge is provided by the language through which they refer to it, a language which constantly links the act of knowing to physical processes. Their understanding of the senses and the ways in which breathing, seeing, speaking, touching and tasting are built into their idea of knowledge means that knowledge for the Turkana is something one incorporates. Their model of knowing binds knowledge, spiritual and social, to the senses and experience – to the body. This knowledge, which operates on all the senses, but privileges none of them, finds a sensory and perceptual unity among the most disparate phenomena. It is this which gives Turkana thought its force and evocative power. It works through metonymies which, like those of poetic imagery, bind thought to immediate experience and the senses. Through these tropes different bodies and phenomena are seen to participate in each other in real and important ways (Broch-Due 1993). To borrow a phrase from Weiner, 'Metaphor is a play of words: poetic image is additionally a play on the world' (1991: 13).

The Turkana universe is conceived of as a series of analogous bodies – bodies which from one perspective fit inside each other, and exist as analogies of each other of differing sizes and scales, related as microcosm to macrocosm. From another perspective they can be inverted or everted versions of each other. The analo-

gies construed between bodies and other entities are complex,
creating precise links between each body part and its analogue.
These bodily analogies interrelate all aspects of their social world
by expanding outward in ever-widening and inclusive circles –
ethnic group, country and cosmos – until, at the outer limit, the
whole world is represented in Earth's image: *Akwap* (Earth),
hanging by its hands like a newborn infant between the outstretched legs of mother-like Sky, *Akuij*. In this imagery the
dome-shaped Sky provides the skeleton (*akai*) and legs; the dry
and hard bones are the non-perishable parts of the body. The
Earth, in contrast, is the more supple flesh.

Most tellingly, the Turkana conception of the world as a living
body writ large, bearing within it sky, landscape and lake, brings
together in a single and subtle image its composite corporeality,
human and animal. For during daylight this containing body is
conceptually carved in human flesh, with hands and legs. When
darkness engulfs the last rays of sunlight, these distinct human
features dissolve and are replaced by a dark surface spotted in
red, *nameri*. This revelation of the starry night sky signifies simultaneously the numerous fires lit by the spirits of the dead and the
colour configuration on the skin of particular cattle which the
Turkana have bred to elicit purposely these effects.

The choice of the female body in Turkana creation stories is
simply because this is the only body capable of creating more
bodies (through childbirth) and being able to contain and deliver
a different body (male babies also come from the female womb).
These two capacities, of multiplying and producing difference, are
at the core of any and all creative work, both everyday and cosmogonic. Physiological cycles cause the feminine continuously to
oscillate between bodily states, wet and dry, singular and plural.
The menstrual cycle is analogous to the moon whose first
crescent comes out of darkness, grows to full, starts to wane, is
drawn back into darkness, seems to die, but is then miraculously
reborn in the next cycle. The imagery associated with *Akuij* (Sky)
is very similar: *Akuij*'s womb gives birth to all life, but also takes
all life back into her womb, only to bring it forth once again, in
an endless cycle which takes us beyond opposites to a eternal
unity. In its pregnant state the body, whether woman or cosmos,
is plural or androgynous.

Akuij is just such an all-embracing spiritual principle, who
appears in several shapes and shifts between female and male.

Sometimes s/he is invoked as Mother, *Ito*, and sometimes as Father, *Apa*, but without ever shedding her feminine garb precisely because s/he is the supreme creator and transformer. Sometimes *Akuij* appears as a menstruating wife, painting the evening sky red with her fertile and flowing blood, a sign which makes earthly women put on garlands of green leaves in order to conceive. Other times *Akuij* appears analogous to a protecting husband, barring the door of the heavenly homestead against howling winds and the dangers of darkness. And sometimes *Akuij* summons the spirits from the wet underworld and sends them out travelling in terrifying thunderstorms. There is a plethora of such spirits, known as *Ekipe*, a name which bears a masculine gender prefix, but which subsumes male and female versions, both of which alter between being harmful and helpful. While these powers are seen as operating separately, Turkana still say that they are *Akuij*. She is simply 'many-one', the core principle not only of the cosmos but also of the camp, in which the paternal and the maternal, male and female, alternate in enveloping each other, in an endless exchange of perspectives. Within a polygamous homestead (*awi*), founded by the common husband and father, each wife is the focus of a separate house and herd (*ekol*).

BODILY STORIES AND BODILY PRACTICES

Let us a take a closer look at how Turkana theories and techniques of transformation (in narratives, rituals and everyday practices) are formed around this feminine physicality. The nature of this continuum of bodies, extending from the human body to the landscape and cosmos, and the transformational relations which relate them, are given narrative form in many myths. The most important is the story of *Nayeche*, the nurturing, female figure who gave birth to all Turkana. She wanders through a wild and barren landscape until she discovers a land which is its exact opposite – bountiful and fertile. She encounters a branded grey bull. The bull represents the bridewealth given in marriage and, by extension, the agnatic clan. Through a symbolic union with the bull (once again, the merging of human and animal) *Nayeche* gives birth to the Turkana and, through a series of acts, tames the wildness and shows them the proper way to live in it and feed from it. *Nayeche* gathers the wild energies of nature, containing them in a landscape which is now imaged as a pregnant body – a cave in a mountain which is a womb within a skeleton. Here she makes her house (*ekol*) – literally 'umbilicus' – and gestates the first Turkana children in an image of 'cooking'. The story of *Nayeche* clearly establishes homologies between animal and human bodies, houses ('umbilicus'), homesteads ('swelling bellies') and the environment – all conceived of as a series of interconnected bodies (Broch-Due 1990a). This version of the creation story celebrates the successful coupling of the female and male, matrifiliation and patriliny.

The vital principles of merging and differentiation which Turkana deduce from feminine physicality and bodily processes are made real, continually created and recreated, not only through narration and naming, but also through the practical activities and structures of everyday life. Just as *Nayeche* created the ordinary homesteads in a bodily image, it is women who build present-day homesteads, draping skins over 'skeletons' to form the house-bodies in which they live. Here wives conceive, cook and feed their children – all creative acts that are coupled in this culture. Similarly the layout of the camp as a whole and its relation to other camps is consistently cast in bodily imagery. The main camp is the 'belly and chest' while the satellite camp is the 'back and buttocks', the two being united to form the complete camp-body when junior herders and their stock return to the main camp at the end of the dry season.

The layout of the camp and the positioning of people within it concretely re-enact the features of physiological processes. Elsewhere I have elaborated on the ways that Turkana conceive of bodily development as a progression from the wet, low and soft (also associated with the east and the rising sun) to the dry, high and hard (associated with the west and the setting sun). While a married man's shelter is always at the centre of the compound, the positioning of women's houses reflects precisely their relative positions in this schema. Young wives, their fertility and age associating them with the wet and low, have their huts on the eastern and 'downward' side of the compound (the lower belly and sex organs) whereas, for instance, the man's mother, 'dry' and 'hard', lives in the 'upper' and western sides of the compound (the dry and airy region of the chest and throat). Thus the activities of everyday life are both channelled by, and recreate, the physiological schema which organizes the Turkana world (Broch-Due 1990a).

Again, the dominant theme is that the world is composed of a series of microcosmic and macrocosmic bodies. These bodies interpenetrate and mutually inform one other, a fact that is enacted and made real for the Turkana through a host of everyday practices. Indeed the main method of discovering what *Akuij* is up to at any given moment – divination – works precisely on this idea of places, groups and bodies contained like concentric circles within each other. States of well-being and disease move effortlessly between all layers of this multidimensional body. Divination finds the perfect image of these multiple worlds in the animal intestines, curled up on themselves within the belly, which the Turkana read to gain information about events in the camp, clan and cosmos. For livestock bear in their bodies an impress of the totality that comprises all that is Turkana. These multiple paths, places and 'bodies', which are physical, social and cosmic, are nested in a map of landscape and living; they are graphically represented in the images found in an animal's belly as a microcosm of the larger world.

This belly microcosm is not, of course, seen as merely a representation or metaphor for the world, but as a body substantively linked to it which registers its fluctuating states in the transient texture of blood bubbles and grains in the animal's stomach and guts. These are visual signs of events and transformations in the external world and are used as a basis to formulate plans and actions. After the body map has been inspected and made known to everyone, it is cooked by the women before being consumed by everyone to ensure that the knowledge gained is stored in the human body. In this culture one comprehends the world by literally ingesting it. Thus, for the Turkana, the world must constantly be verified through ingestion and digestion.

Perhaps because of the recurrent Turkana idea that bodies participate in each other and that the world is a series of bodies within bodies, people share a preoccupation with bodily surfaces which form the more or less permeable bodily boundaries. This is nowhere more evident than with activities aimed at forming and growing a child. The first part of this formative process consists of the mother 'feeding into' the child's body its capacities to feel, know and reflect its social composition (Broch-Due 1990a; 1993). I want to focus on the final stage in this process – turning a child into a reproducer itself. The Turkana child is seen as composed of the acts of both parents, and in this sense is regarded as androgynous. In order to become a reproducer, a child has to be made more one-sidedly male or female and, in that sense, less complete. Completeness is then restored in the heterosexual couple, when single-sexed males and females co-operate to produce children (see Strathern 1993). While girls' bodies are capable of directly reproducing children, boys' bodies are more problematic and thus require particular attention. Most revealing, Turkana turn boys into men by imitating girls' bodily growth. This is done during *Asapan*, the male initiation ritual. A consideration of Turkana initiation rites reveals a complex play in Turkana thought with the idea of androgyny, and the multiple possibilities of sexed bodies. It also reveals the role of the feminine and the female body as central tropes of the Turkana cosmos and transformational forces.

In Turkana, the turning point between being a boy (*esorokit*) and a warrior (*ekajion*) is *Asapan* initiation. Until and unless a man is initiated, he is regarded as a social minor and cannot eat with the elders, speak in meetings, marry or form a homestead (*awi*) – all events that define someone as 'adult man' (*ekile*). Most telling, the group of initiates, all of whom are in their twenties, are collectively called 'the breast-fed ones' (*anaket apey*). The ceremonial logic of *Asapan* is clearly to infuse the young man with the bodily femaleness which will allow him to grow.

On the first day of the ritual, the boy must spear his favourite ox under the supervision of his ceremonial godfather. At sunrise the next day, he enters the house of his ceremonial godmother, who places him on a white cow hide. He sits with legs outstretched, facing east, 'like a baby'. She then strips off his clothes and beads. She shaves part of his hair and smears a mixture of oil, ashes and red clay over his forehead and body. She then puts a red mud-cap on him (which is like a womb) and ties a sinew (*apusit*) around his head, analogous in name and shape to an umbilical cord. Having been given these feminine procreative elements, the initiate is now addressed as *ateran* (bride). He stays in the godmother's yard and sleeps with the immature girls without touching them. At night, he sleeps in a foetal position, covered with a white hide. Nothing could more clearly denote the state of infancy as well as enveloping femininity to which the initiate is being returned. He spends the days in camp together with the women, performing female tasks such as fetching water and firewood, preparing food and watering the livestock under the supervision of the godmother. He is not allowed to do the milking or to sit on other men's chairs. He must constantly call out the names of the various types of animals and artefacts he sees in the compound. When he wakes up on the seventh day, he is placed on the white hide facing east and smeared with oil by his godmother, before he is given the *eropit* animals ('rope', 'path' and 'throat').

During an intermediate period, the boy is returned to his own mother who places him on a white cow hide and feeds him with porridge normally made for newborns. In the final stage of *Asapan*, the god-mother removes the sinew that represents the umbilical cord and puts some green clay on the front of his red mud cap. Green is the colour of men. The initiate has been reborn as a man. He is then taken on a tour of all the female-centred houses (*ekol*) of the homestead (*awi*). To 'renew his breath', the godmother creates a 'life-giving smoke' in the cow-milk container (*akurum*), an artefact with a phallic-shaped neck and a rounded womb shape at its base. This container symbolizes the union of male and female in a concretely androgynous image.

In stories and rituals dealing with metamorphosis, female figures are, thus, either creators or central ceremonial actors. As the examples presented in this paper make clear, this is character-istic of Turkana thought, which systematically intertwines images of transformation with the female body. The choice of uterine images for all processes of growth and creation clearly springs from the capacity of a woman's womb to conceive and grow a child. However, I should emphasize once again that with the dynamic Turkana construction of gender, 'maleness' and 'female-ness' depend on culturally definable acts and not on unchange-able essences. Once the act, and not the biological sex of the individual, becomes the analytic focus, it becomes possible to understand how the Turkana use gender as a technology of trans-action and transformation in a more abstract way in which men and women alike bear both masculine and feminine qualities in an androgynous balance and display these traits in the acts they have learned to perform.

SUBVERSIVE FEMININITY

In terms of spaces, substances and acts, the *Asapan* ritual, condu-cive to the growing and maturing of men's bodies, is a re-enactment of the narrative about *Nayeche* and her creation of the Turkana ethnic group. The imagery of successful creation and the coupling of bodies – physical and social, male and female, animal and human – clearly constitutes the dominant discourse: it is 'high Turkana culture', so to speak. The narrative about *Nayeche* represents a harmonious and normative vision of the state of affairs. Her creative acts ensure that the maternal and paternal elements that constitute persons, ethnic groups and cosmos exist in a perfectly balanced and appropriate blend. However, this constructive androgynous sociality embodied by the good *Nayeche* is counterpoised by a subversive generic female form overflowing with excessive and evil femininity.

These are the sensational and shocking stories about *Napeysekina* (the one-breasted one). As a discursive formation about disruptive femininity, it responds and contributes to the fracturing of social certainties. This is registered in the narrative's insistent ambiguity about core values and their uncertainty about the central issues of gendered identities and bodily transformation. They are texts of turbulent excess, of murderous impulses, simmering treason, passionate and illicit sexuality, eruption and explosions.

Here is one such example, a variation of the earlier story about the heavenly separation. It features *Napeysekina*, rather than *Akuij*, as the driving force. However, what is interesting about such stories is that they turn out in very different ways. Turkana pose the problem through a narrative twist where the evil *Napeysekina*, rather than *Akuij*, plays the leading part in introducing death after a pair of mythical maidens have pushed the sky up. This act sets in motion a series of events leading to inauspicious births.

At dusk a pair of girls herding camels discover that some calves are missing. To avoid punishment, the girls set out the next morning to trace the lost stock, going west. They roam all day, but in vain. At sunset they arrive at a stony cave where an old one-breasted woman lives. *Napeysekina* advises them to stop searching for the night and invites them to sleep in her camp. She asks the girls to build a new *akai* (the wife's dome-shaped night hut) the next morning. At dawn the girls go out and cut wooden poles with which they push the sky high up, before they bring back the long poles to camp. The same things happen for two more days. *Napeysekina*'s son tells the girls not to drink the milk served by his mother. The two girls dig a hole in the ground and pour her milk into it, only drinking the milk brought by the boy. The same happens for two more days. On the third day, the son warns the girls that his mother will kill them the next morning, encircling the night-hut with her tongue. The girls go to sleep near the door. When the tongue begins winding around the hut they run away.

One of the girls forgets her belt in the hut and returns to fetch it. She goes inside, but on the way out she steps on *Napeysekina*'s tongue and wakes her up. She runs after the girl who climbs a tree. *Napeysekina* tells her son to fetch an axe so that she can fell the tree. The child slaughters a camel. She asks again. The son slaughters a cow. She asks a third time. The son comes to the tree, but without bringing the axe. *Napeysekina* leaves him and goes to fetch the axe herself. The son tells the girl to run away as quick as she can. A fat vulture lands on the tree. She fells the tree thinking that the girl is still in the treetop, and the vulture flies away. *Napeysekina* turns into a cow with a calf. Some people take this cow and she lets them milk her in the morning, but in the evening she tells the boy who is milking to leave some for her calf. The boy reports the incident, but the others think he is insane. The same happens for two more days. On the third day, another man hides nearby, listens to the cow and confirms the boy's tale. The cow and calf are both killed and burnt on the fire.

It rains, and the ashes are washed into the river, where subsequently an *Echoke* tree loaded with berries grows. Women are picking the fruits, but they are sour and sting in the mouth. The tree is burnt and the ashes are washed into the river again. The *Edome* tree grows. Men and boys cut the sticks, but the sticks beat them hard and leave them bleeding. The tree is burnt, and the ashes are washed into the river. A woman drinks the water and gets pregnant. After three months the baby inside her womb asks to be let out. Nobody can believe it. In the fourth month of pregnancy, the baby asks the same. Puzzlement. When the child asks again in the fifth month, a man decides to let the baby out. Out he comes and is named *Emoruiemoenit*, 'stony enemy'. The monstrous infant secretly drinks all the cow's milk milked by the mother, for three successive days, but on the third day he is discovered by the husband. At night his parents abandon him. He enters a camel's stomach through its anus, and follows his father and mother, harassing them. The couple leave their animals behind, and another man finds the herd. When crossing a dry area, he decides to eat a goat, but the goat tells him not to eat her. The same is repeated when *Emoruiemoenit* enters different animals. The man arrives at the neighbourhood where the child's parents live and tells his strange story. The father slaughters the animal and finds the monster inside the rumen, killing it with his spear.

Elsewhere, I have provided a detailed analysis of the symbolism in these stories, demonstrating how the narrative structure and central motifs are linked to other Turkana texts, modes of knowledge and a host of everyday practices (Broch-Due 1990a). Here I restrict myself to the most significant elements for the purpose of this chapter.

The temperament and tempo of *Napeysekina* stories are illuminating for the ways she alters between male and female modes. As with other composite and androgynous beings like *Akuij* and *Nayeche*, she never loses her overall femininity. Most stories about this monstrous woman start out calmly. In the dormant state s/he lies like a sleeping snake, with the one breast and the long tongue curled around the flickering flames and glowing embers of the hearth. Here she represents the darker sides of femininity and masculinity contained in an androgynous form which is kept momentarily inactive.

When she is mobilized in the male mode, she is typically armed to the teeth, as in one story where she uproots people with her violent knife and penetrating tongue and turns them into refugees. In this story, her destructive force is subdued by the beneficial force of *Akuij*, also dually gendered. In stories where she is mobilized in the female mode, the typical scenario is of a mother living alone with her daughter. When, as in another story similar to the above, the daughter is visited by some of her young women friends, *Napeyesekina* is progressively revealed to be a grotesque and terrifying destroyer of fertility and of all proper social relations. The story culminates with her own bodily dissolution. Different parts of her body transform themselves into everyday features of the landscape – pools, plants, gourds, trees, animals, and children – with which unsuspecting humans must contend.

The whole corpus of *Napeysekina* stories share the same narrative structure. Following a series of horrible events, the stories always end with her wild body being dismembered or otherwise destroyed and subsequently transformed into elements in the environment. In other words, these stories paint a picture of a wild and untamed landscape formed and animated by the destructive internal energies of an ordinary body which has exploded and been everted. Most significantly, these subversive stories set the stage for the narrative of *Nayeche* – the 'mother' of the Turkana – who gathers the wild energies of *Napeysekina*'s exploded and fragmented bodyscape. She, however, contains them and deploys them to positive ends.

The transgressive power of such texts demands an equivalent alteration in our reading codes and modes of interpretations. The two discursive formations, one about destructive femininity and one about constructive femininity, are clearly bound together in an 'inter-textual' web. From completely different perspectives the texts, the social and subversive, draw on the same elements and create analogies in the most diverse domains of social thought and practice. These fluid and shifting analogies interwoven in the texts also provide the broader context in which the listeners evaluate the puzzles and paradoxes put before them. Yet no resolution is forthcoming, precisely because of the plurality of meanings that are constantly being shifted and shattered in each story, and the changing perspectives on the same event from one story to another.

Napeysekina can be interpreted as reflecting the margins of the stabilizing normative visions contained in the *Nayeche* story. And, as Mary Douglas remarks in *Purity and Danger*, 'margins are dangerous ... if they are pulled this way or that the shape of fundamental experience is altered. Any structure of ideas is vulnerable at its margins' (Douglas 1966: 121). The creation story that centres on *Akuij*, the feminine divinity, also has such discontinuities, absences, uncertainties, both structural and thematic, built into it. Symbolism is not born smoothly from the spiritual womb of *Akuij*. It comes from a conflicting set of historical circumstances and contexts. Turkana symbolism therefore speaks to the real conflicts which exist between the spheres of men and women, young and old, household and clan, agnates and affines, and between different domains of production. People's attitudes can be involved in long-running sequences of strategies and exchanges. These attributes are simultaneously social, economic, political, symbolic and spiritual. And it is at the intersection of controversy and agreement that ideas about creation, feminine divinity and subversive femininity become discursive resources and have consequences in daily life.

PROCREATION, PRODUCTION AND POWER

I would like to end this exposition with another example of how women, through their actions, draw upon these ideas which bind (pro)creative forces (positive and negative) in all domains to femininity. The concern with fertility and its potential failure means that nature's periodicity takes on a profound significance in all spheres. It is the core idiom through which Turkana organize their (re)production cycle and create consonance between their perception of the social and the physical, indeed of all aspects of their lives. The peaks of dry seasons are times of waiting and anxious concern – for, if severe, the ensuing drought will result in miscarriages and misfortune. The month of March, which normally brings the 'long rains' which set the natural growth cycle of grass, calves and children in motion, is the entry point into the local calendar. It is also the start of the season in which unruly parties of pastoral wives roam the countryside in an effort, on the one hand, to receive what is due to them as generators of fertility and, on the other hand, to promote fertility by protesting against and punishing those men singled out as trying to prevent its realization (see Snyder and Blystad, this volume; also Rigby 1968; Snyder 1997; Spencer 1988).

The women visit all the homesteads in the area, singing, dancing and demanding that the senior man slaughter a goat from his own corral and not from any of his wives'. Young unmarried men accompany the women and roast the meat for them. If a man refuses to give a goat, the women abuse him by lifting their leather skirts to expose their sexual organs. In Turkana, this is the most extreme provocation. The goat will usually be immediately forthcoming, particularly since the man's own wives also want these women visitors to stop harassing them and threatening their own fertility.

Most significantly, the women's performance, called *akinyaka-nar*, emulates the dance in which warriors display their war tactics before carrying out cattle raids. These women aim to seize

goats forcefully and they do this in return for their own procreative powers, not only for children already born, but also for
those who might be born in the future. For a wife usually wishes
to have more children than does her husband who must cater for
the children of several wives. 'There are many "pots" (pregnan-
cies) hidden in the bush' is a figure of speech women use to
indicate that they intend to 'cook children' without their
husbands' approval. Another aim of the women's aggressive expeditions and their *akinyakanar* performances is often to extract
pregnancy fines and bridewealth from the families of men who
have illegitimately made their daughters pregnant 'on the dancing
ground'. In these cases their dance is to insist that these daughters be taken as proper wives and that bridewealth be paid.

These gendered dramas surrounding fertility decisions and performances should not be dismissed as peripheral to dominant
power structures, as might be the case in contemporary European
societies. In Turkana, as in most pastoral communities, procreation, marriage and motherhood feature prominently in the
complex topography of prosperity and poverty. Wealth in people
and wealth in livestock are inter-linked. While men's social
powers are constituted more directly through the circulation of
cattle, women's social powers are constituted through children
who provide their mothers with access to cattle wealth. Women's
and men's careers differ slightly in structure and time-scale.

First of all it should be borne in mind that the difficulties of
amassing the exorbitant Turkana bridewealth are such that most
men do not marry before they are well into their thirties (if at
all). However, given the fact of polygamy while most Turkana
women are married, they are all married at a much younger age,
and usually when their male age-mates are still dependant herd
boys. This means that men and women enter their marriage
careers at different points in their lives, bringing to the conjugal
union very different life experiences and expectations. Grooms
have already achieved independence and significant social
standing, while most brides are little more than children suddenly
removed from the mutual bonds of affection they enjoyed with
their own mothers and siblings.

The point of marriage is the point at which a man's career
begins to peak as he starts to gather wives, children and livestock
around him. His career is at its height as his young daughters are
married away and bridewealth flows which allows him to marry

more wives himself. He tries to delay his sons' marriages for as long as possible because, for him, these unions mark the beginning of the end. His homestead will begin to dissolve into its constituent houses, each headed by one of his wives. As his career and animal capital decline, those of his wives begin to flourish. The portion of bridewealth women receive in their own name from their daughters' marriages gradually builds their house's herds. This accumulation of animals will eventually enable the oldest sons to marry, with or without their father's consent.

At this stage in the evolution of many marriages the balance of power between spouses shifts rapidly in favour of the wife – and if the husband has no younger wives, he will feel this power shift all the more intensely. Frequently a wife breaks away from her husband's homestead to set up a separate one with her sons and daughters-in-law, enjoying the privileged position as the seniormost person in the new homestead. At this point we should remember that the husband is becoming an old man while his wives are in their prime, enjoying the material and emotional benefits that come with strong maternal bonds. Even if they did not leave with their married sons, their husbands' deaths would normally come to pass long before their own anyway. For whatever reason, it is when a middle-aged woman has been separated from her husband that wealth, power and influence are at their zenith, while an elderly man, separated from his wife and losing paternal control over sons through the dispersal of the family herd, will often become lonely and bitter.

Thus, husbands and wives reach the peaks of their careers at about the same age, but they do not reach them together – their career cycles are out of rhythm with each other. This is a very important point as it suggests that, in many contexts, seniority may be even more significant than gender. This observation undermines the now familiar (and static) image of pastoral patriarchal relations: a household headed by a senior man, surrounded by his subordinate wives and sons. This image misses the crucial point that this is only a temporary stage in the homestead and herd development cycle. Yet this image has provided *the* stereotype of pastoral gender relations. A more processual account, such as the one I have given here, shows that nothing is static, least of all the ways in which gender relations structure relations of wealth and power.

In everyday life, much hinges on the individual person's

capacity to engage others in prosperous relationships, as well as evincing personal power through the display of their own bodies and the bodies of their beasts and children. In this highly politicized display, there are strong men and women as well as weak and powerless ones. This point leads to another: the power of scale which this form of sociality brings forth is central to situations of dominance in gendered relationships. The person who sees his or her acts echoed and enlarged in the acts of others like themselves – for example, by an age group, or a clan, or indeed by the cosmos – has a better chance of affecting the acts of others. In Marilyn Strathern's words: '[t]he hidden sociological dimension is that collective relations aggrandize individual acts' (1988: 328).

Once again, Turkana reality undermines fixed notions about patriarchal power and women's subordination. When Turkana cosmic narratives prominently feature female agency as a powerful force of both creation and subversion – even *the* prime moving force – they create a template for that female agency which is enacted in key domains of social life and at key points in a woman's life-cycle. It is in these cosmic narratives, I want to suggest, that the Turkana create a conceptual space for the agency of women. The placing of the trope 'woman' within these narratives sets the cultural parameters within which, or outside of which, real women speak and act. If we follow Julia Kristeva (Kristeva and Moi 1986) and conceptualize female agency in terms of *positionality* rather than essence, the positions created within Turkana discourses are plural and potentially very powerful. The contemporary picture is more complex because new and contrastive gender scripts, as well as new ideas about domesticity, have arrived in Turkanaland with the translocal flows of modernity and Christianity. The space constituted by all these ambiguities is a convenient locus to challenge the ordered, gendered certainties – both their own and ours. It is all really a matter of perspective. . . .

REFERENCES

Århem, K. (1991) 'The symbolic world of the Maasai homestead' in A. Jacobson-Widding (ed.). *Body and Space: Symbolic Models of Unity and Division in African Cosmology and Experience* (Uppsala: Acta Universitatis Upsaliensis).

Ash, J. (1990) 'The discursive construction of Christ's body in the later Middle Ages: resistance and autonomy' in T. Threadgold and A. Cranny-Francis (eds) *Feminine, Masculine and Representation* (London: Allen & Unwin).

Auerbach, N. (1982) *Woman and the Demon: The Life of a Victorian Myth* (Cambridge, Ma.: Harvard University Press).

Benjamin, M. (1993) *A Question of Identity: Women, Science, and Literature* (New Brunswick: Rutgers University Press).

Benson, S. (1974) 'A study of religious beliefs and practices of the Maasai tribe and the implications for the work of the Evangelical Lutheran Church of Tanzania', M.Th thesis, Northwestern Lutheran Theological Seminary, Minnesota.

Bianco, B.A. (1991) 'Women and things: Pokot motherhood as political destiny', *American Ethnologist*, 18: 770–85.

Broch-Due, V. (1987) ' "Livestock speak louder than sweet words": changing property and gender relations among the Turkana' in P.T.W. Baxter with R. Hogg (eds) *Property, Poverty and People: Changing Rights in Property and Problems of Pastoral Development* (Manchester: Department of Social Anthropology, Manchester University).

Broch-Due, V. (1990a) 'The bodies within the body: journeys in Turkana thought and practice', PhD thesis, University of Bergen.

Broch-Due, V. (1990b) 'Cattle are companions, goats are gifts: animals and people in Turkana thought' in G. Pálsson (ed.) *From Water to World-Making: African Models and Arid Lands* (Uppsala: Scandinavian Institute of African Studies).

Broch-Due, V. (1993) 'Making meaning out of matter: perceptions of sex, gender and bodies among the Turkana' in V. Broch-Due, I. Rudie and T. Bleie (eds) *Carved Flesh/Cast Selves: Gendered Symbols and Social Practices* (Oxford: Berg).

Broch-Due, V. and I. Rudie. (1993) 'Carved flesh – cast selves: an introduction' in V. Broch-Due, I. Rudie and T. Bleie (eds) *Carved Flesh/Cast Selves: Gendered Symbols and Social Practices* (Oxford: Berg).

Burton, J.W. (1991) 'Representations of the feminine in Nilotic cosmologies' in A. Jacobson-Widding (ed.) *Body and Space: Symbolic Models of Unity and Division in African Cosmology and Experience* (Uppsala: Acta Universitatis Upsaliensis).

Caplan, P. and J.M. Burja (eds) (1978) *Women United, Women Divided: Cross-Cultural Perspectives on Female Solidarity* (London: Tavistock).

Chatman, S.B. (1978) *Story and Discourse: Narrative Structure in Fiction and Film* (Ithaca: Cornell University Press).

Clifford, J. (1988) *The Predicament of Culture: Twentieth-Century Ethnography, Literature, and Art* (Cambridge, MA: Harvard University Press).

Douglas, M. (1966) *Purity and Danger* (London: Routledge & Kegan Paul).

Driberg, J.H. (1932) 'The status of women among the Nilotics and Nilo-Hamitics', *Africa*, 5: 404–21.

Evans-Pritchard, E.E. (1940) *The Nuer* (Oxford: Clarendon).

Fernandez, J.W. (1982) *Bwiti: An Ethnography of the Religious Imagination in Africa* (Princeton: University Press).

Foucault, M. (1972) *The Archaeology of Knowledge*, translated by A.M. Sheridan Smith (New York: Pantheon).

Gatens, M. (1991) *Feminism and Philosophy: Perspectives on Difference and Equality* (Bloomington: Indiana University Press).

Geertz, H. and C. Geertz (1975) *Kinship in Bali* (Chicago: Chicago University Press).

Gulliver, P.H. (1953) *A Preliminary Survey of the Turkana* (Cape Town: University Printers).

Gulliver, P.H. (1955) *The Family Herds: A Study of Two Pastoral Tribes in East Africa, the Jie and Turkana* (London: Routledge & Kegan Paul).

Herskovits, M. (1926) 'The cattle complex in East Africa', *American Anthropologist*, 28: 230–72, 361–88, 494–528, 633–64.

Hodgson, D. (1995) 'The politics of gender, ethnicity and "development": images, interventions, and reconfiguration of Maasai identities, 1916–1993', PhD dissertation, University of Michigan.

Hutchinson, S. (1992) 'The cattle of money and the cattle of girls among the Nuer, 1930–83', *American Ethnologist*,19: 294–316.

Hutchinson, S. (1996) *Nuer Dilemmas: Coping with Money, War and the State* (Berkeley: University of California Press).

Kettel, B. (1986) 'The commoditization of women in Tugen (Kenya) social organization' in C. Robertson and I. Berger (eds) *Women and Class in Africa* (New York: Africana Publishing Company).

Kipury, N. (1989) 'Maasai women in transition: class and gender in the transformation of a pastoral society', PhD dissertation, Temple University.

Kristeva, J. and T. Moi (1986) *A Kristeva Reader* (New York: Columbia University Press).

Lakoff, G. and M. Johnson (1980) *Metaphors We Live By* (Chicago: Chicago University Press).

Lewis, B.A. (1972) *The Murle: Red Chiefs and Black Commoners* (Oxford: Oxford University Press).

Lienhardt, G. (1961) *Divinity and Experience* (Oxford: Clarendon).

Llewelyn-Davies, M. (1978) 'Two contexts of solidarity among pastoral Maasai women' in P. Caplan and J.M. Burja (eds) *Women United, Women Divided* (London: Tavistock).

Moore, H.L. (1988) *Feminism and Anthropology* (Cambridge: Polity).

Moore, H.L. (1994) *A Passion for Difference* (Cambridge: Polity).

Olsson, T. (1989) 'Philosophy of medicine among the Maasai' in A. Jacobson-Widding and D. Westerlund (eds) *Culture, Experience and Pluralism: Essays on African Ideas of Illness and Healing* (Stockholm: Almqvist & Wiksell).

Ortner, S.B. (1974) 'Is female to male as nature is to culture?' in M.Z. Rosaldo and L. Lamphere (eds) *Women, Culture and Society* (Stanford: Stanford University Press).

Rapp, R. (1979) 'Anthropology: a review essay', *Signs*, 4 (3): 497–513.

Rattray, R. (1927) *Religion and Art in Ashanti* (Oxford: Clarendon Press).

Reichel-Dolmatoff, G. (1971) *Amazonian Cosmos: The Sexual and Religious Symbolism of the Tukano Indians* (Chicago: Chicago University Press).

Rigby, P. (1968) 'Some Gogo rituals of "purification": an essay on social and moral categories' in E.R. Leach (ed.) *Dialectic in Practical Religion* (Cambridge: Cambridge University Press).

Rogers, S.C. (1975) 'Female forms of power and the myth of male dominance: model of female/male interaction in peasant societies', *American Ethnologist*, 2: 727–56.

Rosaldo, M.Z. (1980) 'The use and abuse of anthropology: reflections on feminism and cross-cultural understanding', *Signs*, 5 (3): 389–417.

Rosaldo, M.Z. and L. Lamphere (eds) (1974) *Women, Culture and Society* (Stanford: Stanford University Press).

Sanday, P.R. (1981) *Female Power and Male Dominance: On the Origins of Sexual Inequality* (Cambridge: Cambridge University Press).

Snyder, K.A. (1997) 'Elders' authority and women's protest: the *masay* ritual and social change among the Iraqw of Tanzania', *Journal of the Royal Anthropological Institute*, 3: 561–76.

Spencer, P. (1988) *The Maasai of Matapato: A Study of Rituals of Rebellion* (Bloomington: Indiana University Press).

Strathern, M. (1980) 'No nature, no culture: the Hagen case' in C. MacCormack and M. Strathern (eds) *Nature, Culture and Gender* (Cambridge: Cambridge University Press).

Strathern, M. (1988) *The Gender of the Gift: Problems with Women and Problems with Society in Melanesia* (Berkeley: University of California Press).

Strathern, M. (1993) 'Making incomplete' in V. Broch-Due, I. Rudie and T. Bleie (eds) *Carved Flesh/Cast Selves: Gendered Symbols and Social Practices* (Oxford: Berg).

Talle, A. (1987) 'Women as heads of houses: the organization of production and the role of women among the pastoral Maasai in Kenya', *Ethnos*, 52 (1–2): 50–80.

Turnbull, C.M. (1961) *The Forest People* (London: Cape).

Weiner, J.F. (1991) *The Empty Place: Poetry, Space, and Being among the Foi of Papua New Guinea* (Bloomington: Indiana University Press).

Wiener, M.J. (1995) *Visible and Invisible Realms: Power, Magic and Colonial Conquest in Bali* (Chicago: Chicago University Press).

White, H.V. (1987) *The Content of the Form: Narrative Discourse and Historical Representation* (Baltimore: Johns Hopkins University Press).

Wienpahl, J. (1984) 'Women's roles in livestock production among the Turkana of Kenya', *Research in Economic Anthropology*, 6: 193–215.

PART III
GENDER, FERTILITY AND SOCIAL AGENCY

CHAPTER 7

'DEALING WITH MEN'S SPEARS'

DATOOGA PASTORALISTS COMBATING MALE INTRUSION ON FEMALE FERTILITY

ASTRID BLYSTAD

INTRODUCTION

The focus of this chapter is the mobilization of women in *girgwea-geeda gadeemga*, literally the 'wives' meeting', of the pastoral Datooga of Tanzania,[1] where tension related to what is perceived as threats to fundamental procreative processes is the heart of what is at stake. The central notion is that the sanctity of the female fertile body is continually infringed upon by destructive male forces, and that women have a sacred responsibility to collectively respond against the encroachment. Action taken by the *girgwea-geeda gadeemga* may have severe consequences for the offender.

Women's meetings and marches have been described from a large number of societies in sub-Saharan Africa with Ritzentha-ler's (1972) and Ardener's (1975) work on the 'Anlu uprising' in the British Cameroons, and Leith-Ross's (1939), Van Allen's (1972), and Ifeka-Moller's (1975) work on the Women's Wars in Nigeria as the most well known examples. Female protest marches have also been documented from Eastern and Southern Africa (see e.g. Edgerton and Conant 1964; Gluckman 1963; Rigby 1968; Snyder 1997; Spencer 1988; Wipper 1982; 1989).

Diduk (1989: 338) and Wipper (1982; 1989) note that there are some striking similarities between different sub-Saharan female protest movements: women protest against what they feel are infringements on their economic and political prerogatives, their mobilizations start out with a high-pitched sound, they have a substantial collective aura, and public humiliation, singing and dancing with obscene content, and diffuse outcomes, such as lack of rewards for female leaders, have all been recurring themes in protest marches recorded far apart in time and space. Rekdal's (1991) and Snyder's (1997) accounts of women's protest marches among the Iraqw are interesting since the Datooga talk of their Cushitic Iraqw neighbours as ever more frequently joining their own women in *girgweageeda gadeemga*. Snyder (1997: 567) argues that men's ritual activity is increasingly dependent upon legitimation by elder women, but she argues that although the women's protest marches mock the power and abilities of male elders, in effect their protests 'operate to reinforce the authority of the elders by leaving the care of the community in their hands'. We shall see that the *girgweageeda gadeemga* largely conforms with the depiction of female protest marches in sub-Saharan Africa. I shall however argue that although the outcome of Datooga meetings and marches may be diffuse in the sense that it does not challenge the outward image of male authority, the tangible consequences of Datooga female mobilizations are many, and the position of Datooga women is relatively elevated by them. Moreover, in contrast to many previously described female political mobilizations the Datooga *girgweageeda gadeemga* is, despite its *ad hoc* nature, part of a complex framework where different categories of people congregate and act within separate although overlapping institutions. It is also noteworthy that the *girgweageeda gadeemga* mobilise in connection with a large variety of issues and in most diverse settings. In a context where the Datooga community appear increasingly fragile and politically marginal, the female population manage to make themselves heard in a large variety of political settings both within and outside 'local' and 'traditional' contexts.

Except for Klima's (1966) article 'Jural relations between the sexes among the Barabaig', in which women's engagement in the two central institutions *ghadoweeda* and *girgweageeda gadeemga* and the dowry institution were recognized as significant factors in relation to women's relatively high status, and Talle's and Holmqvist's (1979) description of a particular mobilization of the *girgweageeda gadeemga* in their biography on Barheida, the *girgweageeda gadeemga* has received minimal attention in the literature. In the following pages I wish to view the institution in terms of both ideology and practice, and particularly investigate the symbolism of gender and procreation which is so effective in these mobilizations. I shall try to show how the metaphoric use

of the categories male and female and of the bodily processes of
conception, pregnancy and birth, death and dying are primary
symbolic components of the *girgweageeda gadeemga*, and how
these lend themselves with great ease not only to idioms of
change, but to actual transformation.

'Performance' has been a powerful concept in contemporary
anthropological theory, because like the concept of practice it
takes us to the action of culture (Singer 1968; Tambiah 1981;
Turner 1990). Performance theory questions ritual as mere reflective representation and ritual as preserving and static, and
emphasizes the processual, dynamic and productive aspects of
ritual activity. Ritual becomes a significant part of history-
making. Jackson (1983; 1989) has sensitized us to the continuity
between language, knowledge and bodily praxis. Drawing on
empirical material from the ritual life of the Kuranko of Sierra
Leone, he shows us how the use of metaphor in ritual is effica-
cious in a very real sense. He addresses the intimate interconnection between metaphor and embodiment, and argues that:

metaphor must be apprehended non-dualistically and that the
idea of sensation and its bodily compliments (social, mechani-
cal, physiological, geographical, etc.) betoken, not an arbitrary
or rhetorical synthesis of two terms – subject and object, tenor
and vehicle – which can be defined more realistically apart
from each other, but a true interdependence of mind and body,
Self and World (Jackson 1983: 132).

Karin Barber's work on Yoruba ritual is an excellent example of
how religious prose is manipulated and how religious devotees
are highly ingenious at drawing on ideas from a large and hetero-
geneous field of resources, to serve their own expressive and emotional purposes (1990; 1991).

Kelly and Kaplan (1990) counter the emphasis on individual
agency as a key to dynamic ritual forms. They argue that 'the
special power in ritual acts, including their unique ability to
encompass contestation, lies in the *lack* of independence asserted
by a ritual participant even while he or she makes assertions
about authority' (Kelly and Kaplan 1990: 140). They write: 'We
are constantly entering and exiting ritual roles in which our
action is authorized outside of ourselves, and that is how we
remake some forms of authority and disempower others' (p. 41).

In the 'wives' meeting' of the Datooga, the sound of words and the sound of voices do not only call upon but evoke the presence of the spirits, ancestors filled with power of the past. By vitalizing the innate past within the present, they effect the merging of the worlds necessary for a Datooga to articulate the words of the spirits to the human community.

Performance theory has not only heightened the importance of communication, but has enhanced the power of experience in ritual (Laderman and Roseman 1996: 2). A growing engagement with issues of embodiment, experience, sensation and imagination has taken place during the recent decade, and in a number of recent anthropological writings from the African continent, the power of the senses and aesthetic form in performance have been recognized (see, e.g. Devisch 1990; 1991; Kratz 1994; Stoller 1996). Victor Turner's inquiry into what he called the condensation of the 'ideological' and the 'physiological' poles of symbols could be seen as an early formulation of the concern for embodiment. 'It was here, in the ability of the symbol to bring lofty ideological concepts into resonance with bodily or "gut" processes, that Turner located the transformative power of symbols' (Laderman and Roseman 1996: 4). I shall try to show that the flexibility and power of the prose played with, the intense emotion generated through the course of collective performance of song and dance in *girgweageeda gadeemga*, and the divine aura created by the continuous elicitation of prayer, are all crucial aspects in our attempts to understand the transformative qualities and in turn the political outcomes of the meeting's action.

SITUATING THE *GIRGWEAGEEDA GADEEMGA*

We need to locate the *girgweageeda gadeemga* structurally within Datooga society, as this council forms part of a complex institutional setting. The boundaries between the diverging concerns, activities and remedies handled by the different councils and meetings women engage in are hardly clear-cut, but create a broad framework, and give indications about a general division of labour. There are several institutions where 'wives who wear the leather skirt' (*hanang'weanda*) are the key participants and strive to ensure and promote safe procreation of female bodies and to protect life in general through prayers and dance which call upon blessings from the spirits. The *gumdageeta* ('under the tree') is a relatively informal gathering of women where issues of concern are discussed, and where possible action is decided upon. In times of great distress either a *ghadoweeda* or a *lukghmajeega ng'yeang'yiida* may be called for by women in *gumdageeta*. In the *ghadoweeda* (literally 'people seeking blessing') groups of women seek the homes of healers, tombs or other sacred sites for gift-giving, redemption and remedy at times of drought, flooding, death, disease, intrusion of people, and so on: that is, in connection with issues of general concern. The *lukghmajeega ng'yeang'yiida* ('praising the earth') is occasioned by similar threats, but on these ritual occasions the men play more prominent roles with ritual slaughters and consumption of honey mead. In contrast, the *girgweageeda gadeemga* is convened in connection with cases that are perceived as serious male intrusion or infringement on a female and fertile domain. These cases have commonly involved only one direct victim of the offence, but critical to our understanding of Datooga women's religious/political engagement in the *girgweageeda gadeemga* is the notion that threats against one woman's procreative potential is a threat against all female bodies, and is ultimately a threat against the entire Datooga community.

The *girgweageeda gadeemga* must also be located among the Datooga meetings. Rules and regulations are enforced by an elaborate system of ad hoc political meetings where no permanent leadership exists. The most commonly held meetings are those of the open meetings (*geetabwaraku*, or *girgweageeda emeeda*), where all Datooga in principle may participate, but which is a male forum in practice. In these meetings problems and questions of general concern are brought up and discussed. Other central councils are the 'clan meeting' (*girgweageeda doshta* or *hulanda doshta*), the 'neighbourhood meeting' (*girgweageeda gischeuuda*), and the 'youth meeting' (*girgweageeda ghearemaanga*). There are moreover numerous more specific meetings which may be convened when need arises, for example, the meeting which deals with disputes between mother's brother and sister's son (*girgweageeda hulanda ghe ghambagheamwata*). Within any of these meetings a 'secret meeting' (*makchameeda*) may be convened when evidence is difficult and sensitive. The *girgweageeda gadeemga* is as such located among the Datooga meetings, with particular focus on concerns related to infringement on the female domain. Grave offences against the 'female body' lead to *ghoghomnyeanda*, a precarious 'near-death' condition linked to the vulnerability of birth giving.

LIVING WITH 'ENEMIES'

The sense of vulnerability of procreation that we shall see extensively played out in the *girgweageeda gadeemga*, needs to be related to people's notions and experience of living in precarious surroundings. The Datooga pastoralists regard the semi-arid plains above and below the Rift Wall in Hanang and Mbulu districts of Tanzania as their heartland. The number one point of reference in the area is the 3,600-metre high green volcano Hanang, which with its woods and water fountains in Datooga cosmology is a cherished location of their spirits. The environment surrounding the mountain is characterized by strong booms and busts. Green lush grazing land may within a few days be turned to dry dusty steppes by wind, sun or fire, or to flooded valleys replacing blooming and fecundity with disease, drought, death and dying. The rotational movement and the seasonal transformations of this land provide the Datooga with a fundamental source for cultural representation of the life-and-death cycles of people, cattle and land (Blystad 1992).

This land, which not more than half a century ago was solely inhabited by Datooga herders and domestic animals, is today increasingly inhabited by neighbouring peoples such as the Iraqw, Nyaturu, Iramba, and Ihanzu. Teachers, bureaucrats, missionaries and development workers have also moved onto this land. These are people who in Datooga thought and experience have the means to allure and dislodge Datooga land, stock and children and force the Datooga to move. Growing numbers of Datooga withdraw to the margins of the plain or move southwards with their herds, away from intruders and in search of new water sources and pasture. The Datooga are highly reluctant to leave this land which is to them is mythical ground won by the Datooga against wild creatures, and sacred ground inhabited by living spirits in the land below (*utang'yeang'yiida*) (Rekdal and Blystad, forthcoming).

Datooga inter-ethnic relations are characterized by strong antagonisms, and the neighbouring peoples, except for the Cushitic Iraqw, are regarded as their enemies (*haloota*). The *lilichta* ritual hunt has as far back as the Datooga can recall engaged young men in hunting expeditions for the five dangerous mammals: lions, leopards, elephants, buffalo and rhinoceros as well as individuals from 'hostile groups', all perceived as 'enemies

of the people'. Authors have made attempts at explaining the
lilichta tradition with diverse theories varying from impetus for
acquiring a lover (Faust 1969), acquiring a wife (Loiske 1990: 97;
Perham 1976: 103; Umesao 1969: 87) acquiring cattle (Wilson
1952: 44) and gaining status, prestige and honour (Klima 1970:
60).

Among the Datooga a successful *lilichta* is not linked up with
marriage, as has been suggested (Kjærby 1979: 20; Setréus 1991:
20), and it is incorrect rather than merely an 'oversimplification'
to say that a man is compelled to kill to be eligible for marriage.
The custom must at least partly be understood as a response to
the Maasai expansion in the middle of the last century (Blystad
1992: 87; Kjærby 1979: 10; Talle 1974: 13). This is validated by
Barabaig myth, song and tale which talk of the *lilichta* in connection with the search for adequate action against the devastating
Barabaig losses in the wars with the Maasai. One aspect of the
lilichta has thus most likely been an attempt to provide their
society with young skilful soldiers.[2] After the spearing of an
'enemy' the young successful hunter is smeared with butter in
front of a spirit guardian's tomb, he is decorated with women's
paraphernalia and is said to have given birth. The young man
then enters speech- and behaviour-related restrictions, with connotations of a convalescent woman (Blystad 1996b).

In recent years the Datooga have continually been on the
losing side in their encounters with ever-increasing numbers of
neighbours, seeing their land, water sources and herds dwindle.
Moreover, the Datooga are today negatively stereotyped: stigma-
tization and discrimination are part of their everyday experience
(Blystad 1996b; Lane 1991; 1996; Ndagala 1991). The precariousness and threats of the surrounding environment, in both a
physical and socio-political sense experienced by the Datooga,
and the related desire to get rid of 'enemies', create the broad
setting in which Datooga women's meetings and marches must be
situated.

GHOGHOMNYEANDA: THE VULNERABILITY OF LABOUR

The concept *ghoghomnyeanda* is related to the critical stages of
birth-giving and dying, and is hence a condition characterized by
extreme vulnerability and danger. Datooga women say that *ghoghomnyeanda* makes them fearful, silent, and it makes them pray
since in *ghoghomnyeanda* they are near the spirits. The terms

geendewi ghoghomnyeanda ('we are in a state of acute danger') and *geendewi mieeda* ('we have received death') are used interchangeably at such precarious moments. In *ghoghomnyeanda* women will spell out their utter distress to the spirits and they will sing and pray that they are 'the houses that cry in *ghoghomnyeanda*' (*gheeda udawuuta ghoghomnyeanda*), and intensely plead for the blessings of the spirits (*ghawooda*).

The precariousness of pregnancy and birth is the prototypical *ghoghomnyeanda*. Cultural elaboration of processes of conception, pregnancy, birth, convalescence and nursing are common and has been reported from around the world (see e.g. Jordan and Davis-Floyd 1993; Leifer 1980; Linke 1992; MacCormack 1982a; 1982b; Ortner and Whitehead 1981; Powers 1980; Sargent 1990; Snow and Johnson 1978). As among many other peoples, blood and semen are thought by the Datooga to contribute to the child's flesh and bones respectively, revealed in expressions such as 'the baby nurses a mother's blood' or 'the child is the bones of Gidaburga' (a man's name). A pregnant woman is referred to as a 'closed' woman (*bungaroocheanda*), 'closed' pointing to her physical body being closed in the sense that it does not menstruate. The blood is kept inside her womb for the foetus to nurse on until the time of birth when the woman 'opens up', and she lets the child and the spare blood out.

We can also talk in a social sense about a pregnant Datooga woman as 'closed', as her apprehension and thoughts related to her pregnant state are commonly not shared with anyone but the life maturing in her womb. She experiences herself as exposed and vulnerable to surroundings pervaded by human beings, substances and states that can cause harm to both herself and her unborn child. The common strategy for a woman in her condition is to keep her fears to herself, and to lead a limited social life.[3] In order to protect herself and her hidden progeny she will live with a web of restrictions on the way she walks, talks, eats and looks at the habitat around her. The outside impressions and stimuli she allows to affect her are substantially reduced. She will commonly talk with her voice lowered and will choose her words carefully. Her eyes frequently focus on the ground and she takes great care not to kill even a little insect when she walks (Blystad 1992; 1996a).

But, for a pregnant Datooga woman, enemies exist not only in her surroundings. Her body is invaded by an internal enemy growing in her womb, a foe that can make her ill or even bring about her death. In the first stages of the pregnancy the foetus is perceived as a watery parasite nursing on its mother's blood. Itself so vulnerable and dependant, it is also demanding and perilous, and the woman takes great care to keep it satisfied. The pregnant woman will choose her diet carefully, since 'her blood becomes what she eats', and she will take care not to drink much milk or eat much butter so that the child in her womb does not become fat and lazy, and have difficulties getting out. Her leather skirt, which she has worn from the day she got married, is tied tightly around her womb in a manner which pushes her growing belly downwards. In this way the unruly foetus is prevented from engaging in unproductive wild play in her womb. Simultaneously she will be able to prevent her condition from becoming known until the later stages of the pregnancy, and hence limit the danger of evil eyes.

There is a considerable chance that the growing womb will lead to bereavement and pain. The foetus may, in Datooga thought, suddenly cease to develop, in which case the child becomes stuck in the maternal womb (*muldaneeda*). During the months or years the child remains in the womb, it feeds on the flesh and blood of its host, drains her energy, and makes the woman weak and fragile. Miscarriages or deaths of still nursing infants are other potential outcomes. Such deaths are perceived as most frightful as they create severe breaches in the perception of correct development from conception through pregnancy and birth to convalescence and nursing. Such events leave the woman, her children, and to some extent her husband, partial, dirty (*gatmooda gaba ririnyeanda*, literally 'women with dirt/pollution') and socially isolated in separate housing enclosures (*ghawiida*) until a new pregnancy is secured, since such events are said to be contagious and can harm the fertile potential of others. The unproductive milk dripping from the woman's breasts is particularly feared. Abnormal births are also feared, and lead to limited social isolation (*metiida*), and ritual cleansing activity. Women who experience recurring miscarriages or infant deaths may spend years of their lives largely isolated behind high thorn fences. The precariousness of pregnancy and labour are thus not merely cultural constructions, but are harshly experienced by Datooga women.

At the time of labour the Datooga will articulate that 'she is close to the dead' and even that 'she is dying'. Indeed, both the woman in labour as well as the women who pray, sweat, and suffer together with her in her private room close to the burning fire are in *ghoghomnyeanda*. This liminal condition has, if matters proceed smoothly, the potential of an outcome joyous and fecund, since *ghoghomnyeanda* is ideally to lead to birth-giving. Becoming a mother and father is the most desired condition of all among the Datooga. Only with parental status can full adulthood be reached. Moreover men and women who 'have grandchildren from both sons and daughters', who 'have whole bodies', and have 'no bones' – that is, have not killed a fellow Datooga, may become buried and reborn as spirit guardians. Ensuring successful procreation is in Datooga thought ultimately dependent upon the blessings of Aseeta (the supreme being) through Udameeseelgwa (the prime female spirit), which again depend upon moral conduct of the living. As labour proceeds the song calling upon Udameeseelgwa is continually performed:

Udameeseelgwa, hayoyahee (*Udameeseelgwa, hayoyahee*).
The one who does not marry (*Udameegeena*)
Why does she not marry? (*Meegeena ghwasaan?*)
Her powers of benediction do not allow it (*Ghaheawa ghawooda*)
The great blessing (*Ghawooda hau*)
The mother who keeps watch at the precarious time of birth
(*Gheamata galanda ghoghomnyeanda*)
The one who supports without requesting a return (*Uteri mawalla*)
The one who never betrays us (*Mawalla iiseaghwa*)
Mother who gives us strength at the precarious time of birth
(*Gheamata weeteasa aba ghoghomnyeanda*)
She who knows no resentment (*Uda miing'waanjeeda*)
Give us children (*Goona ghameakaasa*)
and the leather slings in which to carry them (*ea hamarooyeeka*)

Not until after the navel cord is cut has a woman 'given birth', and the child received as a precious gift from Udameeseelgwa. At this point the woman enters a new 'liminal' phase (*ghereega*) which implies near total seclusion for a mother and her infant for a period of about three months. Even at the 'celebration of the child' (*werweerga jeapta*) the mother will rarely leave her private room and will merely listen to the singing and peep through cracks in the walls to get glimpses of the dancing women. Convalescent women are referred to as *Udaghereega*, 'Uda' being the prefix for most female names, and despite the fact that convalescence is a new period of precariousness, being *Udaghereega* is perceived as a most precious, worshipped, and highly desired condition by woman. We shall see that like the notion *ghoghomnyeanda*, giving birth (*jeata*) and convalescence (*ghereega*) link up with a whole range of life events and transitions among the Datooga, all highly ambiguous, with potential outcomes of growth and fertility or alternatively of danger and bereavement. The vulnerable state of procreation may thus be removed from the biological reproductive sphere, and symbolically elaborated upon in a manner where these processes may bring meaning to a large number of critical conditions and events in Datooga life. Datooga women will say that they are in *ghoghomnyeanda* when a person is very sick or dying, when young men are circumcised, when they are in the final stages of a funeral, and during men's ritual hunts. *Ghoghomnyeanda* is also a characteristic feature of the condition following male offences against female bodies, especially female procreative bodies. In addition, as a result of chained notions which refer simultaneously to the body, the house, and bodies in the landscape, such as Datooga tombs, it is connected to other diverse religious and reproductive practices.

THE VULNERABILITY OF MARRIAGE

In the above sections we have seen that the environment in Datooga thought is filled with 'enemies', such as disease, drought, non-friendly neighbours ('enemies of the people'), substances or states in the local surroundings, blood-sucking foetuses ('enemies' inside maternal wombs), and enemies that create a precarious habitat. The myth of the creation of cosmos and the myth of the creation of marriage give us some further clues as to the ambivalence and vulnerability which characterizes the lives of married Datooga women, and which induce them to take action.

Long ago, heaven and earth were not separated as now. A man and a woman lived in this habitat. After two children were born to them, calamity caused the woman's death. Aseeta saw the misery of the man and his children, and gave them a promise. The deity showed them a certain patch of grass and told them that the woman would rise from this tuft. The father told the children that if they fed the tuft milk it would one day again bring forth their mother. The children commenced a continuous watch over the grass and poured some milk at its base every day. Some days later the man woke up and saw a strange woman together with his children. The woman got married to the man but she was not told of the promise of Aseeta. One day she called the children to help her in the skinning of a calf, but they didn't answer. When she saw that they were watching a tuft of grass she asked them what they were doing. The children answered that from this tuft of grass their mother would rise. The woman became jealous and angry because of their disrespect for her and furiously shouted that she would put an end to their disobedience. She then took her knife and cut the grass. At this moment blood spurted from the 'wound' with tremendous strength. The blood even reached Aseeta as the deity withdrew upwards and took the skies along. This was how the elements as we know them now were created, and the colour of Aseeta's eye is still visible when the sun sets in the evening.

This is a myth dense with messages and only a few can be commented upon here. In the myth an image is conveyed of a control by Aseeta and the patriclan over the married woman (who is of another clan) and, by the same token, the fertile element which the woman represents. Despite the communication of control over the women's procreative powers, it is a woman who appears to be the agent or 'mover' in the creation of earth, the 'birth' of earth. This 'birth' takes place in the wake of a cutting of the grass sod, or rather, a killing of the first and fertile woman. The act of killing and death, and the act of creation which are so closely connected in the myth give associations of a life-death linkage. In fact, the myth suggests that the first wife was killed by the knife of the second wife; a killing ultimately leading to life. An ambiguous image of women and their reproductive capacity thus seems to be revealed by the two women in the myth: one good and fertile who is greatly missed by her husband and children after her death, and the other destructive and biologically infertile, but none the less vested with immense procreative potential. Moreover the myth points to a distinction between an eternal fertility represented by Aseeta, the clan, men and their offspring, on the one side, and female procreative powers which are temporary and need to be watched and controlled by Aseeta, the husband and his clan on the other. The creation myth appears in contrast to the myth which tells of the circumstances leading to marriage since, in Datooga thought, it is the female spirit Udameeseelgwa, sometimes referred to as Udamwahe in this context, and not Aseeta who laid out the frames which women must relate to throughout their married lives. Udameeseelgwa/Udamwahe assisted women in seducing men to accept marital ties with women, she taught women the intricate craft of sewing their leather skirts to be worn after marriage is consummated, a skirt which is directly related to the procreative performance of women, and, most significantly, she invested the women with the conception of the sanctity of the female body, and women's sacred responsibility to act when this body is threatened by destructive male forces.

At the time marriage did not yet exist, Datooga women were without any influence or power in the society in which they lived. They were moving from homestead to homestead and stayed only for short periods of time with every man. When they bore children the boys remained with the men whereas the girls moved on with their mother. At this time men carried out almost all the work. Cooking, milking and herding were their duties. Women gradually became tired of their inferior and worthless position. They contacted the powerful woman, Udameeseelgwa/Udamwahe, who was famous for her extensive healing and ritual knowledge, to voice their grievances and ask for help. She prepared a remedy and gave the women clear instructions about what to do with it in order that it should influence men's minds. When the men returned to their homesteads wet, cold and tired after a day with heavy rains, they were astonished to see that the women had lit the fires. The women had secretly squirted some of the potion into the fire, and when the men huddled together for warmth in front of the hearth, the concoction started to work. The men became drowsy and tired, and became reluctant to leave their comfortable place. Finally they asked the women to assist them in the milking of the cattle. The women eagerly went out and milked the cattle. While milking they poured some of the secret remedy into the gourds, before they brought them to the men.

The men drank the fresh milk greedily. As they were drinking their thoughts turned to the value and worth of women, and to how good life would be if a woman would live with them permanently. From this time women stayed on in the home with one man. This was how marriage started. From this day men became afraid of losing their women, and started to listen to their words and wishes.[4]

In the initial sequence women were found moving around, having sexual partners apparently without any regulation of the relationships, like animals of the bush. They did no major chores, apart from giving birth and raising girls, while men tended to all the household tasks as well as to herding. With the assistance of the female spirit, the women were brought out of their unworthy position, were given permanent partners, meaningful chores and homes, and were given a say in the household. The homes where this new ordered life was located were in the Datooga housing compound, the *gheeda*. These compounds contain at least one house which must contain 'the men's room' (*hulanda*), 'the wives' public room' (*dodooda*), and 'the wives' private room' (*gah*). More commonly, however, there are a number of structures including a separate man's house, and one or more women's houses (*ghorajeega*). It is in the private quarters that the wives will sleep with their younger children, eat, engage in procreative activity, give birth, cook, and churn butter. No stranger may enter this combined bedroom and kitchen, and only members of the particular woman's house, and the husband, may come and go freely. In fact, even the husband will rarely enter this room except when sneaking away from the men's house for a short period during the night. The room has a large bed (*bulaliideba gah*) covered by a large bull's hide on which conception and birth must take place. The three stones that make up the hearth (*gisheatka*), also located in these private quarters, are in Datooga thought strongly linked to and associated with a husband, wife, and children respectively. The hearth stones, flames and ashes resonate with images of motherhood, caring, and nurturing and giving birth and, simultaneously, with death and dying. Only when a member of the household dies may any of these stones be removed.[5]

Housing compounds, hence, are replete with symbolically significant content, and provide the Datooga with basic structural features which impose a pattern of sexual segregation on those who live in them. Through the practices of everyday life actual relations between men and women, affines and agates, young and old, human and animal populations are continuously created and recreated. The myth imparts an ideal order for Datooga married life, an order in which rights and duties are shared between partners in a fairly stable reproductive unit. But the marriage alliance between men and women, between two clans, and the contributions of each in processes of production and procreation is less obvious and clear-cut in actual life than what is presented in the myth. The ambiguity of masculinity and femininity, and ambiguity related to matri- and patriclan – that is, a mother and her children, symbolized by a woman's house, and father and his children symbolized by the men's house – was not solved once and for all as the mythical representation suggests. Quite the contrary, the relationship between husband and wife is often delicate and fragile – divorce, particularly instigated by women, is common – and an underlying tension seems to be continuously experienced to some extent by every man and woman, which surfaces in daily settings as well as on formal ritual occasions. The themes for dispute are part of a vast field where continual negotiation over boundaries and domains take place, and the members of a household continuously trespass on and in each others' spheres regarding both physical boundaries and chores. Amicable atmospheres and sound co-operation alternate with irritated remarks, quarrels and fights. All are part of life.

OFFENCES AGAINST THE FERTILE FEMALE BODY

Some eruptions in the relationship are experienced as more serious than others, and incidences which women perceive as serious transgressions on the fertile female body impel women to act in the *girgweageeda gadeemga* lest they damage the procreative potential of all Datooga.

Any male interference with the elaborate norms regulating *ghoghomnyeanda*, such as mistreating or quarrelling with a pregnant or convalescent woman, or reacting negatively towards any decision taken by a midwife (a metaphoric Udameeseelgwa), are regarded as particularly serious offences. Sexual harassment, sexually offensive statements, watching the birth of a child (if not specifically summoned to assist as a member of a healing clan), arguing over funds for treating barrenness, miscarriage, or illness related to pregnancy, birth or nursing will also require action.[6] Female animals – not only livestock but also domestic animals such as cats and dogs – are protected in ways parallel to women when they are pregnant or with litters.[7] Male violence inside a Datooga woman's private room or violence directed against any of the central and meaningful material objects inside the room is considered utterly harmful.[8] The most highly valued dairy products, milk, ghee and butter, which are handled solely by girls and women, are also a part of this domain.[9] Male behaviour also quickly comes under women's scrutiny following incidences of male misconduct against women in relation to what is perceived as female sacred activity in such institutions as the gatherings for prayer (ghadoweeda), 'praising the earth' (lukghmajeega ng'yeang'yiida), female wedding ceremonies (nyeangiida), in the 'welcoming of the child' (werweerga jeapta) and so on.

The cultural representations and concepts connected to the female procreative body thus appear to be infiltrated in most diverse aspects of Datooga life, and have entered domains which appear to be far removed from the themes of bodily reproduction and nurturance. As such, we are not merely talking about a set of well defined regulations which protect women from overt misconduct by Datooga men, but a large, complex and ambiguous field where justification for action is largely context dependent, and where the parties are, as we shall see below, female and male more than women and men.

Most significantly, the challenges to the norms of moral conduct experienced among the living penetrate the world of spirits as well. Ideally the spirits are pure and sinless and provide the living with blessings. But despite the fact that it is solely moral individuals who may become spirit guardians, the Datooga know very well that human beings are never entirely moral, and so neither are the spirits. Envy, quarrelling and anger also form part of the 'world below'. This gendered spirit world engages in internal fighting which is revealed during the seances where female mediums (gijoocheanda) evoke the voices of male and female spirits who battle over 'female' and 'male' conduct respectively. The mythic event where Gidamwageera returns from a hunting expedition, approaches a woman, and pleads with her to remove the arrow which is still stuck in his body, is one of the themes that the spirits fight over with such fierceness that glowing coal from the fires fills the air, and the spirit's voices evoked by the female medium turn loud and frightening. The mythical woman refuses to assist the man, but her baby son, who is fastened to her back, reaches out and removes the arrow (Blystad 1992). As such, the spirit world as a moral community is as ambiguous as the morality of the human community. The only entirely moral being is Aseeta, the androgynous deity, the ultimate source of Datooga fecundity. If kept contented, Aseeta will return ample life force to the human community through the spirits.

MOBILIZING THE *GIRGWEAGEEDA GADEEMGA*

With this enhanced knowledge we shall at this point review two concrete cases of mobilization of the *girgweageeda gadeemga* which I was able to follow quite closely. Firstly, the case against Gidamuhaled of Dang'eyda, and secondly, the case against female taxation.[10] I shall not attempt to present these cases in all their incredible richness and complexity, but will merely make an attempt to illustrate some key features of these mobilizations.

CASE I: THE OFFENCE OF GIDAMUHALED

Gidamuhaled not only disapproved of the women's choice of animal, he tried to intrude while the women were choking the goat (*heeyda ghereega*, 'the goat of convalescence'). This goat, which is awarded the female spirit guardian Udameeseelgwa and her earthly mediator, the midwife, after a successful birth, can, according to Datooga norms, in principle be obtained from any man's flock. The impingement on the women's choice was therefore highly unacceptable. After the decision was reached to convene the 'wives' meeting' and *gilbwaheasa gadeemga* (literally, 'everyone on our side') had been called in front of the gates, around fifty women of the community women left their compounds. The women moved through the landscape with the characteristic swaying from the long fringes of their leather skirts. The skirts, *hanang'weanda,* were smeared with ghee and red ochre, and their heavy jewellery was finely polished as they marched through the community with tufts of grass and sticks in their hands. They finally seated themselves under a large tree and initiated a drama that was not to end until three days later.

Intense melodic prayer started the performance. Placed close together in a circle, with their bodies moving rhythmically, the impassioned voice of an old woman called upon the spirits in songs of blessing (*dumda ghawooda/dumda meanga*) starting out with the intensely performed 'song which awakens the earth' (*dumda siheeta ng'yeang'yiida*). The sung prayer was replaced by spoken prayer (*moshta ghawooda*) which with unusual force recollected the violation that had take place. Their vulnerable state due to the encroachment of men were in principle phrases repeated throughout the prayer these days:

SPEAKER: Tell them mother (*Eashiinea iyya*)
SECONDER: Yes (*Oh*)
SP: We are in a state of *ghoghomnyeanda* (*Goong'oyseasa ghoghomnyeanda*)
SE: Yes (Oh)
SP: Datooga women are dealing with the spears of the men (*Datooga* ii *ng'utkeaka headiga*)
SE: Yes (*Oh*)
SP: Please open the heads (wits) of our Datooga men (*Eaniyean ghwaajaachi uhuuda beanda ghaheanda Datoogasa*)
UNISON: We say we, the Datooga, agree with your words (*Ayeena geawaschi Datoogasa*)

With the closing of the prayer the hearings were initiated. In a highly agitated manner, one woman after the other stood in front of the other and presented information about the case, particularly details about Gidamuhaled's many dubious propositions to women. One woman's recollection of the manner in which he in an impassioned and aggressive manner approached both girls and married women, even women of his child's generation set, when he returned drunk from the cattle auction, set off a chain of reactions in the crowd. Evidence suggested that this man had infringed upon the female domain many times before. The present case, interfering with women's gift-giving to Udameeseelgwa, was by far the most serious and threatening to their procreative powers, but the man's continual smaller provocations did not help him in these circumstances. Some close relatives and neighbours carefully tried to interfere with the directions of the proceedings by bringing forth evidence of Gidamuhaled's more favourable sides, but they were hardly convincing in their argumentation, and were scorned, and the audience's distaste for their words was conveyed. The hearing of Gidamuhaled's case and a recollection of cases similar and dissimilar to his went on for hours.

The opportunity to voice complaints was used to the fullest, and a series of experiences of male misconduct were communicated in front of the crowd. Testimony upon testimony created an image of men as intruders, transgressors and violators. Whereas some women made their testimony meekly, others grimaced, raised their voices, beat their sticks on the ground, or waved them in the air. When convincing or forceful the performer was applauded and encouraged to go on. Good memory and knowledge possessed by some, and the skilful oratory and performance of others, were acclaimed and rewarded by excited outbursts of consent and sympathy.

Gidamuhaled's unsuccessful attempts to attract the women's attention were ridiculed, and mocking comments about his failing moves caused laughter and amusement. In this cheerful atmosphere an older woman started out the characteristic melodic 'ohii o hee' initiating the women's songs (*dumda gadeemga*) which brought new vigour to the crowd. The women stood as a series of songs were performed, each one more lewd than the previous. Verses ridiculing men's desire of women, songs mortifying male sexuality and songs of female sexual pleasures with young virile men of good conduct were presented to an increasingly spirited crowd.

Tell the men that they have lost their land due to lust (*Eashiine headiga, beela nirooda ng'eang'yiideang'wa*)
You depend upon women, but you want them all (*Ghwaaghuschi gadeemga nea headiga ghomughuuta*)
You even 'eat' the women of Iramba (*Nda gadeemga eara gea Yeambi ghwaayaaji*)
You court them with Datooga bracelets (*Ghoaloachi muleelga dearoyeeka wangiida*)
But, the Iramba girls don't know the sweetness of the play (*Haweega Yeambi mwanala gissamu ng'alealleeda*)
The dance of the calabash with its mouth pointing downwards (*Dumda gideeshteayda gul ghuuta ng'eanyi hea*)

The dance of the vagina which is not 'eaten' by the dishonest (*Dumda gideeshteayda meaka gijoosajeega*)

It is solely of the young men of truth (*Geeghus gheareemaneeda rukku gea huumwa*)

The ones who are deceitful will not be given anything (*Nea gea marukkuuna gea huumwa ea majeebiiw*)

They are told to get up and to wear their shoes (*Geeruksa ea ghang'eat ghwaalla geekea*)

Each song closed with the women throwing themselves into lively dance where two women faced each other and in intense and rhythmic jumping 'competed for each others husbands' in the 'dance of the penis' (*dumda dumooda*). The one who managed to out-jump the other was jokingly said to 'win the sexual favours of the other's husband'. From time to time, two thin elderly women mimicked and mocked the act of sex while the audience applauded the gaiety and the actors' skill. Stories of male intruders on female meetings who were raped to death by women were presented to the exhilarated crowd. One woman shouted abusive obscenities at a few men who were seated within the women's sight. This greatly amused the crowd and caused outbreaks of laughter. The skilful performances, the intensity of messages and music, the power of the prayer, and the passion of the sweating, dancing bodies moving together in rhythmic jumping in the heat of the day caused trance like states. In this manner the alternating forms and the adding of information from relevant cases continued for two days interrupted only by a few hours' sleep.

After a brief prayer gathering the third morning, the women got up and rushed towards the home of the offender with their sticks held above their heads. As they moved they sang with frightening force 'we have come to collect our hide' (*Hiaghuu orjooda hirigheega*). At this point a number of men as well as Gidamuhaled himself showed up and attempted to block the path by placing themselves between the women and the homestead. They placed tufts of grass on the path trying to 'cool the women down'. The women chased them away, threatened them with their sticks, and presented the men with their decree: Gidamuhaled was fined a large black bull (*ghorjooda gadeemga*, literally 'wives' fine'). Three animals were consecutively brought before the women only to be received by contemptuous laughter, and with boisterous demand for a black oxen, a scarce and most valued animal among the Datooga. When a proper bullock finally was brought forward, the women rushed towards it, beat it with their sticks, and panicked the animal into running through the gate of the offender's homestead. Informants said the 'women attacked the compound of Gidamuhaled' (*gangeasa ghe Gidamuhaled gadeemga*). At this point the women began to sing blessing songs calling upon their spirit guardians. The powerful sound of the women's voices at this point appeared to paralyse all other activity.

Men and women now wrested the large bull to the ground, and suffocated it without drawing blood or breaking any of its bones. After the animal's death the women danced wildly around the carcass singing 'we have given birth' (*sitiniischi*) while touching the dead animal with their sticks. As their dancing ceased, the men collected the sticks, divided up the carcass and made sure that every woman received a large piece of meat. Most of the women at this point hurriedly left the compound bringing with them their portions of meat, while the women of the homestead and the men waited for the men to cook and serve the meat in a collective feast.

In a number of recent cases where Datooga women have convened the council the issues at stake have at face value appeared to be far removed from the concern conveyed by the wives' meeting recollected above. Poor treatment of children in schools, adult education, demand for contribution of maize and beans for schools, appropriation of land for cultivation, extraction of taxes, and so forth, have caused not only distress among women, but have also caused them to march off to meet the appropriate politicians or bureaucrats.[11] What have usually been cases heard under local trees do at times become large scale multi-ethnic protest marches to far-away places, bringing the Datooga into confrontations with people radically different from themselves. Some of these mobilizations are nonetheless referred to as *girgweageeda gadeemga*. We shall take a brief look at the proceedings from one such encounter.

CASE 2: THE OFFENCE OF TANZANIAN POLITICIANS

The prospects of female taxation caught the attention of the Datooga in 1989, and culminated with large-scale protest marches and meetings of women in Hanang and Mbulu Districts of Arusha Region during the spring of 1990. Tax in these two districts at this point consisted of a yearly fee on human and cattle population plus the taxation levied at cattle auctions.[12] Increasing numbers of separate taxes were however demanded for purposes such as secondary schools, vehicles for district bureaucrats, new roads, and so on – artefacts and facilities from which only a small fraction of the district's population experienced any benefit. The total taxation pressure was now experienced to be unreasonably high, and the prospects of having an additional head tax on women was taken as a provocation.

After the women again had run in front of the gates of the compounds shouting 'everyone on our side' women headed for the Basootu Plains. Women wearing leather dress and elaborate brass decoration, 'kanga' and 'vitenge' (colourful cotton dress worn by most rural Tanzanian women), confronted women in high fashion female dress and jewellery, and engaged in debate and intense emotional performance at Darabeambw. The historic encounter occurred above the Basotu ridge for some eight intense days at the end of the 1990 rainy season.

What initially appeared to me, residing in a Datooga community in the south-western corner of Hanang District, to be a locally-convened meeting of married Datooga women, quickly grew to include women living several hundreds of kilometres apart. Approximately a thousand women[13] from every Datooga subsection, Iraqw, Gorowa, and even some Nyaturu women joined in mass mobilization against what was perceived as governmental encroachment on village women. The encounter brought into relief the difference in women's discourses between various ethnic groups in the area, between young and old, men and women, between educated and uneducated, between women trained in the language of the Tanzanian bureaucracy and peasant and pastoral women to whom Katesh and Mbulu life and discourses were highly foreign. The shapes of the arguments and styles of performance presented amazing variation. Despite their distinct mode of communication, their limited knowledge about the literate world surrounding them, as well as their incompetence in Swahili, Datooga women managed to make themselves highly visible throughout the performance and demonstration.

Datooga women initiated the meetings with a sung prayer, followed by a lengthy and intense spoken prayer in which Datooga and Iraqw women brought out the issue at stake (the later type of prayer is called *moshta ghawooda* in Datooga and *firro* in Iraqw). Every message could thus be heard in both Datooga and Iraqw, and later in Swahili as well. Individual women in convincing and forceful oratory conveyed how they feared the burden of the levies that were now to be forced upon them. The rough and disrespectful way the tax collectors fared, particularly among the Datooga, strengthened the wrath and animosity felt against the government and its tax policy. Powerful chorus from hundreds of voices exclaimed consensus to the messages brought forward. Large numbers of women and men arrived throughout the following days, and, without the will or means to return to their homes, slept outside with limited food and shelter. Young men fetched water and firewood and cooked for the large crowd.

The Datooga women filled the air with their characteristic 'prayers for blessing', 'women's songs', the 'dance of the penis', and agitated speech. Laughter and amusement, anger and indignation alternated. Their resentment was communicated in speech acts that bore witness to knowledge and insights that were continually referred to by the women from other ethnic groups. 'We pay taxes through our bodies', 'we give birth', 'our babies are our taxes' an old Datooga woman exclaimed. Another woman called out in agitation that while Datooga women were still in *ghereega* (convalescence) men come to collect money, showing utter disrespect. Their forceful intrusion on the female realm threatened babies and women. The crowd acknowledged these statements with praising cheers. The women demanded to meet with the politicians and bureaucrats responsible for the new governmental decree.

Representatives from the local bureaucracy in Basotu showed up, but were ridiculed and turned down. The women demanded meetings with higher-level politicians. After three days politicians from the district headquarters in Katesh arrived and initiated dialogues. A female representative from Katesh argued that, as a woman, she understood very well their concerns, but said it was significant for women's struggle for influence and equality to contribute to the state economy. Paying taxes signals that women, like men, contribute to the development of Tanzanian society. The Datooga and Iraqw women, quietly supported by a large number of men, responded that taxes would hardly improve their position. To the contrary, taxes would cause conflicts within households over who was to earn the money.

The Datooga and Iraqw women detailed how women in Hanang District had no access to money except what was earned from the sale of a few eggs, chickens, oil and, in cases of utter poverty, firewood. Should these pennies be used for taxes rather than for the treatment of sick babies and women? They maintained that with their dwindling herds and small farm plots, they were frustrated about 'eating cattle needlessly' in order to subsidize a corrupt district-level elite. 'When cattle and calves disappear, so do our children,' they told the bureaucrats.

When the two female representatives from Katesh responded angrily to these accusations, Datooga women made enquiry about their positions. They acknowledged the nicely dressed female bodies of the bureaucrats, but told them that they talked and acted as if they were men. One of the women was single, and she was told that being an unmarried woman, she was indeed more like a man than a woman. As a man she could not possibly understand what women were talking about. The other representative, who was married to a bureaucrat in Katesh, was asked how she could act so self-confidently on behalf of all women (*Kwa nini unaringa?*, Swahili). She was told that, due to her husband's substantial wages, neither was she like other women in the crowd. The representatives were asked if women did not contribute to their country by giving birth. Indeed the bureaucrats from Katesh would not have been there at all if it were not for women, one woman reminded the crowd.

The bureaucrats did indeed appear to listen to the women's complaints and concerns, and they left with a mandate to pursue meticulously the case the women had brought forward in this performance. Datooga and Iraqw women jointly closed the meetings by forcefully performing a sung prayer and blessing. The female head tax has, to date, not been initiated.

THE POWER OF FEMALE WITHDRAWAL AND RE-EMERGENCE IN THE COMPOUND

The issue at stake during the mobilization against female taxation at Darabeambw, the socio-political context in which it took place, the heterogeneity of the participants, the complexity of their orations and languages, and the scale of the meetings were not all that similar to the mobilization against Gidamuhaled in Dang'eyda provided above. But despite the substantial differences, the Datooga would quite easily recognize considerable similarities in form between the two meetings. The solemn sung prayers to the spirits, the spoken prayer, the cheerful songs of mockery, the diverse dance forms, and the lengthy auditions were all central elements of both meetings. Moreover, on closer inspection, it is apparent that the vernacular prose accentuates the 'female body' and emphasizes the vulnerability of its 'procreative potential', as was also the case in the mobilization against Gidamuhaled recounted above. Furthermore, and perhaps most importantly, the Datooga did not perceive these gatherings as fundamentally different from other conventions of the married women's meeting, and referred to the meetings as *girgweageeda gadeemga*.

Let us take a fresh look at the symbolic forms and play which underpin the council, in order that we may enhance our understanding of what takes place during these performances, the apparent flexibility of the institution, as well as of its impact on ongoing Datooga life. The central messages communicated by women in cases handled by the 'wives' meeting' is the manner in which a particular male offence threatens the bearing of children and thus threatens the continuation of life. Throughout the performance Datooga women communicate that their bodies are jeopardized by male forces, and that they are in a liminal state of birth-giving (*ghoghomnyeanda*).

As we have seen, the notion that male inclination to impropriety and brutal conduct poses threats to the female procreative potential and thus to the reproduction of the Datooga, is employed metaphorically on a vast number of issues. It is now common knowledge that in societies where gender is a central organizing idea, one cannot talk about gender as if it were only about relations between men and women (see e.g. Broch-Due and Rudie 1993; Caplan 1987; MacCormack and Strathern 1980; Moore 1994; Strathern 1988; 1993). Men and women are potentially feminine and masculine, and discourse brings about fluctuations in this androgynous balance. The metaphoric use of the male–female distinction may in such societies be used to order other contrasts than those between men and women.

When fertility is jeopardized by male forces, women march in a threatening manner through the community and then withdraw into the bush. Located far away from housing compounds they stand up and cry out their messages of disgust, contempt and anger for the malconduct while waving sticks in the air, and furiously refuse any unacceptable attempt at rapprochement. For several days the women engage in action directed against impending male activity. Male encroachment on the female domain is denounced, male sexuality ridiculed, questioned and challenged, and women gradually appear as powerful sexual beings, as manipulators of sexuality and fertility and as masters of procreative activity. The male contribution in matters of procreation at certain points appears to be effectively eradicated in these performances. But the male contribution in the procreative process never entirely vanishes. Indeed, it is most compellingly and creatively present in these performances. The heterosexual nature of procreation, the productivity and fecundity of male and female merging is acknowledged in a variety of ways.

When women shout and wave their sticks while presenting their allegations they give association of men's conduct in male meetings. When women chase the animal, beat it with their sticks and aggressively penetrate the gate of the compound, they resemble men chasing animals in ritual hunts. A strong male image emerges. But simultaneously, the women remain utterly female. They appear in their finery, sway their leather-dressed bodies to melodic prayer, talk of their wounded, infertile bodies, and dance the 'dance of the penis', hailing sexuality while ridiculing male sexual appetite. A seeming appropriation and manipulation of both male and female components take place. Women in *girgweageeda gadeemga* appear to embody stereotypical constituents of both male and female within themselves.

This play with gender notions by the women can however hardly produce real children, and the council will have to seek ways to reintroduce and reincorporate the female body in the compound and as such reassume the fertile prescription laid down by Udameeseelgwa. The displays thus need to facilitate a political reconciliation between female and male, in order to reassume true procreation.

Let us for a moment return to the cases to see how such a bringing together of the genders is facilitated. The case against Gidamuhaled culminates when the women after their performances in the bush confront the men, chase them together with the bull into the compound, and join them in sacrifice and joint consumption of meat. In the mobilization against female taxation the female element (village women and men) force the male element (bureaucrats, both women and men) to confront them, demand that they listen to their memorandum, threaten them with damaging action, and finally engage in a dialogue which culminates in the peaceful agreement that the representatives pursue their case. The Datooga do in this last case create distinctions between 'female bodies ill-suited for taxation' and 'male bodies liable of taxation'. Hence, in both cases a perceived male violation of female fertility causes injury and harm, and requires a separation, a demanding confrontation, and a successive merging of female and male in order to regain the fertile potential. At the very moment this coupling takes place, the fertile order is re-established, and a union indispensable for continued fertility is revitalized. Gender notions are thus played with, contrasted and combined, in a manner that appears ambiguous and contradictory, but which is simultaneously highly meaningful and highly productive. Through such a frolicking with metaphors of gender and fertility, powerful embodied experiences of transformation are created and, by the same token, these experiences transform.

The recurring concepts of conception, pregnancy and birth-giving, as touched upon above, also involve the manipulation of the powerful notion of life-bringing death. That is to say, just as a birth is perceived as 'a small death', so death may be perceived as a small, or in some cases even a grand birth. The close interconnection between life and death is a central and recurring theme in Datooga thought and practice. In the mythical creation of heaven and earth, the death of a fertile woman facilitated the conception of heaven and earth as we know it now. In the *lilichta* ritual hunt, the successful killer is smeared with butter, wears female attire, observes convalescence-like restrictions and is hailed like a woman who has given birth. The understanding is that by relieving the Datooga community of an enemy, he has by the same token brought new life to it (Bloch 1992; Bloch and Parry 1982; Frazer 1890). In the elaborate public funeral (*bung'eeda*), the dead body is wrapped in a bull's hide, baptized in butter, and is placed in a foetus-like position in the tomb. During the nine-month long funeral the burial mound is enlarged in height and width until the 'begetting of the child' takes place in front of an 'entire Datooga community'. In some cases several thousand people are present this day. Through elaborate play with gender notions, concepts of fertility, birth, life and death, a spirit is born. Again we see a death leading to life.

In the final stages of the *girgweageeda gadeemga* a cherished bull is chased and killed after which the women shout that they have given birth and engage in sung prayer. They have, like men in *lilichta*, rid themselves of an enemy, and by the same token given birth. The life-giving death of the bull was as far as I could understand not a part of the mobilization of Darabeambw. But the productive play with the notions of *ghoghomnyeanda* and *ghereega*, pregnancy and birth, separation and merging of male and female, and the engagement in songs of blessings calling upon the spirits at the final stage of the performance seem also in this mobilization to facilitate a sense of retrieved fertility through the recreation of fecund alliance. Indeed, it is as though the final impassioned engagement in songs of blessing facilitates a powerful sense of recreation of a procreative unit.

THE TRANSFORMATIVE DYNAMICS OF *GIRGWEAGEEDA GADEEMGA*

Jackson (1983), as was recollected above, reminds us that metaphors are ways of doing things, not merely saying things. Now, what kind of impact do these mobilisations have on ongoing social life? The oratory which through song and speech acts makes public details of particular individual's misconduct, questions and ridicules people's character, will necessarily shape the images of and comportment towards these individuals after the meeting.[14] The consequences of a wives' meeting may indeed become quite extreme in cases where a person is not ony fined but cursed, since the female curse (*moshteyda gadeemga*) implies that a social network built up over a life time is lost. A cursed individual tends to move out of the Datooga community. But the most serious outcome of being the target of a wives' meeting is a damaged relationship with the spirit world; the offender will never receive a Datooga funeral since his body can never become spiritually life-giving. The ultimate aim of the *girgweageeda gadeemga* is to facilitate actual transformation of a condition characterized by infertility, danger and dying to a fertile condition of birth-giving. I shall argue that it is the force of the embodied prose played with, the intense emotion generated through the course of collective performance, and the divine aura created by the eliciation of sung and spoken prayer that jointly generate the meeting's substantial political potential. The participants in the wives' meeting appear to sense and embody the distress just as they embody the distress of an adversary in their womb during a pregnancy, and they transform the distress through the course of the performances just as the foetus is transformed through the precarious voyages of pregnancy and birth. During the final state an image of birth is communicated, and simultaneously an embodied experience of birth, growth and fertility is facilitated. Informants talked of this experience in terms of 'calming down' (*sihing'anyi*, 'we have calmed down') and linked it to the embodied experience of relief following labour (*jeata*).

We need to take a closer look at the form of the performance in order to appreciate fully the creative power of embodied experience facilitated throughout the mobilizations. We are dealing with a performance where women for three days or more join in collective speaking, listening, looking, laughing, marching, jumping, bending, tasting, smelling, crying, sweating, touching. To some extent the female participants share sensations of hunger, fatigue, exhaustion, distress, of vigour, mastery, triumph and fertility. Felt qualities, values and virtues are expressed through and evoked by melody and movement throughout the performance. The considerable variation in melodic themes, rhythm, pitch and tempo evoke diverse sensations such as anger, anguish, passion and pain. The light-hearted tunes of lewd and lustful women's songs excite and evoke feelings of gaiety and desire and the enticing character of monotonous sung prayer induces serenity and experience of a divine presence.

By giving particular attention to non-verbal characteristics of culture, ethnographies on music, song and dance have focused anthropology on the body, sentiment and sensation (Barber *et al.* 1997; Blacking and Kealiinohomoku 1979; Chernoff 1979; Feld 1982; Friedson 1996; Kratz 1994; Spencer 1985; Stoller 1996). Attempts to acquire knowledge of the sound and spirit of performances will assist our understanding of their existential force and creative qualities. The intense engagement in the full range of female expressive genres during the *girgweageeda gadeemga,* from marching and running bodies, to swaying, rocking and jumping bodies, generate, I suggest, an embodied knowledge of strength and vigour which entices women to take action.

Csordas (1990; 1994) demonstrates how performance-oriented approaches can be enriched by theories of embodiment, imagination and memory in religious ritual. The inducing character of the musical forms in these female performances, the absorbing bodily movements, and the stirring oratory, evoke emotion and, by the same token, the presence of Datooga ancestor spirits, and in particular female spirituality. The intensely emotional 'songs of blessing' which only with minor variation are reiterated time and again, do in Datooga thought facilitate communication with the spirits and a sense of their presence among the living. The proximity of the spirits bestows the gathering a sacred esteem which is highly respected by men and women, young and old. By resorting to higher levels of authority, the Datooga women engage in an endeavour which could hardly be productive without it.

The vocal genres all take place with a principal orator, who in the case of the prayers for blessing (*moshta ghawooda*) impart personal grievances upon the crowd. The seconder will repeat key messages, a form which facilitates communication of evidence, knowledge, ideas and moral to a listening and attentive audience. At certain intervals all the women will join in and call out 'We the Datooga, agree'. The text is as such performed solo but with a polyphonic humming and repetition of the central moral and meaning. Personal and private concerns of individual 'wives' are in this way brought into the social arena where it is consciously rephrased, questioned, confirmed, strengthened and thus made collective.

It is in such a personal but simultaneously collective, creative but simultaneously divine, context that the play with metaphors of gender and fertility, birth and death take place, and it in this context we must seek to account for the dynamics of transformation of this female performance.

CONCLUDING REMARKS

We have seen that concepts of fertility, the female procreative body and female spirituality conveyed through female performance are the substance of major attention among the Datooga. This concern is hardly unique to the Datooga. Rather the Datooga wives' meeting is preoccupied with issues that are historic concerns of women. It speaks of women's bodily concern with securing fecundity at all times and in all places. In the unique cultural elaboration of the issue among the Datooga pastoralists of Tanzania, the female procreative body attains an almost mystic sacredness, a sanctity which is threatened by male 'enemies'. At the base of this concern is the conception that unless all moral norms are observed, the spirit world will not bestow the living with their blessings, and nature will thus not yield her fruits. A breach in moral conduct requires a reintegration, a fresh bringing together of male and female bodies, and in extension the social body and cosmos in order to recapture the immense potency that for a moment was lost. The most significant feature of the *girgweageeda gadeemga* is this ability to transform the disintegrative, infertile, partial and threatening into positive, fertile integrative wholeness by the rejoining of male and female. I have tried to show that this concept is fluid and flexible and can apply to diverse concerns and contexts. It is with this understanding that a threat of female head tax can appear as an infliction on female wombs.

These ideas may appear abstract, but the abstractness is experientially reinforced and given meaning through women's grounding bodies. To be 'vulnerable', and to be 'invaded by enemies', are familiar sensations to people who throughout their lives experience the dangers of disease and drought, of loss of land and livestock. These themes indeed appear utterly meaningful to women who throughout large parts of their adult lives struggle to safely escort their offspring through pregnancy, birth, infancy and childhood in precarious surroundings. They are part of embodied femalehood.

NOTES

1 The Southern Nilotic Datooga consist of some 13 subsections of which Barabaig is numerically the largest. In the area where I have carried out research (four separate communities in Hanang and Mbulu districts for a period of two years between 1989 and 1998), the Barabaig make up a large majority of the Datooga population. But most of the other Datooga subsections are also well represented in the area of study and have been central informants (particularly members of the Gisamjaanga, Bajuuta, Gidang'oodiga, Rotigeanga, and Isimjeega subsections), hence the use of the label 'Datooga'. The labels are spelled in a number of different ways in the existing literature, but I shall use the terms suggested by the Bible translation project. The size of the Datooga population is estimated at around 100 000 people.

2 In the paper '*Lilichta* and violence: reconsidering Barbayiiga killings' (Blystad 1996c) I show how the ritual hunts are elaborated upon in a manner where they appear as discourses on and transformations of gender and fertility in the premarital state.

3 During my second fieldwork among the Datooga I was pregnant and
gave birth. I was struck by the silence that surrounded my pregnant
state. People did not comment upon the fact that I was expecting a
child, and even in company with women only, people would react
awkwardly if I touched upon my condition.
4 Similar versions of this myth have been recorded by Klima (1970: 88)
and Talle and Holmqvist (1979: 95).
5 See Moore (1986) for an excellent account of the place of the hearth
in Marakwet cosmology and practice.
6 In 1994 a man in Basodesh told his wife that she was 'his child'. Indicating that the husband had a sexual relationship with his child was
so insulting and distasteful that the meeting convened and the man
was fined.
7 In 1991 a man from Wandela beat his dog, which had a large litter,
to death. The *girgweageeda gadeemga* convened and fined the man a
bull, and ordered joint consumption of food. The women threatened
grievous consequences for the man's offspring as well as his cattle if
the verdict was not followed. A large reconciliation rite where dogs
and human beings ate together was carried out shortly after.
8 I have recorded cases where men have set fire to a woman's sacred
leather skirt, destroyed a milking calabash, kicked a woman's bed,
removed a woman's hearth stones, all of which have led to action by
the *girgweageeda gadeemga*.
9 Lane (1991) mentions a case where the women's meeting called men
to account for allowing the sacred land Udawang to be ploughed up
for farming. In 1993 the women of Dang'eyda and beyond were
greatly preoccupied with the case of a young Pentecostal who made a
serious attempt to cut down the 'heathen' tree where Datooga women
gather for meetings. After refusing to pay the fine the man was finally
cursed by the meeting. Throughout our stay in Dang'eyda the man
did not co-operate with anyone but the few members of the local Pentecostal community. There have also been recurring mobilizations of
the meeting in connection with the clearing of land and ploughing
down of graves related to the Tanzania Canada Wheat Project (see
Blystad forthcoming).
10 These cases were recorded in some detail through personal participation, transcription of tapes, and through interviews with participants
as well as with individuals who were not taking part in the mobilizations. The cases took place in Dang'eyda in 1994 and in Darabeambw
in 1990. The name Gidamuhaled is fictitious.
11 In 1994 women in Getanyamba mobilized the meeting against the
school's demands for steadily increasing amounts of maize and beans
for children's school lunches. In 1989, 1991 and in 1993 women in
Wandela convened the meeting against adult education (1989, 1991,
1993). In 1993 the headteacher in Dang'eyda was confronted by with
serious complaints from the wives' meeting of schoolchildren working
extensively on his land, teachers beating the children to force them to
give the names of younger siblings for school enrolment, and seduction of schoolgirls. The women's meeting has also imposed legal sanc-

tions against men who were accused of distributing food aid in a biased manner.

12 In Hanang the income tax was 500 Tanzania shillings (Tsh) in 1990. In addition 200 Tsh was paid to Universal Primary Education, and 100 Tsh to Secondary Aid; totalling 800 Tsh per head. *Ad hoc* taxes would be levied in addition to this sum.

13 The number was fluctuating throughout the days of the mobilizations, but between 300 and 1000 women took part throughout the meetings.

14 See Briggs (1992) for an excellent account of the manner in which individual women's voices in ritual wailing among the Warao strategically challenge expectation about relationships, feelings and experience.

REFERENCES

Ardener, S. (1975) 'Sexual insult and female militancy' in S. Ardener (ed.) *Perceiving women* (London: Malaby (J.M. Dent)).

Barber, K. (1990) 'Oriki, women and the proliferation and merging of Orisa', *Africa*, 60: 313–37.

Barber, K. (1991) *I Could Speak until Tomorrow: Oriki, Women and the Past in a Yoruba Town* (Edinburgh: Edinburgh University Press for the International African Institute).

Barber, K., J. Collins and A. Ricard (1997) *West African Popular Theatre* (Bloomington: Indiana University Press).

Blacking, J. and J.W. Kealiinohomoku (eds) (1979) *The Performing Arts: Music and Dance* (The Hague: Mouton).

Bloch, M. (1992) *Prey into Hunter: The Politics of Religious Experience* (Cambridge: Cambridge University Press).

Bloch, M. and J.P. Parry (eds) (1982) *Death and the Regeneration of Life* (Cambridge: Cambridge University Press).

Blystad, A. (1992) 'The pastoral Barabaig: fertility, recycling and the social order', Cand. Polit. thesis in Social Anthropology, University of Bergen.

Blystad, A. (1996a) '"Do give us children": the problem of fertility among the pastoral Barbayiiga of Tanzania', in A.G.M. Ahmed and H.A. Abdel (eds) *Managing Scarcity: Human Adaptation in East African Drylands* (Addis Ababa: Commercial Printing Enterprise).

Blystad, A. (1996b) 'La chant qui reveille la terre' in T. Dorn (ed.) *Houn-Noukoun: Tambours et Visages* (Paris: Editions Florent-Massot).

Blystad, A. (1996c) '*Lilichta* and violence: reconsidering Barbayiiga killings', paper presented at the seminar 'Varieties of Human Suffering', Harvard University.

Briggs, C.L. (1992) '"Since I am a woman, I will chastise my relatives": gender, reported speech, and the (re)production of social relations in Warao ritual wailing', *American Ethnologist*, 19: 337–61.

Broch-Due, V. and I. Rudie (1993) 'Carved flesh/cast selves: an introduction' in V. Broch-Due, I. Rudie and T. Bleie (eds) *Carved Flesh/Cast Selves: Gendered Symbols and Social Practices* (Oxford: Berg).

Caplan, P. (ed.) (1987) *The Cultural Construction of Sexuality* (London: Tavistock).

Chernoff, J.M. (1979) *African Rhythm and African Sensibility: Aesthetics and Social Action in African Musical Idioms* (Chicago: University of Chicago Press).

Csordas, T.J. (1990) 'Embodiment as a paradigm for anthropology', *Ethos*, 18: 5–47.

Csordas, T.J. (ed.) (1994) *Embodiment and Experience: The Existential Ground of Culture and Self* (Cambridge: Cambridge University Press).

Devisch, R. (1990) 'The human body as a vehicle for emotions' in M. Jackson and I. Karp (eds) *Personhood and Agency: The Expression of Self and Other in African Cultures* (Uppsala: Acta Universitatis Upsaliensis).

Devisch, R. (1991) 'Symbol and symptom among the Yaka of Zaire' in A. Jacobson-Widding (ed.) *Body and Space: Symbolic Models of Unity and Division in African Cosmology and Experience* (Stockholm: Almqvist and Wiksell).

Diduk, S. (1989) 'Women's agricultural production and political action in the Cameroon grassfields', *Africa*, 59: 338–355.

Edgerton, R.B. and F.P. Conant (1964) 'Kilapat: the "shaming party", among the Pokot of East Africa', *Southwestern Journal of Anthropology*, 20: 404–418.

Faust, H. (1969) 'Courtship via murder', *World Encounter*, 6 (3): 1–7.

Feld, S. (1982) *Sound and Sentiment: Birds, Weeping, Poetics, and Song in Kaluli Expression* (Philadelphia: University of Pennsylvania Press).

Frazer, J.G. (1890) *The Golden Bough* (London: MacMillan).

Friedson, S.M. (1996) *Dancing Prophets: Musical Experience in Tumbuka Healing* (Chicago: University of Chicago Press).

Gluckman, M. (1963) *Order and Rebellion in Tribal Africa* (New York: Free Press).

Ifeka-Moller, C. (1975) 'Female militancy and colonial revolt – women's war of 1929 Eastern Nigeria' in S. Ardener (ed.) *Perceiving Women* (London: Malaby).

Jackson, M. (1983) 'Thinking through the body: an essay on understanding metaphor', *Social Analysis*, 14: 127–49.

Jackson, M. (1989) *Paths toward a Clearing: Radical Empiricism and Ethnographic Inquiry* (Bloomington: Indiana University Press).

Jordan, B. and R. Davis-Floyd (1993) *Birth in Four Cultures: A Crosscultural Investigation of Childbirth in Yucatan, Holland, Sweden, and the United States* (Prospect Heights, IL: Waveland).

Kelly, J.D. and M. Kaplan (1990) 'History, structure, and ritual', *Annual Review of Anthropology*, 19: 119–50.

Kjærby, F. (1979) 'The development of agropastoralism among the Barabaig in Hanang District', *BRALUP Research Paper*, 56, University of Dar es Salaam.

Klima, G. (1966) 'Jural relations between the sexes among the Barabaig', *Africa*, 34: 9–20.

Klima, G. (1970) *The Barabaig: East African Cattle-Herders* (New York: Holt).

Kratz, C.A. (1994) *Affecting Performance: Meaning, Movement, and Experience in Okiek Women's Initiation* (Washington DC: Smithsonian Institution Press).

Laderman, C. and M. Roseman (1996) 'Introduction' in C. Laderman and M. Roseman (eds) *The Performance of Healing* (London: Routledge).

Lane, C. (1991) 'Wheat at what cost? CIDA and the Tanzania–Canada wheat program' in J. Swift and B. Tomlinson (eds) *Conflicts of Interest: Canada and the Third World* (Toronto: Between the Lines).

Lane, C. (1996) *Pastures Lost: Barabaig Economy, Resource Tenure, and the Alienation of their Land in Tanzania*, ACTS Drylands Research Series, no. 7 (Nairobi: Initiatives).

Leifer, M. (1980) 'Pregnancy', *Signs: Journal of Women in Culture and Society*, 5: 754–65.

Leith-Ross, S. (1939) *African Women* (London: Faber and Faber).

Linke, U. (1992) 'Manhood, femaleness, and power: a cultural analysis of prehistoric images of reproduction', *Comparative Studies in Society and History*, 34: 579–620.

Loiske, V.M. (1990) 'Political adaptation: The case of the Wabarabaig in Hanang District, Tanzania' in M. Bovin and L. Manger (eds) *Adaptive Strategies in Arid Lands* (Uppsala: Scandinavian Institute of African Studies).

MacCormack, C.P. (1982a) 'Biological, cultural and social adaptation in human fertility and birth: a synthesis' in C.P. MacCormack (ed.) *Ethnography of Fertility and Birth* (London: Academic).

MacCormack, C.P. (ed.) (1982b) *Ethnography of Fertility and Birth* (London: Academic).

MacCormack, C. P. and M. Strathern (eds) (1980) *Nature, Culture and Gender* (Cambridge: Cambridge University Press).

Moore, H.L. (1986) *Space, Text and Gender* (Cambridge: Cambridge University Press).

Moore, H.L. (1994) *A Passion for Difference: Essays in Anthropology and Gender* (Cambridge: Polity).

Ndagala, D.K. (1991) 'The unmaking of the Datoga: decreasing resources and increasing conflict in rural Tanzania', *Nomadic Peoples*, 28: 71–82.

Ortner, S.B. and H. Whitehead (1981) 'Introduction: accounting for sexual meanings' in S.B. Ortner and H. Whitehead (eds) *Sexual Meanings: The Cultural Construction of Gender and Sexuality* (Cambridge: Cambridge University Press).

Perham, M. (1976) *East African Journey: Kenya and Tanganyika, 1929–30* (London: Faber & Faber).

Powers, M.N. (1980) 'Menstruation and reproduction: an Oglala case', *Signs: Journal of Women in Culture and Society*, 6: 54–65.

Rekdal, O.B. (1991) 'Endring og kontinuitet i iraqw samfunn og kultur', Cand. Polit. thesis, University of Bergen.

Rekdal, O.B. and A. Blystad (forthcoming). '"We are as sheep and goats": Iraqw and Datooga discourses on fortune, failure, and the future' in D.M. Anderson and V. Broch-Due (eds) *The Poor are not Us': Poverty and Pastoralism in Eastern Africa* (London: James Currey).

Ritzenthaler, R.E. (1972) 'Anlu: a women's uprising in the British Cameroons' in R. A. Turner and L. M. Killian (eds) *Collective Behaviour* (Englewood, NJ: Prentice Hall).

Rigby, P. (1968) 'Some Gogo rituals of "purification": an essay on social and moral categories' in E.R. Leach (ed.) *Dialectic in Practical Religion* (Cambridge: Cambridge University Press).

Sargent, C. (1990) 'The politics of birth: cultural dimensions of pain, virtue, and control among the Bariba of Benin' in W.P. Handwerker (ed.) *Births and Power: Social Change and the Politics of Reproduction* (Boulder: Westview).

Setréus, J. (1991) 'Datoga – warriors transgressing moral order', unpublished paper, Uppsala University.

Singer, M. (1968) *Krishna: Myths, Rites and Attitudes* (Chicago: Chicago University Press).

Snow, L.F. and S.M. Johnson (1978) 'Folklore, food, female reproductive cycle', *Ecology of Food and Nutrition*, 7: 41–9.

Snyder, K.A. (1997) 'Elders' authority and women's protest: the *masay* ritual and social change among the Iraqw of Tanzania', *Journal of the Royal Anthropological Institute*, 3: 561–76.

Spencer, P. (ed.) (1985) *Society and the Dance* (Cambridge: Cambridge University Press).

Spencer, P. (1988) *The Maasai of Matapato: a Study of Rituals of Rebellion*. Bloomington: Indiana University Press.

Stoller, P. (1996) 'Sounds and things: pulsations of power in Songhay' in C. Laderman and M. Roseman (eds) *The Performance of Healing* (London: Routledge).

Strathern, M. (1988) *The Gender of the Gift: Problems with Women and Problems with Society in Melanesia* (Berkeley: University of California Press).

Strathern, M. (1993) 'Making incomplete' in V. Broch-Due, I. Rudie and T. Bleie (eds) *Carved Flesh/Cast Selves: Gendered Symbols and Social Practices* (Oxford: Berg).

Talle, A. (1974) 'Økonomiske dilemmaer i kombinasjon av buskapshold og økonomisk jordbruk', Mag. Art thesis, University of Oslo.

Talle, A. and S. Holmqvist (1979) *Barheida og dei tre konene hans* (Oslo: Det Norske Samlaget).

Tambiah, S.J. (1981) *A Performative Approach to Ritual* (London: British Academy).

Turner, V.W. (1990) 'Are there universals of performance in myth, ritual, and drama?' in R. Schechner and W. Appel (eds) *By Means of Performance: Intercultural Studies of Theatre and Ritual* (Cambridge: Cambridge University Press).

Umesao, T. (1969) 'Hunting culture of the pastoral Datoga', *Kyoto University African Studies*, 3: 77–92.

Van Allen, J. (1972) ' "Sitting on a man": colonialism and the lost political institutions of Igbo women' (special issue: *The Roles of African*

Women: Past, Present, and Future), *Canadian Journal of African Studies*, 6 (2): 165–81.

Wilson, G.M. (1952) 'The Tatoga of Tanganyika, Part I', *Tanganyika Notes and Records*, 33: 34–47.

Wipper, A. (1982) 'Riot and rebellion among African women: three examples of women's political clout' in J. O'Barr (ed.) *Perspectives on Power: Women in Africa, Asia, and Latin America* (Durham, NC: Duke University Center for International Studies).

Wipper, A. (1989) 'Kikuyu women and the Harry Thuku disturbances: some uniformities of female militancy', *Africa*, 59: 300–37.

CHAPTER 8

GENDER IDEOLOGY, AND THE DOMESTIC AND PUBLIC DOMAINS AMONG THE IRAQW

KATHERINE A. SNYDER

INTRODUCTION

This paper examines gender ideology and its expression in, and relationship to, the domestic and public spheres among the Iraqw of northern Tanzania. The Iraqw are an agro-pastoral, southern-Cushitic-speaking people in north-central Tanzania. In the pre-colonial era they were confined to an area that they now refer to as their homeland and call Irqwa Da'aw (or 'Mama Issara' in Kiswahili), in what is now Mbulu District, between Lakes Manyara and Eyasi. With the colonial pacification of their Maasai and Datooga neighbours, the Iraqw began migrating out of their homeland and now occupy territory about 15 times greater than their original site. Fieldwork on which this paper is based was conducted primarily in the Iraqw homeland.

The anthropology of gender has paid much attention to the domestic/public sphere dichotomy since Rosaldo's and Lamphere's (1974) ground-breaking work, which first posited this division of space and action as a source of women's inequality. Much subsequent work has called into question the notion that such a rigid dichotomy exits or is in any way a cultural universal (c.f. Rapp 1979; Rogers 1975; Rosaldo 1980; for a reworking see Strathern 1981; 1984; 1988). Weiner (1976) emphasized the importance of understanding the power that women can have in their domain of activity and how this power contributes to their valuation in society. MacCormack (1980) cautioned against the universalizing of European categories and values. Strathern (1984) has also observed that, for the Hagen of Papua New Guinea, the domestic sphere and women's connections to it are not constructively viewed through a western perspective which denigrates and devalues this sphere of social life. These reassessments have demonstrated that we must always question whether a domestic/ public dichotomy exists in a given society. If such distinct spheres do in fact exist, analysis should focus on the relationship of the two spheres to one another over time. Synthesizing these debates, Comaroff (1987) pushes the enquiry further by illustrating the ways in which the construction of gender shifts over time with changes in the wider social system in which the domestic and public are embedded. My intention is not to review the domestic/ public debates as Strathern (1984), Comaroff (1987), Moore (1988) and Di Leonardo (1991) have done this with different emphases. Instead, I intend to pick up certain threads from these discussions to explore more fully the relationship of the two spheres to one another and to the concepts of gender. Rather than considering the domestic and public as opposing and asym-metrical categories, I would argue the Iraqw treat them as interre-lated and complementary domains.[1] The Iraqw public is essentially an extension of the Iraqw domestic, which is nested within it rather than standing in binary opposition to it. An indi-vidual's status, whether male or female, within the domestic sphere directly structures his or her status and ability to claim authority and prestige in the public sphere.

It is clear that gender can not be assessed separately from the values, identities and ideologies associated with these social and political-economic domains. As Peletz notes, 'entire ideologies bearing on gender are rarely if ever "about" gender. Because they are also "about" kinship, human nature, and sociality...' (1996: 308). Peletz argues that the categories of 'male' and 'female' do not have much salience on their own but instead must be viewed alongside kinship categories such as 'brother', 'sister', 'husband', 'wife', 'father', and 'mother' (1996: 5). This statement holds true for the Iraqw case as well. Male and female do not have meanings irrespective of other social and kinship categories such as uncircumcised/circumcised, unmarried/married, clan/uterine kin member. And these categories relate directly to roles within the domestic and public spheres.

Among the Iraqw, the complementarity between domestic and public was greater in the pre-colonial era, when men's participa-tion in the public sphere was more directly affected by their status as husbands and fathers. Today, participation in the politi-cal sphere of the Tanzanian State does not depend as greatly on a man's reputation as the head of a household. However, while the relationship between the spheres has changed over time, it still remains a feature of Iraqw discourse and social practice. In focusing on the connections between the two spheres of activity, this discussion aims to expand the ways in which we think about the domestic and the public in Africa.

To unravel gender ideology among the Iraqw, I turn first to an examination of cosmology. As will be seen in the discussion which follows, the Iraqw cosmos is imbued with ideas about gender and 'essential' notions of male and female. Fertility is a central focus of both the domestic and public domains and is a central aspect of gender among the Iraqw. This paper examines fertility as it relates to both cosmology and to social organization and cultural practices. Throughout the paper, I point to divisions in social life that crosscut gender categories, such as age, religious affiliation and prestige markers.

SPIRITS, GHOSTS, AND THE DIVINE

An analysis of Iraqw cosmology makes apparent the ways in which 'gender is played out on a cosmic stage' (Schlegel 1990: 32). The gender categories associated with the supernatural world convey central ideas about identity and gender complementarity around which Iraqw social organization takes place. Iraqw cosmology is based primarily on the juxtaposition of two spiritual forces, one female and considered benevolent, the other male and prone to anger and revenge. *Looaa*, the female creator, is perceived as the mother of the Iraqw people and is represented by the sun. As a mother, she possesses specific character traits such as kindness, gentleness and generosity. Her 'mother love' is manifested in her desire for good health and prosperity for the humans she created. Iraqw pray to *Looaa* during times of need or distress, and she is thanked for good fortune, such as a plentiful harvest, with the brewing of beer and the recitation of special prayers. No sacrifices are made to *Looaa*, for she is said not to require appeasement.

Looaa is said to rarely intervene directly in people's lives except when called upon by specific individuals through a curse (*lo'o*) to deliver justice and punish a wrongdoer. *Looaa* is more remote and uninvolved in Iraqw daily life than *neetlaamee* (*netlangw*, sing.), the earth spirits who dwell below the surface of the earth and in springs, streams and rivers, rocky caves on mountains and special forest groves. These earth spirits are said to be male, to have wives and children, and are more active in the lives of the human population. Iraqw claim that these spirits resemble human beings in appearance and are motivated by similar feelings, such as the desire to protect their households from harm. They are also prone to the more negative aspects of human nature such as jealousy and revenge. *Looaa* and *neetlaamee* inhabit separate spheres and behave very differently. The earth spirits serve as a check on human moral behaviour. *Looaa* and *netlaamee* are said to meet in the dead of the night (around 2 a.m.) to discuss the state of affairs on earth. *Looaa* is then informed of how many people may have been killed by the earth spirits so that she can take measures to increase the number of births to account for these deaths.

Each Iraqw neighbourhood and community (*aya*) is the residence of particular earth spirits and these spirits identify themselves with these specific territories. From time to time they strike out against the human inhabitants of these territories when angered by human transgressions. In particular, they are concerned with moral transgressions, which give rise to states of ritual impurity. Their concern is a selfish one, as they fear that pollution from the human population may infect their own domain. Failure of the rains, spread of disease, death, and attacks by wild animals are all signs of the earth spirits' revenge. When an Iraqw community suffers from such misfortune, the elders gather and perform a community-wide ritual known as *masay* (medicine) to appease the earth spirits and cleanse the community of the pollution.

Gender complementarity is a feature of the supernatural world. Earth spirits are associated with water (below, cool, and dark) while the creator being is associated with the sun (above, warm, and light). These two elements, water and light, are the necessary elements in the growth of plants on which Iraqw depend. The two spirits also balance one another in their actions: the male earth spirits often cause destruction which the female creator spirit then has to fix through stimulating fertility. The clear association of these two spirits with specific genders is important for understanding gender roles in kinship, and in the domestic and public spheres.

Another supernatural force in the lives of Iraqw, though of

much less significance, is the ghosts or *giusee*. Similar to the earth spirits, the ghosts are easily angered and vengeful if not treated with the proper respect. The only ghosts of significance in a person's life are those who were known by the living such as their parents or grandparents. The Iraqw have no concern for distant ancestors. In addition, a man or woman who dies before marriage or before having children will not be a threat to anyone. If a child did not treat a parent well in life, he/she will fear that the ghost of the parent will strike out against him/her after death. The relationship formed between parents and their children continues after the death of the parent, and children should continue to show respect to the ghosts. Clearly, these ideas surrounding ghosts underscore the relationships within and primary to the household.

The afterworld, which the ghosts inhabit, is a world nearly identical to that of the living. It has boundaries, as well as crops and livestock, and it exists in space somewhere below the world of human habitation. When a man dies, the hide of a cow and some of his possessions are buried with him to take to the world of the ghosts. Similarly, a woman is buried with her clothes and perhaps some cooking pots. If a diviner determines that the ghosts are responsible for a person's misfortune, a sacrifice, usually a cow, will be made to appease them.

KINSHIP AND DESCENT

Descent among the Iraqw is patrilineal with clans being the largest corporate grouping, and each is divided into lineages and sub-lineages. Iraqw men feel a strong sense of identity with their clans. As in most African societies, fertility is highly valued for both sub-lineage, lineage and clan perpetuation. Thus, women are important contributors to their husbands' clans through their childbearing capabilities. Their own clan affiliation is less important to their identity than their husband's is to his. Instead, women have a strong association with their uterine kin or *daa'awi*. Previous ethnographers of the Iraqw (Thornton 1980; 1982; Winter 1964; 1966; 1968) have largely ignored the *daa'awi*, though Winter does acknowledge the existence of 'unnamed matrilineages' (1966: 162).[2] However, ideas about the *daa'awi* are crucial for understanding social, kinship and gender relations among the Iraqw. The *daa'awi* links a woman and her children together with her mother, her mother's brothers and sisters, her sister's children, her maternal grandmother and so on. Women therefore perpetuate the *daa'awi* while men perpetuate the clan. So, individuals belong to their father's clan and their mother's *daa'awi*. The *daa'awi* resembles in many ways the *soog* as described by Fortes among the Tallensi, in that this uterine kin group forms 'essentially a personal bond, a bond of mutual interest and concern uniting individual to individual' (Fortes 1949: 37) and does not, unlike agnatic kin, give rise to corporate units.

Conceptually the Iraqw associate the clan with bones and the uterine kin with blood. Thus, the skeleton is the man's contribution to the forming of a child, as his semen is what produces bones and bone marrow. The woman contributes blood and therefore life to the child. The properties of blood (a warm and flowing substance as opposed to a static and hard one like bones) are thought to convey stronger emotional bonds than bones, and the uterine kin group is thus the site of strong affective ties.[3] The blood relationship is seen as nurturing and exerting a greater sway over individuals than that of the clan. Iraqw state that ties to one's uterine kin can be felt physically. For example, if a close member of your uterine kin falls ill, you may also 'feel' this illness as it affects your blood as well. The same is true if a wrong is committed against one of your uterine kin.

The *daa'awi* is an important source of assistance. In times of need, individuals are more likely to go first to their uterine kin for aid before approaching clan members. Ideas surrounding the uterine kin group are closely associated with notions of motherhood. Affective ties among uterine kin members are conceived of as extensions, if dilutions, of the mother/child bond.

Uterine kin are important for social relations in a number of ways. First, the *daa'awi* is a crucial factor in assessing the marriageability of a couple, as it is used to trace their clan relations. For example, elders identify, for both the prospective bride and groom, the clan of the mother, her mother's clan, of her grandmother and so forth, up to eight generations, in order to know which clans are not suitable for marriage. No couple who share a bond through their *daa'awi* may marry. The *daa'awi* is also considered crucial for assessing a person's character and suitability for performing community rituals. If a member of a person's uterine kin has committed a serious offence (such as murder or suicide) all members of his or her *daa'awi* are believed to carry the taint of this pollution.

Connections to and knowledge of the supernatural world are also conveyed through clan and uterine kin affiliation. Divination, which is used to benefit individuals or the community as a whole, calls upon the benevolent power of *Looaa*, and knowledge of divination is passed through clan lines. The anti-social acts of witchcraft and sorcery are linked to the earth spirits, and these skills are passed through uterine kin. Generally, it is more common to find men who are diviners, and there is also a higher proportion of women who are said to be witches than men. These are not exclusive categories, however, and Iraqw state that female diviners tend to be experts in diagnosing and combating witchcraft. There are no female paramount diviners, however, who can work on behalf of the whole community. Fortes suggests that the 'pegging of witchcraft to the uterine line serves to circumvent any danger it might be to the community' (1949: 35). Because uterine kin do not form corporate groups they are not likely to mobilize in defence of their members like a lineage or clan might if so accused of witchcraft.

In an individual's life, the most important kinship ties in daily life are with one's parents, grandparents and siblings, and then with members of *daa'awi* and lineage. Two relatives are of particular importance in rites of passage and in providing assistance: the mother's brother (*mamay*) and the father's sister (*ayshiga*). The mother's brother is particularly important to his sister's children in marriage negotiations as he is responsible for tracing *daa'awi* lines. As is clear from the above description, gender complementarity is an important feature of kinship organization.

CIRCUMCISION, MARRIAGE AND THE HOUSEHOLD

Circumcision is an important rite of passage for Iraqw, transforming children into marriageable youth. The circumcision of boys in pre-colonial Iraqw society was conducted in a communal public ritual. In each neighbourhood, boys in early adolescence would undergo the ritual together. Women were not present at this ritual except to sing songs in celebration after the boys had been cut and were being walked to their homes to heal. Increasingly, these communal rituals are giving way to hospital circumcisions for boys, but it varies according to geographical location.

Iraqw living to the south-west of the homeland, in communities which are either on the border of Datooga territory or which are composed of both Datooga and Iraqw, still maintain the communal rituals.[4] In the homeland, the communal rituals have largely been abandoned.

While male circumcision takes place in the world outside of the household, female circumcision occurs within their homes, and girls undergo the operation alone or with a sister. A mother decides when her daughters are ready for the operation and summons a local female circumcision specialist to perform the operation. The men and boys of the household are sent away for the time that it takes to perform the operation. The girl remains in seclusion in the home and is cared for by her mother and sisters until she heals. Her seclusion is designed to protect her from harm, which could befall her in her vulnerable state if she were to cross the threshold of the house and enter the public world. There is little ceremony to female circumcision. All Iraqw consider circumcision for both boys and girls crucial. One young woman described in great detail the pain and distress she underwent in circumcision. I asked her whether she would choose not to have her daughter circumcised. She replied without hesitation that her daughter would certainly have the operation as 'it was important' that all girls as well as boys do so to become marriageable adults. Some women interviewed who lived in the district capital and who had attended secondary school reiterated national policy on such practices and stated that the practice was harmful and should be abandoned for girls. In the homeland, a few young women and men told me that they pressured their parents into getting the operation performed so they would not be the subjects of ridicule among their peers.

In the pre-colonial era, Iraqw girls underwent an initiation ritual called *marmo* in which they were secluded as a group in a special house for several months to a year (Wada 1984). During this time, they did not bathe or cut their hair, but cleansed themselves through sweat baths. They were not allowed to feed themselves but were instead fed by either elder women or younger female attendants. Elder women instructed the girls about adulthood and marriage. Once the period of seclusion and instruction was deemed sufficient, a celebration was held in which the girls presented themselves to the community and were called from that point onwards by the teknonym *Deena*. Chief Michael Ahho declared the ritual backward and 'uncivilized' and abolished *marmo* in the 1930s. According to elder women who underwent the ritual, it has not been performed since that time.

Marriage is the most important rite of passage into adulthood for both men and women. It is considered a disgrace if a man or woman does not marry, and he or she will not be accorded the respect and status which married adults receive. Instead, an unmarried person will continue to be called by his or her first name, or the teknonyms used for boys and girls. Today, women begin to use the teknonym *Deena* or *Ama* when they marry and they cease to be called by their first names. So, a woman would be called Ama Burra for example, meaning the wife of Burra.

As Ortner and Whitehead (1981) have observed, prestige, which they define loosely as 'social honour' or 'social value', has significant implications for gender. For the Iraqw, a woman's identity and prestige are bound up in her being a wife and eventually mother, and her reputation is very closely linked to that of her husband. A man depends on marrying a wife to increase his status but also to establish his independence from his father.[5] How he manages his household is very important to his prestige and his authority in the community, as will be seen more clearly in the sections which follow.

In Iraqw weddings, the fertility of the couple, and particularly of the bride, is a focal point of the ceremony. For example, during the wedding festivities, when the bride is led up to the compound of the groom, a ewe and perhaps a ewe and her lamb meet her. This sheep is considered hers and its fertility is meant to represent her own. The bride's fertility serves the interest of the groom's lineage, but the uterine kin also have a stake in her bearing children as she will be perpetuating the *daa'awi* as well. If a woman remains childless, a man will usually take another wife to try and ensure progeny. A childless woman does not have the same status and respect as one who is able to bear children. However, her husband or kin rarely abandon her.

The household is the most important unit of production and reproduction in Iraqw society. When a man and woman marry, unless the husband is the last born, residence follows a neolocal pattern with the new couple building a house on land allocated to the new husband by his father or clan or acquired independently. In the pre-colonial era sons often sought land in neighbouring communities or ventured forth to form new communities. Now that there is increased population pressure on the land throughout the region it is becoming harder for young men to migrate. The last-born son is expected to build a house near that of his father so he can care for his parents in their old age. He will be allotted some land to cultivate and will inherit his father's plots when he dies. Each household then is responsible for their own fields and their own livestock.

The division of labour within the household is marked but complementary. Women are responsible for domestic chores such as house cleaning, childcare and cooking. They also work in the fields, planting, weeding and harvesting, and they milk the cows. Men are responsible for the heavier farm work, for herding the livestock and for house construction. Iraqw do not place more value on men's work than on women's. Yet the products of that labour are valued differently. Livestock, particularly cattle, are the primary form of wealth and symbolic capital. Agricultural produce, even when it is sold for cash on the market, does not carry the same prestige. While decision-making within households varies greatly according to the relationship between a husband and wife, both men and women state that ultimately men have the final say over household decisions. Men's control over livestock clearly indicates their position in the social hierarchy. Ultimately men have greater authority over domestic production matters because they are the owners of land and livestock and it is through them that resources are passed on to the next generation.

Today, more women are involved in income-earning activities outside of the household such as beer-brewing, mat- and basket-making, trade in foodstuffs and making and selling charcoal. Women complain that men are working less in the fields and that they instead have to do more of the agricultural labour. In the pre-colonial era, men were responsible for clearing the fields and shared the other tasks of weeding and harvesting while women focused on planting. Increasingly, women can be seen doing much of the heavier work usually considered the work of men. The decline in male labour on the farms was publicly acknowledged at a local village meeting in 1991. The ward officer gave a speech admonishing the men on their laziness, stating that women are becoming 'the donkeys' of the community as they carry goods on their backs to the district capital market. Men are spending more time seeking work in the towns or spending hours at the local bar with their friends. Interestingly, with the decline in pollution beliefs, which confined women more strictly to the household environs, the workload of women has increased. While in the pre-colonial past it was men who journeyed to areas outside of the homeland to seek food assistance in times of drought or crop failure, women are now seen on the roads and paths of the district travelling great distances to request aid in food from relatives.

While women take up tasks which were formerly those of men, it does not mean that this shift allows them greater authority within the household. In taking up roles or activities that are more 'male', given Iraqw gender conceptions, women are not, by extension considered 'male'. Instead, they are viewed as being good wives and mothers because they are acting on behalf of their household. Both women and men criticize men for what is seen as irresponsible, lazy, and selfish behaviour, which ignores the needs of the household.

Women use the cash from their activities primarily to meet household needs for such things as school uniforms and school supplies, and essentials such as salt, soap, cooking fat, blankets, clothing and possibly kerosene and sugar. Their income is directed towards children and the commensual needs of the household, while men tend to spend money on farm implements (hoes, axes), livestock needs, or beer. Women complain that men quite often demand the cash that women earn to buy beer or to spend on their own needs. They are rarely able to refuse husband's demands as to do so would be to risk receiving a beating. While the activities of men and women are complementary, decisions about household income or expenditures are the husband's. As one woman said, 'If my husband wants to sell a cow and use the money on beer, there is little I can do about it.' Men stated that women often resort to 'cleverness' to circumvent their husband's control. As one man related, 'If my wife hides part of the harvest and sells it, I may never know.' Land and livestock are the property of men and thus any products from these resources are ultimately the property of men, even if it is women's labour that has produced them.

Women can go too far in taking on 'male' roles, as the following incident attests. Village service is a requirement of young men and women. One young man in his early thirties was called upon, along with other youths in the community, to guard the village offices and health dispensary at night. He refused to show up for duty, claiming he was ill. The next day he was fined a chicken and told that he would still be expected to show up the following evening. The village delegation that informed him of their expectations took one of the household chickens as they left the compound. This man has not yet married and lives with his parents. The young man's mother, who is in her sixties, was very angry that they had confiscated the chicken. In response, that evening at dusk she marched down to the village offices with a stave and a spear. Iraqw men carry staves when they walk, and use these staves as well as spears for hunting and defence against attack. Young men are expected to show up for guard duty with a stave and a spear. When she arrived, the ward officer who was at the office was astounded and began berating her for carrying a spear. He said this behaviour was truly 'shameful' and that she should go back to her home immediately. She at first refused, saying the chicken had been hers and thus she would do the guarding. She eventually gave in as other male village officials joined in and jeered at her. The ward officer explained that her behaviour was disgraceful on two counts: (1) that she was carrying a spear which only men do, and (2) she was offering to stay outside at night as only men do. Thus, clearly this invasion of the male domain (physical defence, hunting, and unrestricted travel and movement at night), in which a woman is acting as a male, is on a different level from a woman entering into economic activities outside of the household to meet her household's needs.

As mothers, women are viewed as having an intrinsic understanding of their household's needs. Both men and women state that husbands rarely understand what problems may exist within the household, and expect to be informed by the wife. In the same way, women act as overseers of the community's well-being by marching in protest when they think the elders have failed to address important problems which have led to the failure of the rains or to attacks by wild animals (Snyder 1997). As mothers, and thus like *Looaa*, they are assumed to be concerned with the welfare of their children and thus of the children of the entire community in a way in which men are not. The blood they share with their children connects them in an affective understanding not shared by husbands and fathers.

This perception of women which views them as interested in

the greater good of the community is rooted in their concern for their children. While children contribute to the lineage of their fathers, for mothers they represent social insurance. Women depend on their children to take care of them in their old age and to guard their interests in the face of their husband's kin if their husbands die before them. Thus, concern for social good in this case could also be seen as self-interest, for a woman depends on her children for her status and for her welfare in later years.

Iraqw moral ideology links community welfare with the welfare of individual households. The two are inseparable and reciprocal. While women are seen as being more attuned to the needs and problems of their households and by extension those of the community, they are also viewed, by men and women alike, as being more susceptible to harm and to negative impulses such as envy, jealousy, gossip and the anti-social acts associated with these emotions, such as witchcraft and sorcery.[6] These are not emotions which are associated solely with women, but Iraqw men in particular do state that women are more susceptible to these emotions. As Strathern (1981) notes regarding the Hagen in New Guinea, there are values of self-interest and social good which cut across gender lines and, while often having greater association with either males or females, are not exclusive to gender.

While both men and women may be witches, the Iraqw believe that women are more often witches than men are. Certainly the number of witchcraft accusations with which I was familiar during fieldwork were mainly levelled at women. And, as witchcraft travels through uterine kin and through the substance of blood, it is more closely associated with women. During my fieldwork, the majority of the accusations were levelled against women who were childless or who had few children by Iraqw standards. These women were thought to be bewitching women who were their neighbours and who were pregnant or who had many children (six or more). Fertility thus is a strong magnet for witchcraft. Because women's status depends directly on their fertility, it makes women more likely targets for witchcraft accusations.

Women's perceived susceptibility to emotion, which is linked to their association with blood and its heat, is believed to make them weaker or 'softer' than men. They are thought to be easily swayed or coerced. Woman are sometimes compared to sheep, they are said to be 'soft' in nature like sheep's wool and, like the animal, can easily be persuaded to follow a particular path.[7] This vulnerability is not seen as a negative attribute but is used to explain why women are not involved in decision-making or other specific actions and roles in the public sphere. In a sense, as *Looaa* remains remote and not directly involved in the lives of her human creations, so are women not involved in decision-making in the public sphere, except when it comes to monitoring women's affairs such as participation in work groups or in the community women's council.

The association of the domestic sphere with females begins at birth. When a child is born, if it is a girl, an announcement is made that a child who will 'fetch water' has been born (*hheekuu-so'o*) while a boy is referred to as a child 'of the bush' (*hhee sla/a*).[8] These distinctions pervade Iraqw gender ideology. Girls and women are supposed to stick close to home and to stray from the compound is discouraged as immoral and unseemly behaviour and is also considered quite dangerous for them. These concepts about the proper domain for women are intimately linked to ideas surrounding pollution.

POLLUTION BELIEFS (*MEETA*)

Pollution beliefs and practices are the focus of some tension in Iraqw communities today as Christians and young people denounce such concepts as 'backward' and 'of the past'. However, there are still many Iraqw, particularly men and women over 40, who believe in and follow many of the practices designed to contain pollution. Thus, even those who themselves reject pollution beliefs may modify their behaviour to avoid offending their relatives and neighbours who do.

Pollution results from misfortunes that threaten fertility and prosperity. Pollution itself is not specifically gendered, though women, believed to be physically weaker, are thought to be in greater danger of contracting pollution than men. It is not that women's bodies and their bodily substances are seen as creating pollution as in other societies (c.f. Delaney 1988).[9] It is aborted fertility which causes pollution and which must be quarantined. Menstruating women are not considered impure, but are in some ways dangerous, as their menses symbolize fertility. For example, they should not pick wild greens while menstruating as this may cause the plants to dry up. In addition, they should not have intercourse with their husbands at this time. Otherwise, they carry on with their activities as usual. This idea of fertility as potentially threatening appears again in the case of the ewe given to a bride at her wedding. While the ewe is the property of the bride, it should not be housed in the same compound as the bride for it may produce more offspring than the woman and thus pose a threat to her own. These examples of fertility as dangerous or powerful are similar to Gottlieb's findings among the Beng of Ivory Coast. Gottlieb analyses the cosmological connections between human and subsistence fertility and observes that the 'essential aspect of this cosmology is that to the extent that human fertility and forest/field fertility are seen as parallel, to the same extent they must be separated' (1988: 65). Among the Iraqw, the fertility of the land, the livestock and the human population are similarly interdependent, but, as the cases above indicate, must be kept separate.

The most dangerous types of pollution are those which affect the family unit and threaten its perpetuation such as (1) miscarriage or the death of a stillborn child; (2) the death of a child who is still nursing; (3) an unmarried woman giving birth inside her natal home.[10] In the first two instances, the household enters into a social and physical isolation or quarantine (*meeta*). Whatever has caused the deaths must be contained so as to prevent the misfortune spreading to neighbouring households and the entire community. During the quarantine, the family cannot fetch water from the streams or springs but must rely on a neighbour to assist them in obtaining water and placing it at a safe (for the neighbour) distance from the home where the family can collect it. The household members must avoid all contact with the earth spirits who live in water sources because the spirits will feel themselves and their families threatened by the pollution that the family is carrying and will strike out in anger at those who break their quarantine.

Men are less restricted under quarantine practices than women. Although they should not eat or drink with other people, they can go outside of the household boundaries and interact with others. Women are believed to suffer a double pollution at the death of a child: that of the death itself and that of the milk still in their breasts.[11] The quarantine ends when the couple successfully delivers another child. One older woman, now a grandmother, described the quarantine that she had experienced many years back when she lost her 9-month-old son:

> My husband was away studying agriculture in Mwanza (western Tanzania) and I lived in quarantine together with my other children. No one visited my home. If friends or relatives passed near the house they would sit a 'safe' distance away and would turn their heads away from me while speaking to me. It was very difficult. I lived like this for three years until my husband returned from his studies and we were able to have another child.

One young couple lost two children, one through miscarriage in the final months of pregnancy and another through stillbirth. Although Catholic, and adamant that they did not believe in such things, they still followed some of the quarantine rules. For example, they gathered water from a source separate from their neighbours, and they did not visit friends or families at their homes nor eat with others. Both of them, however, did attend Catholic mass on Sundays. When asked why they followed these practices, the young woman responded:

> We are Catholics and do not believe in *meeta*, but many people here still do, so we have to follow the rules or people will be angry with us. Many of our friends who are Catholics live with their parents or grandparents and do not want to anger their relatives by refusing to observe the quarantine. Their relatives are afraid they will bring the pollution into their households.

The focus of fertility is on women, and it is their fertility, that gives them status in the community. Thus, quarantine practices are concerned with protecting this fertility. Because of their vulnerability, women should always limit their contact with others outside the household (who may themselves be carrying some pollution) and should also avoid water sources after they are married. Once married, it is the husband's job, and then the children's, to fetch water.[12]

In the pre-colonial era, if an unmarried woman became pregnant she was banished to the bush where she would have to fend for herself. She also had the option of fleeing to a neighbouring area and marrying someone from another ethnic group.

In addition, she might try to get the child adopted by a family from a neighbouring ethnic community. Today, practices surrounding this form of pollution have changed. Instead of being sent to the bush (little of which really exists today), the young woman is sent to town which serves as a figurative 'bush', not fully social, as is an Iraqw rural community.

Some Christian families may also take in an unmarried woman who is pregnant and care for her until she has successfully delivered her child and is well enough to return home. Because of implications of incest, such a woman must not deliver her child within her natal home because to do so would suggest that her father is also the child's father, if born in his house. In the village where I lived, an old childless Catholic widow took in women and sometimes couples who were in a polluted state. Her home was never without residents, many of them Christian as well. All of the boarders followed certain of the ritual prohibitions surrounding pollution and quarantine, and the old woman was insistent on this practice. Most of the villagers carefully avoided this house for fear of contracting pollution.

All Iraqw, both Christian and non-Christian, consider the growing incidence of unwed mothers to be a problem. Non-Christians blame the lenient attitudes towards unwed mothers by the churches, claiming that the pre-colonial policy of banishment was a much more effective deterrent. Older women also suggested that if the female initiation were still performed there would be fewer occurrences of unwed mothers. In many cases, unwed mothers who have no prospective husbands at the time of their pregnancy never marry because the taint of pollution is not easy to discard. Both Christians and non-Christians state that women are very susceptible to seduction and persuasion by men. Clearly, the important message in these beliefs is that fertility should be properly controlled. Quarantines protect a family and the community at large from the dangers of aborted fertility or, in the case of unwed mothers, of uncontrolled and improperly directed fertility. Women's fertility is legitimate and revered when it produces offspring for the lineage and clan, but is disapproved of when it does not. Children born to unmarried mothers receive no clan name and thus have no rights to patrilineal membership or inheritance. These children are known as *doroway* and carry the stigma of their illegitimacy throughout their lives. Gottlieb (1990) observes that patrilineal societies show a greater emphasis on female pollution, which corresponds to the sociological marginality of women in these societies. However, while, among the Iraqw, women are more susceptible to pollution, it is not a specifically gendered concept.

Because of women's perceived vulnerability to pollution, it is customary for men and women to eat in separate spaces and with separate utensils and vessels. The wife cooks the food and serves the husband's portion to him in vessels separate from those she uses and shares with her children. Usually, women and children eat near the hearth fire. This separation prevents any impurity, which the husband may have encountered in his interactions outside of the household, from spreading to his wife and children. Even most Christians still follow this separation in eating space.

As is evident from this description, pollution beliefs place greater restrictions on the lives of women and girls than on the men. They reinforce notions of women as properly confined to the domestic sphere. Colonial officers and church officials discouraged pollution beliefs, denouncing them as ignorant and backward. Elders voice their dissatisfaction at such external meddling, but younger Iraqw are increasingly drawn to membership in the Christian churches which they see as a important markers of their identity as 'modern' Tanzanians. A 150-household survey conducted in 1990 showed that 48.4 per cent of the sample were Christian while 51.6 per cent remained non-Christian. The split occurs primarily by age, with older people following 'traditional' Iraqw beliefs and younger people joining churches (Snyder 1997).

The Catholic Church is the oldest Christian church in the area and has the largest following.[13] More recently, several evangelical churches have moved into the area. Younger women are increasingly drawn to these churches. Elders complain that the practices of these churches are leading to the spread of pollution in the community and the resulting misfortunes of drought, wild animal attacks and disease as the earth spirits strike out in anger. The Pentecostal church is in the habit of baptizing its converts in the rivers (where earth spirits reside) and elders note that many of these converts are women who may be in a state of pollution and are thus breaching quarantine practices. Again, it is the earth spirits who strike out against individuals and the community when breaches of quarantine occur, because they are responding to threats to their own fertility. Elders also clearly feel their authority and power is threatened by the churches which are usurping their role as moral guardians of the community and promoting a break with the past and the 'traditions' on which much of the elders' status and prestige is founded (Snyder 1997).

One case with which I was familiar seemed to support elders' beliefs that it is those women suffering some form of pollution who are drawn to the evangelical churches. One such woman, who was married and in her thirties, was living in quarantine in the house run by the Catholic widow. She had two healthy young children, but her last child had died while an infant. So, she moved out of her home to the widow's house to observe *meeta*. Her husband and children stayed at home (which is not a very strict adherence to 'traditional' quarantine practices).[14] Her husband left her at the widow's, rarely visited and told her that he did not want her to return home. She was quite desperate to see her children and despaired of her situation because if her husband refused to visit her, and more specifically to sleep with her, she was unlikely to become pregnant again and have the quarantine end. She began attending the Pentecostal church services in the area and was told by the pastor that if she converted, and 'was saved', she would no longer be in a polluted state and her husband would take her back and she could live at home again. She did then become 'saved' and went back to her home to live with her family, simply ignoring her husband's insistence that she leave because she was not allowed to live with them in a polluted state.

THE PUBLIC SPHERE

As I have discussed elsewhere (Snyder 1997), in times of crisis, such as during a drought, elder Iraqw women gather in a group and march in protest around the community to prod the elders to action. Usually their protest focuses on spurring elders to perform the *masay* ritual designed to rid the community of pollution and thus to appease the earth spirits and lay the proper foundation for the rains, good health and good fortune for the community's members. When these women march in protest, they threaten to abandon their homes and 'sleep in the bush' unless the men heed their wishes. The 'bush' is considered dangerous, both spiritually and practically (wild animals), and women rarely venture into the 'bush' while men are able to travel through it, carrying spears and staves for self-defence. As mothers and caretakers of the home, women wield considerable power within this domain and have many responsibilities. Their threats to withdraw from the home are taken seriously. Ultimately the issues with which these women are concerned focus on fertility. Fertility of the land is crucial for the fertility of the livestock and the human population. Because women achieve power and status in both the household and the wider community through their role as mothers, they clearly have a stake in the wider fertility of natural resources. In the marches that I witnessed in Mbulu District, the participants were all non-Christian married women and all were mothers, most of whom were over thirty. Marriage was the criterion for participation in the women's council, as unmarried women are not considered fully adult. The level of participation in women's councils today points to the necessity of avoiding sweeping generalizations about 'women' among the Iraqw. Younger married Christian women did not participate in these marches, largely because the churches in the area to which most of them belonged denounced the marches as backward 'pagan' practices.

Women's protest marches are public events and are observed by all community residents. In 1991, even the national English language newspaper, the *Daily News* ran a story on these protests:

> Some 150 women from Rhotia and Mbulumbulu wards in Mbulu District have gathered ... to discuss their society's problems as well as pray for rain.... The women will stay here for over a week, they will sleep outside and food will be brought to them only by younger women.[15]

In the Iraqw homeland, women marched for hours around the community until they finally ended up either at the house of the elders' council leader or at a public meeting place where they demanded that the men's elders' council meet with them. During their marches, they paused before crossing any river or stream and said prayers to *Looaa* asking her to protect them from the earth spirits. They also sang songs as they marched. The lyrics of one of these songs told the story of a young man who attempted to spy on the secret affairs of the *marmo* initiation. He was seen by the women in charge of *marmo* and was caught and beaten to death. This tale underscores the aggressive tone of these marches. The women threaten to tear down the house of the elders' council leader if he fails to act quickly in response to their demands. During my fieldwork, I heard several accounts of women in various communities in the Iraqw homeland and in other areas demolishing these leaders' houses. In one community, Iraqw women teamed up with Datooga women to destroy the house of the elders' council leader because they believed that, instead of taking cows to the diviner to *bring* rain, he was actually requesting the diviner to *withhold* rain from the community.

In one march in 1994, the women gathered on the field in front of the ward government offices to complain about the reallocation of a widow's land by the local government. The widow had taken over the lands of her husband when he died but had left several acres in the valley bottom fallow for a few years. The government, responding to requests for land allocation, divided this land up and parcelled it out to local residents. The widow protested but the officials refused to change their decision. In response, she took a cow to a paramount diviner and asked him to prevent the rains from falling. As the community had been suffering a drought for months, the women assumed that the diviner had been successful. Thus they decided to march and camp out in front of the ward offices and force the government officers to demand that the officials give the land back to the widow. The government officer in charge of the ward literally hid inside his office and sent for two of the most respected elders in the ward to communicate with the women. The elders had food brought to the group and told them that they would pressure the government to give the land back to the woman. The local officials were reluctant to discuss the matter with the elders so the elders' council instead took matters into their own hands and asked those who had been allotted land to give it back to the widow. All who had been given plots agreed and the widow went to the diviner again with another cow to ask him to now remove what medicine he had used to prevent the rains. Not long after, the drought ended and the women saw no need to march again (Snyder 1997).

In 1993, leopard attacks spurred elder women to take action again. A leopard had been plaguing the area for over a year. Stories varied about how many people had been killed. At least one young boy had been mauled, another killed and various livestock eaten. The source of these calamities was rumoured to be a local diviner. This man had married a woman from the clan of paramount diviners and had bought 'medicine' from them. He had boasted publicly of his newly acquired powers and demanded that he be treated with the respect normally accorded the paramount diviners. In particular, he requested gifts of livestock and labour assistance in his fields. No one recognized his claims so he began threatening them with leopard attacks. When a leopard began harming people in the area, he was heard in the local bars proudly taking credit for the disasters. Residents of the area claimed that game officers had been called in to hunt the animal but gave up when they realized it was not a 'normal' leopard, but had been sent by a diviner. Finally, the elder women of several of the communities where attacks had occurred gathered and marched to the elders' council leader of the community where the culprit lived. They insisted he accompany them to capture the diviner and take him to the district police station. They proceeded, with all the women carrying staves like men, surrounded the diviner at a local bar and marched him off to police headquarters. They waited outside of the station until dusk when finally officials convinced them to disperse. The man was initially released because the government had no evidence on which to hold him. Later, however, when the women voiced their outrage at his release, he was arrested and convicted for disturbing the peace and was imprisoned for a few months.

These protest marches illustrate the ways in which women enter, and take action in, the public sphere. Their very ability to be effective rests on the authority and respect given to them as wives and mothers. As is clear in pollution beliefs and in ritual, the fertility of land, livestock, and women are all interconnected in Iraqw thought. Women play a vital role in lineage and clan perpetuation and in household reproduction from both a physical and subsistence point of view. Withdrawal from the domestic sphere is taken seriously as a threat to this reproduction and to subsistence. Their contribution of labour is critical to the economic prosperity of the household. In addition, because men do not participate at all in food preparation, they are quite helpless if there are no female children old enough to take over these duties during the mother's absence.

The power of women within the public sphere is, however, limited and mirrors their power within the domestic sphere.

While the leader of one of the elder women's groups boasted that men would not know what to do about community welfare unless women told them, women are still barred from actual participation in the community's *masay* ritual on the grounds that they may be harbouring some pollution which would damage the effectiveness of the medicine. Men claimed that women might have miscarried and not made this information public or perhaps they had not even recognized that they had miscarried. Therefore, they could not attend the ritual. Women, however, never voiced any interest in attending.

When women act in a group, they are rarely challenged. The curse of women and the curse of mothers are considered very powerful. When the women positioned themselves in front of the government offices to protest the widow's land case, an elder man, who was returning from a local bar rather inebriated, passed the group of women and insulted them. He told them they did not know what they were doing and that if they wanted to protest properly they would really go to the bush. The women interpreted this statement as a curse. As the woman's leader explained, 'by telling us to go to the bush, it was the same as telling us to go die in the wilderness'. The man was fined a goat. An elder man elaborated on the event: 'you can't refuse the women if they all, in unison, claim that you have wronged them. You must pay retribution.' To refuse to pay the fine would mean ostracism (*bayni*) by the entire community.

The status and roles that both women and men have in the public sphere are closely related to their roles within the domestic sphere. The men whose voices carry more authority in elders' council meetings are those who have good reputations for managing the affairs of their households (having a 'peaceful' household without arguments and dissent) and those who have amassed wealth for their households, primarily in the form of cattle. These features, together with their expertise in oratory (which is also seen to aid in their household affairs), make some elders more persuasive than others in community affairs. The elders are referred to, by both men and women, as the 'fathers' of the community and should act on behalf of the community as husbands and fathers act for their households. Women also interact in the wider community as wives and mothers and are respected for their reputation in their household. The association of the household with the community (*aya*) appears constantly in

THOSE WHO PLAY WITH FIRE

Iraqw discourse. As Thornton notes, 'In ritual, the *aya* and the domestic group are symbolically equated in order that the immediacy of the relationship of cohabitation and siblingship can be used in political rhetoric' (1980: 47).

In the pre-colonial era the men's elders' council was responsible for overseeing the affairs of the community such as distributing land, settling disputes, setting fines and performing community rituals. Today, the councils are largely relegated to the ritual sphere, as state government has taken control of legal and political matters. Selected elders are asked to serve as advisors to the local government on various matters such as local disputes and land allocation.

CONCLUSION

This chapter has demonstrated the ways in which gender roles are linked to cosmology and pollution beliefs, which are in turn part of the wider system of Iraqw cultural beliefs and practices formed in the pre-colonial era. They remain a significant influence in Iraqw life today, but the Christian churches and the Tanzanian state are providing alternative ideologies in which gender takes on different formulations. Since independence, the political rhetoric of Tanzania has encouraged equality for women and women's active participation in the public sphere. In the administrative wards where I conducted fieldwork, there were no female government officials who were Iraqw. The very few women who had government jobs usually came from outside the community and had married in.[16] There were a few women primary school teachers, but they were a minority. As Iyam observes among the Biase of Nigeria, the 'exclusion of women from political authority as a means of protecting a male-defined status hierarchy does not diminish women's enthusiasm for excelling in the economic sphere' (1996: 405). Among Iraqw, women support men's action in the public sphere in the same way that they rely on men's action (as husbands and fathers) in the domestic domain. Women's participation in the economic sphere is viewed as a contribution to the household, not as a threat to male authority within the household. Their activities revolve around marketing of agricultural crops, or handicrafts traditionally made by women. They rarely participate in wage labour and do not control livestock.

The Tanzanian government has recognized the vital contribution which women make to the household economy and survival. In the late 1980s, women around the country protested the head tax, stating that they should be exempted from paying this tax. In Mbulu District, women argued that, as they had no livestock, they had no means of raising the cash sufficient to pay this tax, and any earnings they did have from the sale of produce and crafts was directed towards the family's survival. The head tax for women was eventually repealed. Women argued against paying the tax by emphasizing their vital contribution to the household. If they had to find ways to raise the money necessary to pay the tax, the entire household would suffer.

Women are increasingly taking an active role in participation in Christian churches in the area. At any Catholic mass I attended, women were generally in the slight majority of those attending. Attendance at these services, as in all public meetings, is strictly divided by sex with women sitting on the left side of the church (or grounds) and men sitting on the right. This association with left and right is also found in the household where women sleep on the left side and men on the right. Women are active in various roles within church, as Sunday school teachers or as assistants to the priests. Participation in the local churches provides a way for women to take more active roles in the public sphere. For young women, church also provides a popular outlet for socializing outside of the confines on the household.

Another benefit in belonging to local churches is in their opposition to pollution beliefs, which place considerable restrictions on women's movements outside of the household. Ironically, as women are less confined by pollution beliefs and practices, they also have to take up more work as men relinquish their control over trade and travel. However, while women move into areas of activity previously open only to men, the ultimate control over finances and household decisions still rests with men.

Among the Iraqw, gender ideology confers specific identities and roles. These identities are crosscut by other social categories related to age and marital status (uncircumcised, and unmarriageable versus circumcised and married for example). Central to these identities is their relationship to the household/domestic domain, whether as unmarried and thus under the authority of the male head of household, or as married adults with their own households. Adult status, which is based on marriage, and prestige status, which is based in part on household fertility (for women as mothers and for men as fathers and as wealthy in livestock) confer status and authority in the public domain. The rights and limitations of these roles in the public sphere are linked to the ideology of gender. While changes in the local and national political economy and culture have affected roles of men and women within the domestic and public spheres, the domestic sphere remains the crucial location for the construction of gender and the basis for participation in the public domain.

NOTES

1 For a similar situation of complementarity from New Guinea see McDowell (1984).
2 In fact, *daa'awi* are named after its founder.
3 Beidelman (1980) notes the same concepts among the matrilineal Kaguru in south-eastern Tanzania.
4 The Datooga are a pastoralist community who live to the south-west of the Iraqw. Iraqw have migrated into their territory, and have intermarried. See Blystad in this volume.
5 See Collier and Rosaldo (1981) for other examples of this feature of bridewealth societies in Africa.
6 Men who are prone to gossip are said to be behaving 'like a woman'. This association of women with gossip is widespread in East Africa and figures in many of the sayings found on *kangas*, the cloths which women tie around their waists and shoulders.
7 Sheep are important animals for sacrifice and are perceived as representing important aspects of Iraqw identity (see Snyder 1997).
8 For Iraqw in the homeland, water sources are plentiful and nearby, and do not require long journeys.
9 See Buckley and Gottlieb (1988) for a review of the literature on menstrual taboos and female pollution.
10 See Snyder (1993) and Thornton (1980) for a complete discussion of pollution types.
11 Among the neighbouring Datooga, Blystad (1992) found similar ideas about pollution and the breast-milk of a woman who had lost a child. The Iraqw believe that the milk of cows whose calf has died is similarly polluted.
12 The degree to which people follow these practices varies by household and by the age, religious affiliation and geographical location of its members. In the homeland, all households that I was familiar with followed the custom regarding fetching water, yet, in part, it may have had as much to do with women's desire to lessen their work burden than a belief that they were in danger from the spirits.
13 In the 1890s, the White Fathers founded the first mission in Mbulu (Iliffe 1979: 217). While conversion appears to have been slow and

limited as reported by Thornton (1980) in the mid-1970s, the last twenty years has seen a marked increase in the number of adherents in Mbulu District (Snyder 1997).
14 Unlike her husband and children, she was carrying the pollution of her child's death in the unused milk in her breasts.
15 *Daily News*, 4 February, 1991.
16 Most of these women came from Kilimanjaro region.

REFERENCES

Beidelman, T.O. (1980) 'Women and men in two East African societies' in I. Karp and C. Bird (eds) *Explorations in African Systems of Thought* (Bloomington: Indiana University Press).
Blystad, A. (1992) 'The pastoral Barabaig: fertility, recycling and the social order', Cand. Polit. Thesis, Department of Anthropology, University of Bergen.
Buckley, T. and A. Gottlieb (eds) (1988) *The Anthropology of Menstruation* (Berkeley: University of California Press).
Collier, J. F. and M. Z. Rosaldo (1981) 'Politics and gender in simple societies' in S. B. Ortner and A. Whitehead (eds) *Sexual Meanings: The Cultural Construction of Gender and Sexuality* (Cambridge: Cambridge University Press).
Comaroff, J. (1987) '*Sui generis*: feminism, kinship theory, and structural "domains"' in J. F. Collier and S. J. Yanagisako (eds) *Gender and Kinship: Essays Toward a Unified Analysis* (Stanford: Stanford University Press).
Delaney, C. (1988) 'Mortal flow: menstruation in Turkish village society' in T. Buckley and A. Gottlieb (eds) *Blood Magic: The Anthropology of Menstruation* (Berkeley: University of California Press).
Di Leonardo, M. (ed.) (1991) *Gender at the Crossroads of Knowledge: Feminist Anthropology in the Postmodern Era* (Berkeley: University of California Press).
Fortes, M. (1949) *The Web of Kinship among the Tallensi* (London: Oxford University Press).
Gottlieb, A. (1988) 'Menstrual cosmology among the Beng of Ivory Coast' in T. Buckley and A. Gottlieb (eds) *Blood Magic: The Anthropology of Menstruation* (Berkeley: University of California Press).
Gottlieb, A. (1990) 'Rethinking female pollution: the Beng case (Côte d'Ivoire)' in P. R. Sanday and R. G. Goodenough (eds) *Beyond the Second Sex: New Directions in the Anthropology of Gender* (Philadelphia: University of Pennsylvania Press).
Iliffe, J. (1979) *A Modern History of Tanganyika* (Cambridge: Cambridge University Press).
Iyam, D. (1996) '"Full" men and "powerful" women: the reconstruction of gender status among the Biase of Southeastern Nigeria', *Canadian Journal of African Studies*, 30 (3): 387–408.
MacCormack, C.P. (1980) 'Nature, culture and gender: a critique' in C.

P. MacCormack and M. Strathern (eds) *Nature, Culture and Gender* (Cambridge: Cambridge University Press).

McDowell, N. (1984) 'Complementarity: the relationship between female and male in the East Sepik village of Bun, Papua New Guinea' in D. O'Brien and S. W. Tiffany (eds) *Rethinking Women's Roles: Perspectives from the Pacific* (Berkeley: University of California Press).

Moore, H.L. (1988) *Feminism and Anthropology* (Cambridge: Polity).

Moore, H.L. (1994) *A Passion for Difference: Essays in Anthropology and Gender* (Cambridge: Polity).

Ortner, S. B. (1996) 'Gender hegemonies' in *Making Gender: The Politics and Erotics of Culture* (Boston: Beacon).

Ortner, S.B. and H. Whitehead (eds) (1981) *Sexual Meanings: The Cultural Construction of Gender and Sexuality* (Cambridge: Cambridge University Press).

Peletz, M. G. (1996) *Reason and Passion: Representations of Gender in a Malay Society* (Berkeley: University of California Press).

Rapp, R. (1979) 'Anthropology: a review essay', *Signs*, 4 (3): 497–513.

Rogers, S.C. (1975) 'Female forms of power and the myth of male dominance: model of female/male interaction in peasant society', *American Ethnologist*, 2: 727–57.

Rosaldo, M.Z. (1980) 'The use and abuse of anthropology: reflections on feminism and cross-cultural understanding', *Signs*, 5: 395–417.

Rosaldo, M.Z. and L. Lamphere (eds) (1974) *Women, Culture and Society* (Stanford: Stanford University Press).

Schlegel, A. (1990) 'Gender meanings: general and specific' in P. R. Sanday and R.G. Goodenough (eds) *Beyond the Second Sex: New Directions in the Anthropology of Gender* (Philadelphia: University of Pennsylvania Press).

Snyder, K.A. (1993) '"Like water and honey": moral ideology and the construction of community among the Iraqw of northern Tanzania', PhD dissertation, Yale University.

Snyder, K.A. (1997) 'Elders' authority and women's protest: the *masay* ritual and social change among the Iraqw of Tanzania', *Journal of the Royal Anthropological Institute*, 3 (3): 561–76.

Strathern, M. (1981) 'Self-interest and the social good' in S. B. Ortner and H. Whitehead (eds) *Sexual Meanings: The Cultural Construction of Gender and Sexuality* (Cambridge: Cambridge University Press).

Strathern, M. (1984) 'Domesticity and the denigration of women' in D. O'Brien and S.W. Tiffany (eds) *Rethinking Women's Roles: Perspectives from the Pacific* (Berkeley: University of California Press).

Strathern, M. (1988) *The Gender of the Gift: Problems with Women and Problems with Society in Melanesia* (Berkeley: University of California Press).

Thornton, R.J. (1980) *Space, Time, and Culture among the Iraqw of Tanzania* (New York: Academic).

Thornton, R.J. (1982) 'Modelling of spatial relations in a boundary-making ritual of the Iraqw of Tanzania', *Man*, 17: 528–45.

Wada, S. (1984) 'Female initiation rites of the Iraqw and the Gorowa', *Senri Ethnological Studies*, 15: 187–97.

Weiner, A.B. (1976) *Women of Value, Men of Renown: New Perspectives in Trobriand Exchange* (Austin: University of Texas Press).

Winter, E.H. (1964) 'The slaughter of a bull: a study of cosmology and ritual' in R.S. Manners (ed.) *Process and Pattern in Culture* (Chicago: Aldine).

Winter, E.H. (1966) 'Territorial groupings and religion among the Iraqw' in M.P. Banton (ed.) *Anthropological Approaches to the Study of Religion* (London: Tavistock).

Winter, E.H. (1968) 'Some aspects of political organization and land tenure among the Iraqw' *Kyoto University African Studies*, 2: 1–29.

CHAPTER 9

WOMEN'S WORK IS WEEPING

CONSTRUCTIONS OF GENDER IN A CATHOLIC COMMUNITY[1]

MAIA GREEN

This chapter explores constructions of gender and transformation among the groups of people defining themselves as Pogoro, Bantu-speaking agriculturalists who occupy the central highlands section of Ulanga District, southern Tanzania. The vast majority of them are at least nominally affiliated to the Roman Catholic Church which has a presence in the area stretching back almost a century (Larson 1976; Green 1993). Despite the attempts of the institutional church to impose uniformity on its congregations, popular Pogoro Catholicism is eclectic and tolerant of a range of practices defined by the Church as non-Christian. Pogoro Catholics participate in both Christian and non-Christian activities and, as they define themselves as Christian, perceive no contradiction between them (Green 1995). While both men and women are involved in popular Catholicism and participate to a varying extent in the formal institutional structures of the Church, degrees of religiosity and the mode of its expression vary according to age and gender. As in some other Catholic communities, popular religiosity and personal piety are largely the domains of older women (Christian 1972; Rushton 1982; Davis 1984; Pina-Cabral 1986; Taylor 1995; Stirrat 1992; Scheper-Hughes 1992).

I argue that the religiosity of older Pogoro Catholic women stems from their particular experience of gender and age, through which the female person is progressively transformed from a mere girl into a fertile mother and, ultimately, into a woman who has 'dried out', past childbearing years. This process inevitably brings a woman into intimate contact with the physical and emotional aspects of reproduction and death, which are conceptualized as so fundamentally affecting those closely associated with them as to effect transformations in the very substance of a person's physical and emotional make-up. These changes ultimately empower a person to assume specific ritual roles on future occasions at which reproduction and death are central. Women's experience of loving and caring for others, and of managing death and sorrow, forms the basis of a distinctly female religiosity, premised on the maintenance of intense and empathetic relationships with the Catholic divinities through the figure of Mary.

For Pogoro Catholics ideational constructions of gender exist not only at the abstract level of symbolic discourse, but are enacted and experienced through specific ritual roles of gendered interdependencies (cf. Kratz 1994). These roles centre on a division of labour between men and certain categories of women who assume responsibility for dealing with the potentially dangerous powers generated through fertility and death. Gender and personhood are conceptualized and experienced in processual terms, effected through the dynamic of ageing as it is culturally constructed (cf. Beidelman 1997: 3; Lutkehaus 1995). A person moves from the raw physicality of the neonate through the sequence of growth, adulthood and death to become, ultimately, a spirit. Time alone is insufficient to effect this transformation. Ageing is conceptualised as a process of growth, literally 'becoming', through which a person's physical substance is altered. This is not viewed as a natural process. It must be mediated by rituals which effect the physical transformation of people's bodies in gender-appropriate ways, through contact with the cosmological powers generated by life and death and the ingestion and incorporation of special substances endowed with power as 'medicines' (Green 1996).

The successful completion of the life course is facilitated by the gendered interdependency of male and female persons in the enactment of the specific life-crisis rituals on which the process of becoming depends. Male and female are differentiated through rituals which effect the constitution of their physical substance, facilitating a cumulative gender differentiation on which the ritual division of labour, premised on age and sex, is founded. This process begins with a rite of female initiation (*unyago*) in which pubescent girls are endowed with the capacity to reproduce themselves and sustain the growth and becoming of their offspring. The capacity for human reproduction entails inevitable physical transformations in women's bodies contingent on motherhood and menstruation, which are imagined as ultimately empowering them to assume ritual responsibilities for dealing with the cosmological powers generated by the reproduction of others. The physical changes in female substance engendered by reproduction are paralleled by equivalent changes in both male and female bodies effected through close contact with death. Bereavement fundamentally alters the state of the person, lessening their vulnerability to the powers released by the deaths of others, and enabling them to undertake specific duties at funeral events.

The embodiment of power leads to ritual empowerment, determining future roles in life crisis rituals. Because the powers generated by human reproductive capacity and death are released through life processes there is a fundamental identity between them (cf. Bloch 1992; Douglas 1966). This identity has implications for constructions of gender and the kinds of ritual obligations women are accorded. A particular construction of the female body as the locus of reproductive potential implies that women's bodies have a greater capacity to be affected by participation in life processes than male bodies are. As women age they assume increasing ritual responsibilities at life crisis rituals concerned with the management of reproduction and death. The changes in a person's substance brought about by close contact with reproduction and mourning are not confined to a person's physical body. They also affect a person's emotional and affective development, augmenting their ability to love and feel pity. Older women have special obligations to mourn the dead, as well as dealing with the ambiguous powers generated by death and decomposition. Women's association with death and the emotional labour of mourning carries over into popular Catholicism which centres on the remembrance of the crucified Christ through compassion for his bereaved mother, Mary.

GENDER AND THE DIVISION OF LABOUR

Like other rural communities in southern Tanzania, the vast majority of Pogoro people struggle to make their living from small-scale farming, mainly of maize, rice, bananas, sweet potatoes and cassava, supplemented by migrant labour, petty trade and handicraft production. Few people keep livestock. Agricultural land is formally owned by the national government, but village administrations have the authority to allocate usufruct rights for farm and residential holdings in their designated areas. Although land tends to get passed on within families, land shortage is only acute in the immediate vicinity of villages where population densities are high. Elsewhere, land is widely available. The ready availability of agricultural land has implications for female autonomy. Women and men have equal rights to land from village governments, irrespective of marital status. Women are allocated fields to farm in their own right, and do not depend on the support of male kin for their livelihoods. Any woman can potentially acquire her own farmland and establish her own household should she choose to do so, without recourse to marriage. Not surprisingly in this situation, a substantial proportion of households are female headed, due to a combination of widowhood, separation, choice and labour migration.

Marriage, though a desirable goal for young women, is neither essential for adult status nor for the constitution of kinship relations. Women are recognized as autonomous adults, capable of managing their own affairs without reliance on male kin or spouses (cf. Harris 1981). Pogoro kinship recognizes potential rights of filiation through the paternal or maternal line. A man can claim rights of paternal affiliation with his children, whether or not he is the husband of their mother, through specific payments for rights in his offspring and the provision of medicines from his own place of origin. Unclaimed children remain affiliated to the family of their mother's father, or if she has no social father, her mother's brother (Green n.d. (a)). Fertility is highly valued, and many women remain unmarried with offspring from different fathers. Others marry after their fertility has been proven through a relationship with another man. Formal marriage is constituted through the transfer of cash from the groom's to the bride's family, which may, or may not, be followed by a Christian marriage.[2] The transfer of bridewealth gives a man certain rights over his children, as well as obligations towards them. Male rights over women are more ambiguous. Women never lose their latent rights to reside with natal families. And, while a wife is expected to cook and provide food for her husband, he is equally obliged to ensure that she is clothed and has access to the things which she needs. Failure on either side to meet appropriate standards of behaviour is accepted as sufficient grounds for separation. Should this occur prior to the birth of children, bridewealth is repaid.

Like women elsewhere in Tanzania, Pogoro women are discriminated against in terms of access to national labour markets and education. However, they have a high degree of potential equality with, and autonomy from, men. They can engage in trade and participate in village government and local organizations. In practice, the achievement of this kind of equality is founded on, and implies, inequality within the household. Successful women household heads generally enjoy access to off-farm income and control over the labour of others, freeing them from the domestic duties which restrict the freedoms of their less fortunate counterparts. Agricultural work is divided between men and women, according to the quality of the relationship between co-operating individuals. Some couples farm shared land together. Others maintain separate plots tended by each partner. Although clearing fields is said to be men's work, women participate in heavy agricultural labour, often for others, and both men and women plant, weed and harvest.

Conventions regarding the sexual division of labour mean that women bear the brunt of domestic chores. Fetching water, food processing, food preparation and childcare all fall on women's shoulders. Although this increases women's workload, it has advantages for some women, who, unlike men, can sustain their own households without recourse to the labour of the opposite sex. Women can also trade in the domestic skills which they have practised since childhood, making money from brewing, food processing and preparation. Beyond infancy, boys and girls are encouraged to behave in what are considered to be gender-appropriate ways and to learn and acquire the skills and styles of behaviour associated with adult men and women. Girls spend time helping female relatives in domestic and agricultural chores, look after younger siblings and, once they reach puberty, must ostentatiously display 'shame' (soni) in the presence of male seniors. Boys are encouraged to spend time with men, to participate in hunting and housebuilding, and to spend time alone on their own enterprises developing a strong sense of autonomy.

The emphasis on female sociability and male autonomy persists throughout adulthood. Women are always involved in caring for others and collective activities, to the extent that they are said to have a natural capacity for 'love' and pity. Men of all ages expect to be recipients of this care, at the same time as their capacity for emotional self-containment is a source of strength both for themselves and their dependents. Women's association with the responsibilities of tending home, men, guests and children directly involves them in the duties of emotional and physical care, which are regarded as essential attributes of being female. These duties include tending the sick, mourning the dead and praying for others, dead and living. The separation of the sexes is especially marked on public occasions where semi-autonomous but interdependent spheres of male and female influence are demarcated.

HEAT AND LIFE

Like other communities in sub-Saharan Africa, Pogoro people imagine human life to depend on the maintenance of social relationships between existing and preceding generations, which entails the construction of chains of continuity between living people and those from whom they are descended (Middleton 1982; Beidelman 1986; 1997; Wilson 1957; Fernandez 1982; Boyer 1990). Dead and living are conceptualized as being physically linked through co-residence and the sharing of food and substance (cf. Lan 1985), just as paternal kinship as a social relationship is created in the present through the transmission of a medicine called *shirala* from a father to his children, incorporating substance from his place of origin into his children's bodies (Green 1993; 1996; cf. Wilson 1957: 105). Relations between people and spirits are effected through offerings of food and beer, which both sides partake of, and which serve to ensure the generalized fertility of crops and people. What matters is the possibility of continuity, of ensuring that humans can reproduce themselves and perpetuate the relationships between people, land and spirits through time. This rests in turn on the management of human reproductive capacities through the careful manipulation of the cosmological powers generated by the life process itself.

Pogoro cosmology centres on fundamental ideas about the life process as a transition between person (*muntu*) and spirit (*lihoka*). Both represent different aspects of being human; people have bodies which implicate them in the physical processes of life. Spirits (*mahoka*) retain shades of their living identity but, having lost the flesh and blood bodies of their human form, exist in a parallel dimension, divorced from the kinds of participation in life processes with which people are associated. Retaining a material presence, they talk, walk and wear shroudcloth on their bodies, but their existence is defined in opposition to that of living people. They occupy a contiguous domain to the living, but are rarely in the same space at the same time. Spirits occupy forest and bush land, are active at night and appear to the living in dreams. The relational existence of the spirit community expresses the fundamental dynamism of the dialectic between life and death. People die and become spirits, just as settlements are abandoned and return to bush, day follows night, and waking follows sleeping. Occasions when domains merge are sought periodically by either party, either through possession when spirits take hold of living people's bodies or appear in dreams, or when living people make offerings and invoke spirits to receive them.

Having abandoned their physical bodies in the earth, spirits are far removed from the biological processes with which living people are associated. The state of the spirits of the dead and territorial shrines is conceptualized as one of essential cold, like the places and times with which they are associated. Territorial spirits reside in the pools of still water which constitute their shrines, deep in sections of unviolated forest. Human habitation is forbidden and people may only enter the area in the company of a male shrine diviner (*mbui*). Spirits demand that those seeking to approach them avoid close contact with processes and people who have become implicated in activities concerning reproduction and death. These processes, centring on sex, birth and death, are said to make a person hot and dirty, as well as generating cosmological powers which can be transmitted to others thereby affecting their fertility and mortality. Prior to making offerings or entering shrine forests both men and women must abstain from sexual intercourse to ensure that their bodies are sufficiently cool so as not to pollute the shrine area. Women who are menstruating, have recently given birth or are wearing the shroudcloth neckbands on their bodies which indicate a state of mourning are not permitted to enter the forest area surrounding territorial shrines.

The contrast between heat and cold, human and spirit, under-lies the idiom of blessing as a relation between spirits and people. Its ultimate objective is *shimba izizimiri*, that 'the body be cool', and it is often carried out by the application of water to a person's body. While the idiom of cooling connotes association with spirits, as well as good health and emotional calm (cf. Jacobson-Widding 1987), the request that the body be cool is not merely concerned with the temporary achievement of well-being, but with the proper completion of the life course as a process of gradual reduction in the heat of biological activity. Cooling down is a key element of life crisis rituals (cf. Beidelman 1997: 175; Jacobson-Widding 1987: 1), which seek to deal appropriately with the physical changes brought about in persons through participation in the biological processes of living and dying. These centre on reducing and removing some of the heat and dirt which inevitably periodically accumulate in people's bodies through being alive and growing older.

As the existence and attributes of spirits are defined in terms of what living people are not, ideas about the human body and the processes with which its is associated come to assume cosmological significance. The processes of birth and death which ultimately engender spirithood have the capacity to release dynamic powers necessary for human development, but which must be carefully controlled and allowed to dissipate lest they jeopardize the life process itself. These powers are conceptualized as forces which inhere in the bodies of people. They centre on two contrasting notions, on the one hand the power of death, and, on the other, the power of life experienced as the capacity for human fertility. Neither the subject of explicit discourse on the nature of life and death, nor abstracted as concepts, powers are given reality through being experienced as immaterial essences which have material effects. They can be transmitted to others through vectors which are conceptualized as having properties analogous to the powers themselves (cf. Herbert 1993: 226). The most usual vectors are fire and water, which are incorporated into food and ultimately into the bodies of others. Actions can also transmit power, in particular sexual intercourse which is symbolically associated with heat and firemaking (Herbert 1993; Richards 1982).

When a person dies, their death generates a potential power to transmit death to all those who have been in contact with the corpse and participated in the burial. The contagiousness of death is carefully managed by ensuring that those leaving a burial are adequately cleansed, washing their faces, hands and feet in water, and by restrictions on who may handle the corpse and its belongings so that only those who have acquired some immunity to death power through previous close associating with death come into immediate contact with them. The power of death is not only transmissable between persons, but can alter their very substance and, if properly managed, enhance their capacity to deal with death power in future. This is achieved through a series of post-burial practices which aim to effect the containment of death power in the bodies of close relatives of the dead, thereby shortcircuiting its transmissibility. The power of life generated through the processes associated with birth and the emergence of female reproductive potential is intimately associated with female fertility and conveys the capacity for human reproduction. Like death power, it is similarly transmissible, but affects men and women in different ways. While both men and women can pass on this power to others, only women are affected by its transmission, either as recipients of the powers of others or as those from whom the powers of female fertility have been stolen away. The transmissibility of the power of life has implications for the ritual management of female fertility and the particular roles of older women who have a duty to contain it, thereby protecting a woman's capacity to give birth.

As the powers generated by life and death epitomize excessive physicality in contrast to the state of the spirits, there is an identity between them. This identity is expressed through the idiom of 'dirt' generated by life processes and which adheres to the bodies of those affected by them. They are not in themselves polluting, in the sense that contact with them implies the social devaluation of the person, nor is 'dirt' inevitably regarded as something which must be removed. The notion of 'dirt' is context dependant, a ritual state, which enables the symbolic representation of its antithesis, the state of the spirits. Identity in one context can become incompatibility in another. On occasions where life and death are in obvious contradiction the powers associated with each must be kept separate or they will cancel each other out: thus, for example, pregnant women must keep away from close participation in funeral activities or their unborn children could die. Similarly, fire and water are both vectors for the transmission of powers and, on occasion, opposite forces capable of reversing the effects of one or other kind of power (cf. Jacobson-Widding 1987: 1). Consequently, water applied to the body is used to purify and reverse states of excessive heat through cooling, while ideas about the life process itself acknowledge the interdependency and necessity of access to both heat and wetness to the generation and regeneration of life.

Pogoro people conceptualise ageing as a process of gradual drying out, a transition from fertile wetness to brittle old age effected through implication in 'heat'. Women and men experience this transition differently and at different rates. Although men gradually lose their vitality, they never totally lose their capacity for fertility and sex. Women, wetter to begin with, dry out more quickly. After the menopause they are no longer fertile and are said to have 'left off things of reproduction', implying that they no longer have sexual intercourse. The supposed non- involvement of older women in sexual activity has implications for their capacity to act as containers of cosmological powers, which they will not transit to others. As the power released by reproduction is identical in some contexts to that released by death, older women whose bodies have already been altered by engagement in reproductive processes have a special capacity to deal with the powers of death and decomposition. The category of women who carry the greatest burden of ritual responsibilities are the *wamakolu*, women who have reached the menopause and, having lost somebody close to them, been fully involved in the mourning process. Older women who have themselves embodied the powers of birth and death can embody the powers generated by others' involvement in these processes with impunity. The fact that having 'dried out' they are no longer engaged in reproductive processes means that they will not become vectors for the transmission of power to others, either draining away the fertility of others or passing on the contagiousness of death.

HUMAN REPRODUCTIVE CAPACITY AND THE FERTILITY OF WOMEN

The specific duties and obligations accorded older women in the management of life processes stem, in part, from ideas about human reproduction which accord men and women different capacities for fertility. Neither men nor women are inherently fertile and capable of successful reproduction. Human reproduction is viewed as a long-term process, encompassing the successful birth and maturity of offspring. The capacity to reproduce ultimately depends on the establishment of paternal kinship via the transmission of *shirala* medicines to babies of either sex shortly after birth (Green n.d. (a)). Boys receive *shirala* medicine only once in their lifetimes. Girls receive another dose on the occasion of their first period and if one of their children dies before them. *Shirala* in itself is insufficient to ensure female fertility. Although in the local idiom of conception, a woman is merely a vessel for the man's seed, the logic of the plant metaphor implies that the ground must be properly prepared if the seed is to flourish. This is achieved through performance of a series of rituals called *unyago* aimed at establishing and safeguarding female fertility.

The series of ceremonies which comprise the *unyago* are similar in structure and detail to those performed by peoples throughout south-east and central Africa (Swantz 1966; 1970; Richards 1982; Turner 1968; Beidelman 1964; 1997; Wilson 1957; Brain 1978; Caplan 1976). Among Pogoro people the practices associated with the puberty of girls are not primarily concerned with nubility as a precursor to fertility as Richards described for the Bemba's *chisungu* and related rites among Lunda peoples in central Africa (1982: 170–86). They are concerned with fertility itself, with ensuring it through the giving of medicine, and with containing the excess potency that the girl's first period entails so that it is unable to escape and be lost for ever. As the timing of the ceremonies is triggered by physiological puberty they are performed for individual girls. On the occasion of their first or second period young girls are secluded inside the house and taught various obligations by older women instructors. These obligations emphasize the duties of caring for others which being a proper woman entails. A novice is given a young child to accompany her and look after, and a laying hen to tend like a child. The continuity of relationships through female reproductive capacity is a recurrent theme of the *unyago* ceremonies, which express a long-term view of reproduction in which the successful upbringing of a child is not completed until the child has reproduced themselves. Particular emphasis is given to feeding people, in particular husbands, because feeding is an idiom through which social relationships are established and maintained. As in other African communities, the capacity to feed and ensure the nurturance of others is regarded as a characteristically female attribute and duty (Beidelman 1997: 83).

Up to the 1930s, the *unyago* ceremonies were part of a successive series of events focused on seclusion and the 'teaching' of girls which led directly to a girl's betrothal, marriage and the birth of her first child. Girls remained in seclusion for months, even years if a partner was not found, although the Church gradually appropriated the seclusion of Christian girls in a boarding school, even going so far as to arrange their marriages with Christian men, and on occasion, receiving bridewealth for them.[3]

The link with marriage now severed, girls remain in seclusion for weeks, or days, due to the demands of primary school and a general consensus that the role of the school is somehow equivalent to seclusion as a place of instruction for the novice. The emphasis of *unyago* ceremonies is no longer on instruction, but on establishing and safeguarding a young woman's ability to bear and bring up children. The period of seclusion is followed by a formal coming out, after a day-long ritual in which the girl is taken sleeping from the house and publicly washed and cooled down in the courtyard. These activities are managed and supervised by *wamakolu*, older women past their reproductive years, under the direction of an instructress cum midwife figure, the *mnyagu*. As in other puberty and initiation rituals, the symbolic drama of events is structured around the transition of the novice from a state mirroring the passivity and asociality of death and birth to that of a person whose state and status enable her to fully participate in social activity (cf. Turner 1967; 1968; Comaroff 1985; Beidelman 1964; Godelier 1986; Bloch 1986; 1992). For the duration of her seclusion a novice is a *mwali kam numba*, a maiden of the inside of the house. She is kept inside the house surrounded by women, like a corpse prior to burial. Contact with men and boys, even if they are related, is forbidden. If for some reason she must leave her house, she is covered in cloths, with only her feet visible. The novice is not permitted to speak and may only communicate in gestures. The prohibition on speech is fundamental, for silence is equated with death and the anti-sociality of witches and corpses (Green 1997). Other prohibitions applying to the novice and those resident in her household are significant for an understanding of the nature of power and the role of women in containing it. These centre on items which can act as vectors for female fertility: fire, water, and a paste made from ground cucumber seeds (*ntanga*) which has transformative power, as 'medicine' (Green 1996).

During the girls' first period and initial seclusion, special restrictions are imposed on all the residents of her household in order to protect her fertility. They must abstain from sex. Fire and water cannot be given to people from other households, nor can fire be taken from neighbours' hearths. The novice herself must not eat food which has been cooked on other people's fires, and food cooked on her fire can only be given to older women past childbearing age. Even they, however, should not be given fire from the house of the *mwali*, lest they pass it on to others who are sexually active, and with it the young woman's fertility. This is talked about in terms of 'depriving her of giving birth'. Not only could people use the fire, water and food to pass harmful medicine to the girls, the restriction on fire is crucial in that it prevents the *mwali* from 'drying out'. Fire is a potential vector of the girl's fertility, which could be dissipated further if those who receive it have sexual relations. The restrictions on food, fire and water apply only while the girl is actually bleeding. Only cooked food is involved, because its preparation involves fire. After the first, and sometimes the second period, apart from a prohibition on intercourse, no other domestic prohibitions apply to menstruating women or their households, although certain restrictions apply with regard to access to territorial shrines and participation in ritual occasions which seek to establish contact with spirits of the dead and those associated with territory. The various prohibitions on the menstruating *mwali* are not concerned with preventing the contamination of others, as Wilson suggests for the menstrual taboos of the Nyakyusa (1957: 131), nor with protecting the woman herself from her own pollution (Buckley and Gottlieb 1988: 11), but with safeguarding her fertility. Protection of female reproductive power is, however, insufficient to ensure the future reproductive capacity of the novice. This capacity must first be established through the incorporation of *shirala* medicine into the young woman's body. While *shirala* medicine makes girls fertile, the establishment of fertility generates a volatile power which could be lost to others if not carefully controlled. This is achieved through its incorporation into the bodies of older non-sexually active women through the manipulation of another medicine made from ground cucumber seeds (*ntanga*).

Cucumbers are a common feature of girls' puberty rites in the area (Swantz 1970: 236; Turner 1968: 241). They reproduce quickly. More than their phallic shape, it is the numerous seeds inside the fruit which make them particularly suited to an equation with fertility in general, and female fertility in particular. The entire sequence of the *unyago* is structured around two contrasting occasions on which *ntanga* are eaten. On the first, at the beginning of seclusion, a girl is fed a portion of the ground-up roasted seeds in a thick paste, during a ritual which primarily involves older women as both participants and audience. What paste remains is shared out among women who are either past the menopause or are not sexually active, who are under an obligation to eat it. Men and sexually active people cannot eat the cucumber seeds on this occasion because it is feared they would transit the power of female fertility to other women through sexual activity, thereby, as women explained it, 'depriving the *mwali* of giving birth'. After the first lot of *ntanga* has been eaten, the girl returns to the house until her formal coming out ceremony, an event which culminates in the public eating of another portion of *ntanga* paste.

In contrast to the eating of the *ntanga* at the start of the seclusion period, the eating of the second lot of *ntanga* is open to men and women of all ages, and is the culmination of the series of events which effect the 'bringing out' of the girl into the community. After elaborate sequences of washing, mime and dance, accompanied by songs of instruction, the girl is again fed *ntanga* while seated passively on a mat between the knees of an older female relative. This time, a large portion of the seeds are prepared, cooked into a lump of paste the size of a football, which the novice is made to grasp in her hands while the instructress breaks off pieces which the audience snatches, mimicking the leering hunger of dogs or hyenas. Close female kin snatch first, followed by other women and men. Men, women and children participate, dancing up to the *mnyagu*'s proffered hands and greedily wolfing down sticky chunks of seed paste. Turner describes a similar sequence for the Ndembu, in which people mimic hyenas, snatching the food as scavengers, which he interprets as stealing some of the girl's mother's fertility (1968: 226). This interpretation does not apply to the Pogoro rite, the whole point of which emphasizes that the girls' fertility is no longer vulnerable to predation. The snatching of the *ntanga* by predatory dogs makes explicit the fact that there is no restriction on who may eat the *ntanga* nor, by extension, on the girl's participation in sexual activity. This state is, however, shortlived. Volatility returns with the powers generated by each birth, which are managed through identical restrictions on the exchange of food, fire and sex that apply to the house of a *mwali*.

Although washing the *mwali* is an essential prerequisite to the public eating of the *ntanga*, and her cooling down is significant, the first eating of the *ntanga* by the *mwali* herself and the older non-sexually active women is what makes possible its general consumption weeks or even months later. Without their ingestion, the *mwali* would be unable to successfully carry, bear and bring up children. Unlike the *shirala* medicine, which coveys the capacity for fertility in a direct and immediate way, the cucumber seeds do not in themselves make the novice fertile. Without puberty and *shirala* they have no power. Rather, what they seem to do is to augment female fertility and then absorb the excess, which can then be contained in other people's bodies and made safe. Therefore the prohibitions which apply to the consumption of the first lot of *ntanga* paste are identical to those on fire, water and sexual contact which apply during the girl's first period. *Wamakolu*, as older non-sexually active women, have an obligation to eat the first lot of *ntanga*, containing within their bodies the fertility of the novice and preventing its dissipation.

FUNERAL PRACTICES

The embodied containment of contagious power is also a feature of funerary practices, together with the notion that containment cumulatively changes a person's substance. Adult women in general, and *wamakolu* in particular, have special responsibilities at funerals concerning the physical embodiment of death. The funeral process is structured around the imagined transition of a dead person into a spirit, achieved through the manipulation of a series of parallel identifications between the dead person and the circle of key mourners, who are most closely identified with the body (cf. Goody 1962: 188; Wilson 1957: 49). It is the extent of this identification which makes possible the series of repeat funerals which constitute the funeral process, without, as in the case of the secondary burials described by Hertz (1960), an actual body to rebury. These consist of the burial itself, and two post burial regroupings of mourners, one, called *toa tatu*, shortly after the burial and the other, *sadaka ya mwisho*, around a year later, after which mourning restrictions are lifted. The identification between mourners and the deceased is most pronounced for the main female mourners, closely related to the dead, who must wear around their necks strips of cloth (*lijemba*) representing both corpse and shroud, until the funeral process is over.

Bodies are usually buried the day after death if at all possible. When a person dies, his or her body is placed on a bed inside a house. Close male and female relatives of the dead remain inside the room with the body until it is taken out for burial. Women, both kin and non-kin, stay inside the house with the corpse. Male mourners, with the exception of the children, siblings and spouses of the deceased, remain outside, sitting apart from women who could either not find room in the house or who are engaged in preparing food for the mourners. Women funeral-goers cry, wail and sing the kinds of Christian songs which have come to constitute an expression of mourning. These are the 'songs of suffering' (*nyimbo za mateso*), which graphically recount the suffering and crucifixion of Jesus. Men prepare the coffin and grave, and collect cash and food contributions from mourners. Sexual abstinence is compulsory for all those attending a funeral and staying at the funeral house. It is also an obligation of people in mourning, and, as older women mourn longer, of the older female main mourners who will continue to be physically identified with the deceased long after the body is buried.

The bodies of men are washed and prepared for burial by older men and the bodies of women by older women. Those who prepare bodies for burial or handle vessels used in the preparation must have already been bereaved themselves. For others to do so could transmit the power of death to their families and homes. While both men and women who have already been bereaved can contain the death power released by the deaths of others, women's obligations to contain death exceed those of men, even of those men most closely related to and thus identified with the corpse. These obligations commence at the very event which is said to open the funeral, after which mourning can formally begin. The activities associated with mourning do not begin automatically at the moment of death. A funeral has to be opened once mourners begin to assemble, at an event called *lugutu* from the verb -*guta* to cry or mourn. This involves a real or classificatory sister of the dead person killing a chicken of the same sex as the deceased on the threshold of the house, while a male elder implores the general spirits of the dead to allow the events to proceed without discord. In contrast to the usual way of killing chickens by cutting their throats, the *lugutu* chicken is killed by smashing its head against the doorframe of the house so that it dies without shedding blood.

The chicken is left where it lies for a time, before being taken away, plucked and cooked. Its meat is eaten by the old people who have already been 'died on' and who, because of their age, think of themselves as being close to death and to the dead. If the young and those not yet exposed to death were to eat it they could bring death to their houses and families. It is said that old women are particularly suited to eating this meat. Not only have they already been 'died on', but, having 'dried out', proximity with death will not harm their fertility.

As in the *unyago*, when the novice is given a hen to tend as a child, chickens can stand for people in certain contexts and on certain occasions. The chicken at *lugutu* stands for the dead person, much as in Nuer sacrifice cattle are identified with the person on whose behalf the sacrifice is made (Evans-Pritchard 1956: 263). However, the killing of the *lugutu* chicken is not a sacrifice or an offering to the dead. Rather, it is a replication of the death of the person who has already died in order that the powers released by death may be safely contained. The spirits of the dead want blood because blood is the stuff of life. Spilled blood is death. The bloodless killing of the chicken is a way of containing death by having a death without blood, which is further contained physically by the already bereaved who consume its meat, just as the potent fertility of the *mwali* is contained by the *wamakolu* when they eat the first lot of cucumber seeds.

For the period prior to burial, the roles of male and female main mourners are similar. They remain with the body, dress in rags and, like others more distantly related to the dead, mark their faces with flour to signify the existence of a relationship. They may not drink or eat until the body has been buried. After the burial main mourners and other relatives who choose to do so have their heads shaved and their bodies washed with medicinal water to cool them down, and mark out their status as mourners. Once the body is taken out of the house for burial differentiation between the roles of male and female main mourners is evident. Men carry out the body for burial, in a procession led by the main female mourners. After the body come the men as a group, followed by a collectivity of women. Men dig the grave and gently lower the body in. Before the body is taken outside, some strips of the shroud used to wrap the body are torn off, and tied around the heads of the main female mourners. Once the body is buried, they lower them to their necks, like a necklace. These pieces of shroud-cloth are called *lijemba*. They are gradually removed in successive stages which differentiate between the closeness to the deceased of various categories of female mourners. The circle of core bereaved progressively shrinks at the series of repeat funerals following the burial of the body.

The first removal occurs after an event called shasangira, on the second morning after the burial. *Shasangira*, which means, literally, things thrown away, refers to the preparation and eating of a meal during the night by those gathered at the funeral house. It concerns only the relatives of the dead person who have remained at the house of the deceased. Other people return to their homes after participating in a meal immediately after the burial. The *shasangira* meal is cooked and prepared by women who have remained inside the house after the burial. Before the meal is served, some handfuls of food are picked up by a main female mourner, past reproductive years, and silently scattered into the corners of the house. The food is left to lie where it falls. This is a kind of offering to the generalized and unnamed dead who continue to hover around the homestead, inside the very house itself, attracted by the death. It parallels what happens to the corpse who has, like the food, been discarded. Before dawn, in the cool of the morning on the cusp of daylight, the women then depart for a muddy riverbank or place by water, and dig a grave for their shroud pieces. As these are laid to rest, the women spit blessing on them on them with flour and water left over from the daubing of faces and ask that the body cool.

After *shasangira*, female kin who are less close to the deceased do not replace their shroudcloth with fresh pieces of old cloth. Those closer to the dead do so, donning replacement strips, tied around their necks just like the original shroud. Depending on the woman's relation to the deceased, these are worn until around two weeks after the burial, at a collective meal called *toa tatu*, which consists of eating and mourning, replicating in its sequence of events and allocation of space the events on the day of the burial. In essence, *toa tatu* is a regrouping of mourners who were present at the burial. The core bereaved remain at the house until *toa tau* is finished. With the exception of the main female mourners, women wearing *lijemba* remove them and bury them by water prior to the funeral meal. Only the main female mourner continues to wear hers until the funeral is finally ended, as much a year later at an event called *sadaka ya mwisho*. This event formally marks the transition of deceased person to spirit of the dead, and offerings of beer are made to the *mahoka*.

CONTAINED POWER AND EMPOWERMENT

Pogoro funeral practices mirror female puberty rites in several obvious ways, including sequences of seclusion, purification and the re-emergence of those identified with the corpse into the community. Both accord older women special roles and responsibilities which centre on the physical containment of power in such a way that it cannot then be transmitted to others. Although in the case of funeral rituals, female mourners eventually lose their identification with the corpse, bereavement, as a life experience, leaves a cumulative trace in people's bodies. This affects both men and women. The once-bereaved acquire a degree of immunity from the ravages of death power, and can assist in the preparation of corpses.

This notion of cumulative changes in a person's make-up informs our understanding of the ritual obligations of women past their reproductive years, as mediators of both life and death. The fundamental identity between the powers of life and death implies that women's bodies can better contain these kinds of powers than male bodies can, because they have already been exposed to them, through their engagement in reproductive processes and participation at funeral events which constitute essential elements of female growth. In the case of the *wamakolu*, who are no longer involved in reproduction, the powers associated with life and death cease to be antithetical because they will neither transmit them to others through sexual activity nor affect their own fertility. While the embodiment of cosmological powers associated with the life process empowers women to assume specific ritual statuses in the management of reproduction and death, it also precludes their assumption of the status of shrine medium (*mbui*). This is only available to men who live their lives in a state as close as possible to that of the spirits. Shrine mediums dress in cloth representing ancestral clothing and adhere to a range of prohibitions restricting their participation in funerals and life processes. The nature of female bodies, with their capacity to absorb power and be transformed by it, means that women cannot achieve the separation from life processes that being a shrine diviner entails. Even after the menopause, women continue to be involved in the life processes of others, as containers of both death pollution and female fertility. Consequently, in contrast to the transmission of mediumship among the Shona, where female power gradually ebbs away leaving women's bodies appropriate vessels for possession by royal ancestor spirits (Lan 1985), Pogoro women never lose their association with life processes, and indeed, have specific ritual duties concerning the life processes of others.

A person's social experience of ageing and growth not only changes their bodily substance, but is recognized as enhancing their emotional capacities. Women are expected to become progressively more able to take on the burden of suffering as they get older, for themselves and for others. The cultural emphasis on suffering as a value is doubtless influenced by Catholicism in which women's childbearing role is intimately related to the pain and fleshly suffering which parallels that borne by Christ on the cross. Women are thought to be better able to deal with suffering than men are, both their own and other people's. Women's capacity to endure and feel empathy for the suffering of others is taken as an index of their capacity to love, and stems from their culturally accorded role as mothers, who have a duty to care for other people, physically and emotionally. Motherhood is premised on a particular experience of one's own body as a nurturer and carrier of the bodies of others, of children in the womb and on one's back, and later, of the shroud representing the body of a loved one. Motherhood in rural Africa involves excruciating pain and suffering, incredible patience and, often, almost unbearable loss. Love, loss and pain are the core emotional experience of being female, as it is culturally constructed. This particular construction of femininity is experienced cumulatively through everyday living and participation in the gendered rituals which emphasize women's duties as carers and caretakers of life and death. The personal experience of caring and loss creates empathy for the suffering of others, heightened by the emotional resonance of ritual occasions which acknowledge the vagaries of death and life. It is this experience (cf. Bynum 1987: 281), rather than symbolic constructions of gender, which forms the basis of Pogoro women's Catholic religiosity, centred on intense personal relationships with Mary and remembering the dead.

CUMULATIVE COMPASSION AND CHRISTIANITY

Among the Pogoro communities of the Mahenge highlands, popular Catholic religiosity is largely the domain of older women, who attend church or services when they can, participate enthusiastically in Christian festivals and maintain highly personal relationships at home with the Virgin Mary. While men also attend church services, wear rosaries and pray at home, women's participation in Christian practices is more extensive, and certainly more intense. Women comprise the majority of participants in all-night vigils held for Mary and those conducted at home as part of the funeral process, where members of the group singing hymns inside the house are mostly female, in contrast to the mixed-sex group dancing what are locally described as 'traditional' songs outside it. Weekday masses attract women in larger numbers than men. Women are more involved in the Legion of Mary and church-sponsored lay organizations than their male counterparts, and regularly pray in their houses on behalf of family members, dead and living.

The most important Christian festival for Pogoro Catholics, male and female is Easter, when church attendance peaks for the period between Maundy Thursday and Easter Sunday. Easter Sunday is a family occasion, attracting large numbers of men, women and children for the celebratory masses held in a decorated church to acknowledge the resurrection. Services held on Good Friday are dominated by women who sing songs of suffering, the very same songs which have come to constitute the legitimate expression of mourning at funeral events, when they are sung for hours at a time. Because these songs are associated with funerals, singing them and hearing them evokes memories of the funerals of others and the pain of personal loss, creating an atmosphere of palpable sadness in the church. Good Friday is not only an occasion for the remembrance and re-experiencing of other funerals. It is also understood as Christ's funeral, which the structure of the service replicates (cf. Taussig 1980: 105; Rushton 1982: 156–7). The crucified Christ is taken down from his high position behind the altar and laid at its foot, for people to file up to and kiss, just as they bid farewell to a dead person immediately prior to burial by filing past the coffin and laying a hand on the cold forehead of the corpse.

Although the events of Good Friday focus on the crucifixion of Christ, the re-enactment of his funeral in establishing the occasion of his death simultaneously effects the establishment of Mary as a bereaved mother. This understanding of Mary as a mother who has lost a son, and of Christ's death, rather than his life, as significant,[4] is fundamental to women's core experience of Catholicism, founded on a relation of empathetic understanding between themselves and Mary. Valued as a mother, rather than a virgin, Mary is imagined as a real person, able to empathize with the experience of others and women in particular. Unlike Christ, who died and was resurrected into Heaven, Mary occupies heaven and earth simultaneously. An ordinary woman, Mary's life is tragic, as a mother who both loved and lost a son. Mary thus understands the plight of women, and feels pity and compassion for them, just as women feel compassion for Mary and help her to remember Christ through mourning. Mary is not merely an intercessor with Christ and God, but a divine being in her own right to whom prayers and conversations can be directed. Unlike the figures of God and Christ, to whom one prays (-sali) or begs (-omba) Mary's humanity means that the conversational exchange is possible. People 'talk' to Mary (-ongea), and she listens because, understanding the suffering of others, she feels pity, just as women feel pity for Mary's own suffering (Green n.d. (b)).

The relation of compassion with Mary is founded on a perception of Mary as an ordinary woman, made extra-ordinary only through her selection by God (cf. Bloch 1993). Tales of Mary's extraordinary nature stress her compassion and kindness, rather than her piety. The kinds of cultural elaborations of Mary as pure and without sin, so common in European Catholicism, are largely absent. Mary is not perceived as a unique kind of woman without sin and sex, who has managed to transcend the ultimate contradiction between spirit and flesh which formal Catholic theology proposes. On the contrary, Pogoro women's representations of Mary emphasize her humanity as a bereaved mother, as a person who has had intimate contact with both birth and death, and who can therefore empathize with the suffering of others (cf. Bynum 1987: 269).

GENDER, EMOTION AND EXPERIENCE

Contemporary Pogoro women's relationships with Mary cannot be explained away either by the history of the Catholic Church in Europe (Davis 1984), or by symbolic constructions of gender in which Mary is thought to appeal to women as a kind of role model of purity and transcendence of original sin (Rushton 1982; Warner 1976). Pogoro women do not regard Mary as a symbol of motherhood or virginity, but as a real woman who has lost a son and with whom a relationship of mutual compassion is possible. Similarly, women do not see themselves as being merely representatives of different gender attributes when they participate in gendered rituals. The whole point about such rituals is that the processes of transformation they effect do not occur at an abstract ideational level, divorced from the people who perform them (cf. Bloch 1992). Participation in rituals associated with fertility and death is imagined as physically and emotionally transforming those undergoing them and determines their capacities to assume gender-specific ritual roles in the future.

In Africa, as elsewhere in the world, gender is experienced as a process of gradual transformation in a person's physical and emotional being. Bodies *matter*, and are made to matter through the repetitions and reiterations which performatively effect gendered personhood (cf. Butler 1993: 9). For Pogoro Catholics, bodies are given meaning at the level of experience through a twofold process of incorporation. Symbolic constructions of gender are embodied and incorporated into male and female persons through specific rituals which establish and consolidate gendered identities through the manipulation of what are constructed as physical substances and cosmological powers capable of affecting the body. Participation in these rituals is not merely experienced in the symbolic terms of representations, but as progressively emotionally affecting those who participate. Older women's involvement in funerary rituals and obligations as mourners conveys an emotional resonance (cf. Kratz 1994: 130) which makes possible the cumulative experience of compassion on which their special relationship with Mary, the mother of a dead son, is founded. This cumulative gender differentiation which the embodiment of power entails means that Pogoro women never become more 'like men' as they age and lose their reproductive capacity, which Herbert has suggested accounts for the special ritual roles of post-menopausal women in African societies (1993: 231). On the contrary, through exposure to the powers released by the life process and an enhanced capacity to empathize, older women embody *par excellence* the female characteristics of nurturance, love and pity. Women's capacity for suffering and the expression of love, achieved through age and experience of involvement in life processes is the culmination of their becoming, and of their identification with Mary as the basis of a personal piety founded on the imitation not of Christ, at his moment of death (Bynum 1987: 257), but of his mother.

NOTES

1 This chapter is based on fieldwork carried out between 1989 and 1991. I am grateful to the ESRC and the University of Manchester for their financial support and to the Tanzanian Commission for Science and Technology for granting research clearance. I wish to thank the people of Mahenge for their support and assistance.
2 Up to the 1930s, brideservice, supplemented by the transfer of wealth items rather than livestock, constituted the basis of marriage transactions.
3 See Green (1993).
4 Sallnow remarks on a similar emphasis in Latin American Catholicism, where Christ's crucifixion is emphasized to the extent that the cult of Christ is essentially a 'cult of death' (1987: 49).

REFERENCES

Beidelman, T.O. (1964) 'Pig (*guluwe*): an essay on Ngulu sexual symbolism and ceremony', *Southwestern Journal of Anthropology*, 20: 359–93.
Beidelman, T.O. (1986) *Moral Imagination in Kaguru Modes of Thought* (Washington DC: Smithsonian Institution Press).
Beidelman, T.O. (1997) *The Cool Knife: Imagery of Gender, Sexuality, and Moral Education in Kaguru Initiation Ritual* (Washington DC: Smithsonian Institution Press).
Bloch, M. (1986) *From Blessing to Violence: History and Ideology in the Circumcision Ritual of the Merina of Madagascar* (Cambridge: Cambridge University Press).
Bloch, M. (1992) *Prey into Hunter: The Politics of Religious Experience* (Cambridge: Cambridge University Press).
Bloch, M. (1993) 'The queen, the slaves and Mary in the slums of Antanarivo' in C. Humphrey and N. Thomas (eds) *Shamanism, History and the State* (Ann Arbor: University of Michigan Press).
Boyer, P. (1990) *Tradition as Truth and Communication: A Cognitive Description of Traditional Discourse* (Cambridge: Cambridge University Press).
Brain, J.L. (1978) 'Symbolic rebirth: the *mwali* rite among the Luguru of eastern Tanzania', *Africa*, 48 (2): 177–88.
Buckley, T. and Gottlieb, A. (1988) 'A critical appraisal of theories of menstrual symbolism' in T. Buckley and A. Gottlieb (eds) *Blood Magic: The Anthropology of Menstruation* (Berkeley: University of California Press).
Butler, J. (1993) *Bodies that Matter: On the Discursive Limits of 'Sex'* (New York: Routledge).

Bynum, C.W. (1987) *Holy Feast and Holy Fast: the Religious Significance of Food to Medieval Women.* Berkeley: University of California Press.

Caplan, A.P. (1976) 'Boys' circumcision and girls' puberty rites among the Swahili of Mafia Island, Tanzania', *Africa,* 46 (1): 21–33.

Christian, W.A. (1972) *Person and God in a Spanish Valley.* New York: Seminar Press.

Comaroff, J. (1985) *Body of Power, Spirit of Resistance: The Culture and History of a South African People* (Chicago: University of Chicago Press).

Davis, J. (1984) 'The sexual division of religious labour in the Mediterranean' in E.R. Wolf (ed.) *Religion, Power and Protest in Local Communities: The Northern Shore of the Mediterranean* (The Hague: Mouton).

Douglas, M. (1966) *Purity and Danger: An Analysis of Concepts of Pollution and Taboo* (London: Routledge & Kegan Paul).

Evans-Pritchard, E.E. (1956) *Nuer Religion* (Oxford: Clarendon).

Fernandez, J.W. (1982) *Bwiti: An Ethnography of the Religious Imagination in Africa* (Princeton: Princeton University Press).

Godelier, M. (1986) *The Making of Great Men: Male Domination and Power among the New Guinea Baruya* (Cambridge: Cambridge University Press).

Goody, J. (1962) *Death, Property and the Ancestors: A Study of the Mortuary Customs of the LoDagaa of West Africa* (London: Tavistock).

Green, M. (1993) 'The construction of "religion" and the perpetuation of "tradition" among Pogoro Catholics, southern Tanzania', PhD thesis, London School of Economics.

Green, M. (1995) 'Why Christianity is the religion of business: perceptions of the church among Pogoro Catholics, southern Tanzania', *Journal of Religion in Africa,* 25 (1): 26–47.

Green, M. (1996) 'Medicines and the embodiment of substances among Pogoro Catholics, southern Tanzania', *Journal of the Royal Anthropological Institute,* 2: 1–14.

Green, M. (1997) 'Witchcraft suppression practices and movements: public politics and the logic of purification', *Comparative Studies in Society and History,* 39 (2): 319–45.

Green, M. n.d. (*a*). 'Overcoming the absent father: procreation theories and practical kinship in southern Tanzania' in P. Loizos and P. Heady (eds) *Conceiving Persons: Ethnographies of Procreation* (London: Athlone).

Green, M. m.s. (*b*). 'Remembering Christ and talking to Mary: words and things in Pogoro Christianity'.

Harris, O. (1981) 'Households as natural units' in K. Young *et al.* (eds) *Of Marriage and the Market* (London: CSE).

Herbert, E. (1993) *Iron, Gender and Power: Rituals of Transformation in African Societies* (Bloomington: Indiana University Press).

Hertz, R. (1960) 'A contribution to the study of the collective representation of death' in *Death and the Right Hand,* translated by R. and C. Needham (London: Cohen and West).

Kratz, C.A. (1994) *Affecting Performance: Meaning, Movement, and*

Experience in Okiek Women's Initiation (Washington DC: Smithsonian Institution Press).

Jacobson-Widding, A. (1987) *Notions of Heat and Fever among the Manyika of Zimbabwe*, Working Papers in African Studies 34, African Studies Programme, University of Uppsala.

Lan, D. (1985) *Guns and Rain: Guerillas and Spirit Mediums in Zimbabwe* (London: James Currey).

Larson, L.E. (1976) 'A history of the Mahenge (Ulanga District), 1860–1957', PhD thesis, University of Dar es Salaam.

Lutkehaus, N. (1995) 'Feminist anthropology and female initiation in Melanesia' in N. Lutkehaus and P. Roscoe (eds) *Gender Rituals: Female Initiation in Melanesia* (New York: Routledge).

Middleton, J. (1982) 'Lugbara death' in M. Bloch and J. Parry (eds) *Death and the Regeneration of Life* (Cambridge: Cambridge University Press).

Pina-Cabral, J. de (1986) *Sons of Adam, Daughters of Eve: The Peasant Worldview of the Alto Minho* (Oxford: Clarendon).

Richards, A.I. (1982) *Chisungu: A Girl's Initiation Ceremony among the Bemba of Zambia* (London: Routledge).

Rushton, L. (1982) 'Religion and identity in a rural Greek community', PhD thesis, University of Sussex.

Sallnow, M.J. (1987) *Pilgrims of the Andes: Regional Cults in Cusco* (Washington DC: Smithsonian Institution Press).

Scheper-Hughes, N. (1992) *Death without Weeping: The Violence of Everyday Life in Brazil* (Berkeley: University of California Press).

Stirrat, R.L. (1992) *Power and Religiosity in a Post-Colonial Setting: Sinhala Catholics in Contemporary Sri Lanka* (Cambridge: Cambridge University Press).

Swantz, M. L. (1966) 'Religious and magical rites of Bantu women in Tanzania', dissertation, University of Dar es Salaam.

Swantz, M.L. (1970) *Ritual and Symbol in Transitional Zaramo Society, with Special Reference to Women* (Uppsala: Scandinavian Institute of African Studies).

Taussig, M.T. (1980) *The Devil and Commodity Fetishism in South America* (Chapel Hill: University of North Carolina Press).

Taylor, L.J. (1995) *Occasions of Faith: Anthropology of Irish Catholics* (Philadelphia: University of Pennsylvania Press).

Turner, V.W. (1967) *The Forest of Symbols* (Ithaca: Cornell).

Turner, V.W. (1968) *The Drums of Affliction: A Study of Religious Processes among the Ndembu of Zambia* (Oxford: Clarendon).

Warner, M. (1976) *Alone of all her Sex: The Myth and Cult of the Virgin Mary* (London: Weidenfeld and Nicholson).

Wilson, M. (1957) *Rituals of Kinship among the Nyakyusa* (London: Oxford University Press).

PART IV
AFTERWORD

CHAPTER 10

CHAOS AND CREATIVITY

THE TRANSFORMATIVE SYMBOLISM OF FUSED CATEGORIES

ANITA JACOBSON-WIDDING

In the past, anthropologists writing about African cultures tended to focus on structure and order, rather than on anti-structure and disorder. Their prime interest seems to have been with normative and sometimes rather strict classifications of social categories in these societies, while their descriptions of everyday life were designed to fit within the norms of the dominant structures. When they discovered deviations from the orthodox order – such as witchcraft accusations, evidence of 'unorthodox' spiritual experiences, or the ritual display of sexual licence – they tended to define such 'anomalies' either in terms of 'custom' and 'religion', or in terms of 'deviation' and 'rebellion'. Few seemed to realize that there may be several layers of recognition of social relationships and existential realities.

Today, the world that Africanist anthropologists describe is not nearly as well structured. Beliefs and behaviours that do not fit with the normative ideology are no longer explained away as 'custom', 'religion' or 'rebellion'. Instead, such beliefs and acts are taken seriously by many anthropologists, who now acknowledge the existence of various kinds of 'muted structures' apart from the 'dominant structures' depicted in public discourses on normative principles.

Thus, a new generation of anthropologists attempts to apply different perspectives on the fissures in the well-structured, apparently seamless whole that is presented to them by those knowledgeable elderly men who often wish to represent their society and culture in terms of general principles. The new attempts at understanding the different kinds of deviance from the explicit models may take the form of an analysis of a particular situation or of a particular person's background. Or they may take the form of an analysis of implicit, 'muted' models of social relationships and existential conditions, paying close attention to the way that such 'muted structures' may be revealed in narrative and myth, in ritual action and informal interaction. Hence the new picture of African societies that is emerging is one where several kinds of 'muted structures' or 'implicit models' are taken into account. In many cases, the 'muted structures' are not explicitly articulated, but rather implicitly referred to in ritual action and myth. In particular, sacred rituals that take place 'backstage' may be pregnant with implicit messages about the existential conditions of human beings.

In this book we find descriptions of a wide variation of such rituals, from initiation rites that are connected with personal transformation, to communal rituals addressed to ancestral spirits that aim to redress abnormal situations during periods of disease or catastrophe. What these rituals have in common is not only that they are performed in situations that may be defined as 'abnormal'. They are all concerned with transformation, or with issues of re-creation, rebirth and reproduction. They may thus be interpreted as fertility rites.

Why, then, would fertility loom so large in African rituals of transformation? Why would fertility feature centrally in those rituals that are performed when people are faced with catastrophe and disease, and not only in connection with rites celebrating young people's sexual maturity? Why would fertility symbolism be central when a chief is initiated into office, or in many other kinds of *rites de passage* which are not immediately concerned with biological conception or sexual reproduction?

First, we must bear in mind that the concept of fertility may refer to a wider spectrum of creative potential than simply a woman's capacity to give birth. Second, there may be particular, culturally specific reasons for the frequent use of sexual metaphors in connection with reproduction writ large. With respect to agricultural societies in Africa, one such reason that has sometimes been suggested is the importance of agricultural fertility in societies where subsistence is entirely dependent upon the productivity of the land. However, as is shown in this book, the fertility theme seems to be just as important in pastoral societies, and even in hunting and gathering communities. Thus if we are to understand why fertility metaphors are so prevalent in African transformative rituals, we must move beyond explanations based on mundane utility and the practical concerns in everyday life.

Another recurring feature in such rituals is the central focus on gender. This may of course be seen as a result of the emphasis on fertility symbolism. Such an interpretation seems to be self-evident – at least as far as 'gender' is interpreted in terms of sexual characteristics, and thus associated with biological reproduction. However, there is reason to pause before interpreting ritual attention to gender and fertility as mere reference to procreation in a narrow biological sense. There are other components inherent in transformative rites that point in the direction of a broader interpretation of the symbolic fusion of the genders as a precondition for fertility writ large.

One of these features is the fact that we often find that a fusion of different generations is symbolically enacted alongside the symbolic demonstration of the fusion of the genders (see Sanders, this volume). Hence the symbolic fusion of the genders – whether represented by the lighting of a fire with a firedrill, or by rituals in which women are supposed to behave as men or vice versa – may not be a matter of symbolizing the mere sexual preconditions for the regeneration of life. Rather, the connection between rituals of transformation and the symbolism of gender and fertility may deserve an interpretation that goes beyond that of sexuality (see Broch-Due, this volume; and Kaspin, this volume).

Several chapters in this book suggest that the fusion of the genders in transformative rites should be interpreted as a comment upon the complementarity of the genders. This notion, I suspect, may resonate strongly with many anthropologists' intuitive interpretations, especially when considered in the light of everyday practices. It may also fit quite nicely with the cosmological classifications of the genders in many African societies. More often than not we find that the genders occupy complementary niches in the instituted models of male/female. Such classifications may take the shape of high/low, centre/periphery, hard/soft, heaven/earth, and so on (Jacobson-Widding 1991; Jacobson-Widding and van Beek 1990). Man and woman may be placed on more or less equal footing, as is often the case in the predominantly bilineal societies in West Africa. Or, the male domain may be explicitly linked with superiority, as is often the case in the patrilineal societies of Southern Africa. However, whatever values are ascribed to male and female domains, the binary classification of the genders found in such overtly depicted ideologies is invariably concerned with the complementarity of the genders. In binary classifications, in short, there is always a strong element of complementarity. One term is defined in contrast to, and thus as a complementary of, the other.

Considering the fact that, first, these cosmological classifications are overt, and made explicit whenever people refer to the dominant structure of their society, we should ask ourselves why the cosmology of complementarity would be the central theme in rituals of transformation that take place as discourses on 'muted structures' in less public 'backstage' arenas. Second, these binary classifications presuppose a distinction between opposite, complementary terms rather than their fusion. Complementarity thus appears to be a matter of overt recognition of structure and order, rather than a covert representation of an implicit anti-structure and 'disorder'.

I would suggest that the theme of 'fusion' – between genders, generations, or whatever – should be interpreted in terms of anti-structure, rather than in terms of structure. The 'complementarity' ideology belongs to the domain of a society's dominant structure, whereas the idea of a 'fusion' of distinct categories belongs to its muted structures.

CREATIVE THINKING AND CULTURAL IMAGINATION

However, if the fusion of separate categories belongs to the muted structures of any given society's cultural imagination, why, then, is this idea accorded such a conspicuous position in rituals of transformation? As has been shown in this book, the theme of fusion recurs time and again in rituals of transformation that are connected to initiation, or to personal or social crisis. It is as if a symbolic fusion would have to be enacted ritually in any *rite de passage*, or in any situation where people pause momentarily to catch their breath before embarking on a new phase in their personal lives, or before society returns to a 'normal' state of affairs. Perhaps this is where we should return to the symbolism of creation and re-creation, birth and rebirth, reproduction and fertility.

In Africa, virtually every creation myth stresses the primordial fusion of the worlds. The fusion may concern the distinct categories of heaven and earth, day and night, dry and wet, gods and humans, men and women. In most African creation myths, the primordial state is depicted in terms of a unity between heaven and earth, which is represented by a rope uniting the two (see Blystad, this volume; Kaare, this volume). In other myths, the primordial state is presented as an upside-down world, where women behave as men in a 'wild' non-structured existence (Burton 1991). However, whatever shape this primordial chaos may take, there is in African symbolism of the original state a heavy emphasis on fusion of the genders. In most of the essays in this book, there is reference to the androgynous symbolism in creation myths and re-creation rituals.

The German ethnologist Hermann Baumann devoted two major books to demonstrating the wide prevalence of androgynous representations in myth and ritual (Baumann 1936; 1955). In one of these books (1936) he focused on creation myths in Africa. The dominant feature of these myths is the idea of an original fusion of male and female, and of other distinctive categories as well. In Baumann's later book (1955) the particular focus was on bisexual representations of creative power in myth and ritual all across the world, even if there was still an emphasis on African cultures. In Chapter III of that work, the author examined what he called 'Kult-Transvestitismus' as a typical feature of fertility rituals and as a matter of 'exchange of life powers' (*Austausch der Leben-skräfte*). He interpreted this exchange of powers as a 'magic poten-tialization', or 'eine Potenzierung oder Erweiterung des eigenen Geschlechts' (Baumann 1955: 355).

If we were to interpret androgynous representations from a universalist semiotic perspective, we might perceive a connection between such metaphors and the idea of creation in many senses of the word (see Power and Watts, this volume). Just as symbols of androgyny are prevalent in many myths of creation, we often find that the state prior to creation is depicted as a one of chaos. There is a lack of differentiation between heaven and earth, night and day, water and land, and so on. Before cosmos, there is chaos (cf. Eliade 1974). In the New Testament (John 1), 'the word' roams about in chaos without distinctions until God distin-guishes darkness from light, water from land, and so on. In the Old Testament, the Garden of Eden is a place where Adam and Eve walk around with no awareness of any sexual distinction. In ancient Egyptian mythology, the lack of sexual distinction assumes an androgynous shape, while androgynous mythical figures are linked to creative power and sacred kingship: 'Male and female function (in the same person) is the basic duality through which regeneration of the creative power of the kingship is accomplished' (Troy 1986: 149).

In a similar vein, Luc de Heusch has interpreted the sacred king in Africa as an ambivalent figure, whose dual character is demonstrated through royal incest (de Heusch 1958). In western and central Africa, creative androgynous power is symbolized by a Janus figure with a male and a female face, which is somtimes identified with a 'magical' red snake with two heads (Jacobson-Widding 1979: 59ff; cf. Tastevin 1934: 250; Bittremieux 1936: 25; de Jonghe 1924: 555; Baumann 1955: 247ff; Hagenbucher-Sacripanti 1973: 113). These and other androgynous metaphors of 'magical' power are intimately linked to ideas about creation, re-creation, and thus fertility.

Androgynous representations of a primordial chaos prior to cosmos thus appear to be a more or less universal feature of creation myths. This may be interpreted in a structural, or even in a structural-functional perspective: a chaotic world is contrasted with the order and structure that was created by God, or by the first culture hero. Correspondingly, as soon as an 'abnormal' state of disorder enters the scene, the original process of creation must be repeated in order to produce a new order. By fusing distinct social categories such as the genders or different generations in a ritual enactment of the creation process, the 'normal' order is recreated. At the same time the dead structure is infused with 'magic potentialization', as Baumann expressed it.

This all makes sense from a traditional, socio-structural perspective, as well as from a functionalist perspective. However, we should not forget that when chaos is symbolized in myth or ritual, there is not only a fusion of *social* categories. Quite often, in fact, there is also a reference to other conceptual categories, like heaven and earth, dry and wet, divine and human, and so on. In short, there is often a transcendental imagination involved that goes far beyond the conception of social categories. This implies that in the symbolization of a primordial chaos that precedes the ordered cosmos, we are faced with representations of deep existential conundrums as well.

No matter where we live in the world, or in what kind of society we have been enculturated, we may recognize this existential dilemma. We all know that, in certain crisis situations in our own lives, we may feel as though we would be lost in chaos where we are unable to make any analytical distinctions. We may feel this way, for instance, when experiencing profound grief or powerful passions, or when suffering from identity crises, or when we simply feel a sense of 'misfit' in relation to what is supposed to be the 'normal order' of things. Further, as every creative artist or researcher knows, there is often a particular stage in the creative process when one feels a need temporarily to dwell in, rather than escape from, a 'creative chaos'. Before being able to rethink certain conventions, or to reshape one's ontology, it is necessary to lose oneself for a while in the chaos, in search of a new conceptual order. Chaos tends to precede rethinking and restructuring, just as emotion and intuition precede new and fertile analyses. Thus it seems that the same kind of processes would be at work, irrespective of whether we attempt to produce new thought patterns, or are about to pass into a new stage in our life-cycle. This process might be termed an 'existential transformation'.

The experiences that we have as *bricoleurs*, as creators or as re-creators, seem to be parallelled by the process that neurologists have defined as the co-operation between the two hemispheres of the brain. As has been known for about twenty years, analysis and spatial and conceptual distinctions are made in the brain's left hemisphere. Hence, this seems to be the part of the brain where 'structure' is conceived. The brain's right hemisphere, in contrast, is where we have visions of whole *Gestalts*, and where we perceive and organize synthesis and body movements. We might call this part of the brain the site of intuition and feeling, or maybe even the site of 'anti-structural' perceptions.

From neurologists and psychologists we have learned that we require access to both of these hemispheres in our daily lives. There is normally a constant alternation between the brain's two hemispheres during productive, 'fertile' thoughts. This would thus be part of a 'neurological condition', although we may just as well call it an 'existential condition'. We all require these two aspects – thought and feeling – in order to continue with our own lives and with our social universe.

STRUCTURE AND ANTI-STRUCTURE

In African societies, the recognition of this existential and social condition is amply demonstrated in both creation myths and in transformative rituals. In virtually every African society south of the Sahara, we find a rich symbolic language to express the alternation between structure and anti-structure, order and chaos, rationality and irrationality.

First, there is of course the conspicuous demonstration of the anti-structural state that Victor Turner has defined as 'communitas' (Turner 1969). This kind of anti-structural state is enacted in all kinds of initiation rituals, that is, in rituals of transformation of personal identity – whether this concerns a new stage in the individual life-cycle, a new stage in a chief's career, or the new identity of a patient who becomes a healer. The common features of such rituals are: (1) a temporary seclusion, that is, a demarcation of marginality in relation to the 'normal' social order; (2) nakedness, indicating that the individual is deprived of social personhood; (3) an ostentatious demonstration of equality in cases of collective initiation rituals. This implies that structural distinctions are temporarily dispensed with.

Second, there are annual rain rituals that belong to the savannah cultures in Africa. These rituals are usually carried out in the bush or atop a mountain, out of sight of the general public, thus 'backstage'. They usually include joking performances of androgyny, pretended sexual licence, and an ostentatious 'playing with the fire'. In this context, those who play with fire are the joking, temporarily 'abnormal' participants in the ritual, who turn gender roles upside-down and who indulge in a symbolic, incestuous intercourse. The symbolic intercourse is enacted via the fire-drill, which is assumed to represent sex between siblings (that is, members of the same clan) who are structurally equivalent. Rather than interpreting this symbolic fusion as an act of complementarity, I think it is more accurate to interpret it as a demonstration of the unity of siblings, and as a symbolic annulment of conventional gender distinctions (Jacobson-Widding 1999).

Third, the equivalence of normally distinct social categories is also demonstrated when joking partners are engaged as ritual officiants in ancestral rites that are designed so as to transform an abnormal situation into a normal one. The re-creation of 'normality' is brought about via symbolic indulgence in 'abnormality': by the co-operation between grandparents and grandchildren, their structural equivalence is emphasized ritually. Thus structure is momentarily denied in order to give way for the creation of a new structure – or for the re-creation of the 'normal' structure.

Fourth, a corresponding symbolic pattern may be recognized in funerary rites all over Africa south of Sahara. While walking to the grave, people wear clothes upside-down or inside-out, or carry out other kinds of reversals (Jacobson-Widding 1988). Joking partners such as the grandchildren of the deceased (Congo), or the daughters-in-law (Zimbabwe) attempt to obstruct the march to the grave, while the other participants are supposed to laugh. At death, normal life structures are reversed. The normality of the social order is denied in the midst of emotional and existential crisis. However, from there, a new order will give way to structure. The corpse has its body placed in the shape of a foetus, which is buried in a round womb, from where new life can once again emerge.

In African rituals of transformation, symbols of chaos form a recurrent theme; within this theme, two representational forms prove dominant. The first is construed around temperature, while the second employs colour imagery.

Colour symbolism is particularly salient in central Africa, where we find that the colour red is ritually contrasted with white and black (Jacobson-Widding 1979). In 'normal life' – the life of structure and order, and of the rationality of analytical thought – we find that black and white are employed to designate determinate categories. It may be the categories of night and day, this life and the next, humans and spirits, individuality versus collective identity, wrong versus right, false versus true, or loser versus winner in a profane, judicial procedure. In such contexts the colour red is de-emphasized. Instead the colour red is used to anoint the bodies of initiands, who are 'betwixt and between', or newborn babies who are not yet real persons, or corpses.

The colour red is thus employed to denote states of marginality, states that may be defined as 'betwixt and between', states that defy easy classification into any of the opposed analytical categories associated with black and white, respectively. Being a symbol of that which is neither right nor wrong, neither true nor false, neither this nor that, the colour red assumes a dynamic potential and is pregnant with 'magic'. It may work in either direction, like the figure zero, with which either miracles or disasters may be created. Accordingly, the colour red is used to denote powerful emotions and magic power, chaos and anomaly, or any potentially creative force. In transformation rituals in Central Africa, the colour red is amply used to denote the state of affairs that defies classification according to rational categories of thought. It thereby becomes the colour of ecstasy, potential fertility and creativity, the creative chaos before the ordered cosmos enters the scene.

Just as the colour red is contrasted with the analytical categories of two-value logic defined by black and white, the irrationality of the right side of the brain is usually interpreted by westerners as the opposite of the 'rationality' characteristic of the brain's left side. Rather, we tend to see emotion and analytical thought as opposites, not as complementary mental processes. In certain situations there seems to be a clear division between the two, for instance when we experience the most powerful emotions in life, like passion or grief. When experiencing such emotional states, we feel incapable of strictly analytical thought operations. We may feel as if the 'heat' of a fire has fused all distinct categories, and thrown us into a world of irrationality. Perhaps we have to remain there for some time, in order to gain the means by which to recreate the world.

African folk philosophers like healers and ritual specialists seem to be well aware of this universal, existential condition. By using symbols grounded in the senses, they have created an idiom by which humans are able to express some of the deepest conundrums in life. While anointing their bodies with the colour red, or while playing with the fire – thus by reversing the normal categories, or mixing up separate genders and generations – people are able to live out their existential conditions, rather than articulating them. A temporary fusion of the worlds is a matter of transcendental experience that allows us to cope with an apparently senseless, ordered life, where complementarity is a matter of profane co-operation between distinct categories.

REFERENCES

Baumann, H. (1936) *Schöpfung und Urzeit des Menschen im Mythus der afrikanischen Völker* (Berlin: Dietrich Reimer).

Baumann, H. (1955) *Das Doppelte Geschlecht: Ethnologische Studien zur Bisexualität in Ritus und Mythos* (Berlin: Dietrich Reimer).

Bittremieux, L. (1936) *La Société Secrète des Bakhimba au Mayombe* (Bruxelles: Institut Royal Colonial Belge, Section des Sciences Morales et Politiques, Mém. 5: 3).

Burton, J. (1991) 'Representations of the feminine in Nilotic cosmologies' in A. Jacobson-Widding (ed.) *Body and Space: Symbolic Models of*

Unity and Division in African Cosmology, Uppsala Studies in Cultural Anthropology 16 (Uppsala: Acta Universitatis Upsaliensis).

De Heusch, L. (1958) *Essays sur le Symbolisme de l'Incest Royale en Afrique* (Bruxelles: Institut de Sociologie Solvay).

Eliade, M. (1974) *The Myth of the Eternal Return, or, Cosmos and History* (Princeton: Princeton University Press).

Hagenbucher-Sacripanti, F. (1973) *Les Fondements Spirituels du Pouvoir au Royaume de Loango* (Paris: ORSTOM, Mém. no. 67).

Jacobson-Widding, A. (1979) *Red-White-Black as a Mode of Thought: A Study of Triadic Classification by Colours in the Ritual Symbolism and Cognitive Thought of the Peoples of the Lower Congo,* Uppsala Studies in Cultural Anthropology 1 (Uppsala: Acta Universitatis Upsaliensis).

Jacobson-Widding, A. (1988) 'Death rituals as inversions of life structures: a comparison of Swedish and African funerals' in S. Cederroth, U. Corlin and J. Lindström (eds) *On the Meaning of Death: Essays on Mortuary Rituals and Eschatological Beliefs,* Uppsala Studies in Cultural Anthropology 8 (Uppsala: Acta Universitatis Upsaliensis).

Jacobson-Widding, A. (1991) 'Subjective body, objective space – an introduction' in A. Jacobson-Widding (ed.) *Body and Space: Symbolic Models of Unity and Division in African Cosmology and Experience,* Uppsala Studies in Cultural Anthropology 16 (Uppsala: Acta Universitatis Upsaliensis).

Jacobson-Widding, A. (1999) *Chapungu, the Bird that Never Drops a Feather: Male and Female Identities in an African Society.* (forthcoming).

Jacobson-Widding A. and W. van Beek (1990) 'Chaos, order and communion in the creation and sustenance of life' in A. Jacobson-Widding and W. van Beek (ed.) *The Creative Communion: African Folk Models of Fertility and the Regeneration of Life,* Uppsala Studies in Cultural Anthropology 15 (Uppsala: Acta Universitatis Upsaliensis).

de Jonghe, E. (1924) *Les Soctiétés Secrètes du Bas-Congo* (Bruxelles: Institut Royal Colonial Belge, Section des Science Morales et Politiques).

Tastevin, C. (1934) 'Les idées religieuses des africains', *La Géographie,* 62 (5–6): 243–70.

Troy, L. (1986) *Patterns of Queenship in Ancient Egyptian Myth and History* (Stockholm: Almqvist and Wiksell).

Turner, V.W. (1969) *The Ritual Process: Structure and Anti-Structure* (Chicago: Aldine).

INDEX

Herbert, E.W., 7, 29(*6n*), 30(*17n*),
33, 262, 277, 279; ritual symbols,
50, 78, 139, 145–6, 151
Herders/herding, 163, 170, 192, 199
Herdt, G.H., 105, 120–1, 129
Herskovits, M., 156, 157, 183
Hertz, R., 29(*7n*), 33, 269, 279
Hewitt, R.L., 110, 112–14,
118–19, 121–2, 129
Hill, J.D., 47, 78
Historical background and
anthropological theory, 8–9
Hodgson, D.L., 158, 183
Hodgson, D.L. and McCurdy, S.,
42, 78
Hoernlé, A.W., 117, 129
Holas, B., 41–2, 78
Hollis, A.C., 101, 130
Holy, L., 47, 78
Holy, L. and Stuchlick, M., 6, 33
Homosexuality, 103
Honey-gathering, 133–4, 139–40
Hood–Williams, J. and Cealey, W.,
74(*5n*), 78
Household management, 11, 16, 20,
40, 48–9; the Datooga, 199–200;
the Iraqw, 231–8, 247–8; the
Pogoro, 259–60; the Turkana,
170
Houseman, M., 4, 33
Howell, P.P., 41–2, 78
Huffman, T., 110, 130
Hughes, A. and Witz, A., 74(*5n*), 78
Human body, *see* Body, Human
Humphreys, A.J.B., 130
Hunter, M., 41–2, 78
Hunters/hunting, 20–4, 44, 192–3,
213, 284–5; the Akie, 133, 137,
140, 144–7; Chewa ritual, 84–5,
89–95; the Datooga, 192, 197,
202–3; Khoisan ritual, 105–15,
118–23; the Pogoro, 259; the
Turkana, 163
Hutchinson, S., 158, 183

Ideational accounts and
anthropological theory, 3, 7, 44–
5
Ifeka–Moller, C., 187, 200

Ihanzu, the, 45–73
Iliffe, J., 250–1(*13n*), 251
Illness/disease, 192, 201–2, 217; the
Datooga, 194–5, 202, 217; the
Ihanzu, 50–66; the Iraqw, 228,
230; the Ndembu 84; the Pogoro,
260
Incwala (ritual), 139
Infertility, 84, 198, 201–2, 214, 217;
the Akie, 139, 147–8; the Iraqw,
233
Inheritance, 41–2, 241, 258
Initiation rituals, *see* Female
initiation; Male initiation
Inkosazana (deity), 18
Iraqw, the, 188, 192, 208–10, 225–
50
Irigaray, L., 29(*7n*), 33
Ivory Coast, 239
Iyam, D., 248, 251

Jackson, M., 6, 9, 14, 29(*8n*), 33,
189, 214, 220
Jacobson–Widding, A., 3, 4, 6,
29(*6n*), 34, 283–92, 293;
biographical details, vii–viii;
fertility and social agency, 261–
3, 280; ritual symbols, 47, 68, 70,
78, 84, 98, 181
Jacobson–Widding, A. and van
Beek, W., 29(*2/6n*), 34, 135, 137,
151, 285, 293
Jaggar, A. and Bordo, S., 29(*7n*),
34
James, W., 18–19, 34
Jaques, A.A., 41–2, 78
Jeffreys, M.D.W., 41–2, 79
Jellicoe, M., 75(*10n*), 79
Jesus Christ, 162, 257, 270, 274,
275–6
Jie, the, 153–4
Jonghe, E. de, 288, 293
Jordan, B. and Davis–Floyd, R.,
194, 220
Ju/'hoan, the, 105–20

Kaare, B., 7, 15–17, 25–6,
133–50, 163, 287; biographical
details, viii

Loiske, V.M., 193, 221
Looaa (creator), 227–8, 236, 238, 244
Lunda, the, 265
Lutkehaus, N., 256, 280

Maasai, the, 133, 139, 147, 155–8, 163, 225
McCall, D.F., 130
MacCormack, C.P., 194, 221, 225, 251
MacCormack, C.P. and Strathern, M., 211, 221
McDougall, L., 6, 34
McDowell, N., 250(*1n*), 252
McKnight, J.D., 68, 79
Magic, 84, 126, 231, 287, 291, *see also* Witchcraft
Malawi, 93
Male initiation, 25, 101, 118–21, 188; the Chewa, 90; the Iraqw, 231–2; the Turkana, 172–3
Malinowski, B., 137, 152, 154
Maluti, the, 105, 108
Mandeville, E., 41–2, 79
Manicom, L., 43, 79
Marakwet, the, 15
Marches, protest, 187–8, 193, 207–8, 244–6
Marmo initiation, 232, 244–5
Marriage, 16, 26, 41, 105; the Akie 134, 140; the Datooga, 193, 197–201; the Iraqw, 230, 231–41, 244, 249–50; the Pogoro, 258, 265–6; the Turkana, 155–7, 169, 179, 179–81
Marshall, L., 30(*19n*), 34, 112–17, 130
Martin, E., 96, 98
Marwick, M., 30(*18n*), 34
Marxism, 157
Masay ritual, 243–4, 247
Masculinity, 16–20, 24–5, 28, 201; the Akie, 138, 141–5; the Ihanzu, 46–50, 68–73; the Iraqw, 227, 235, 236, 237; the Khoisan, 101–5, 121–3; the Pogoro, 256, 264; the Turkana, 158–60, 169, 173

Masks, 85–94, 97, 119
Massai, the, 193
Maternal figure, 19–21, 25–6
Matriarchy/matrilineage, 18–19, 26; the Ihanzu, 46; the Iraqw, 229–31
Maxwell, K., 25–6, 34
Mazel, A., 105, 130
Mbui (shrine mediums), 273
Mbusa (sacred emblems), 11–13
Mbuti, the, 161
Medicine, 85, 228, 247, 256, 264–9
Medicine dances, 105
Mediums, 202–3, 273
Meigs, A., 31(*24n*), 35, 43, 47, 79
Melanesia, 26, 43
Menopause, 264, 268
Menstruation, 22, 115–17; the Chewa, 83–5, 90–96; the Iraqw, 238–9; the Ju/'hoan, 111; the Khoisan, 105–12, 118–22, 123; and male initiation, 89, 101, 118–22; the Pogoro, 256–7, 261, 264, 266–7; the Turkana, 168–9
Merleau-Ponty, M., 8–10, 29(*9n*), 35
Metaphors, 13–15, 84, 284–5, 288; Akie ritual 145; appropriation of female qualities, 122; Datooga wives' council, 188–9, 201, 211; first menstruation, 108; genitalia, 21; the Pogoro, 264–5; sexual intercourse, 70; trance death, 105, 117; the Turkana, 159–60; woman and nature, 166–8; women as prey, 111
Middleton, J., 260, 280
Midwives, 201, 203, 266
Mind, 13, 157, 189
Miscarriages, 140, 178; the Datooga, 195, 201–2; the Iraqw, 239, 240, 247
Mnemonics, 10, 12–13
Moon, 107–8, 112–13, 121, 123, 168
Moore, H.L., 3–28, 29(*4/11n*), 31(*24/25n*), 35, 218(*5n*), 221;

Political mobilization, 187–217
Political structures and
anthropological theory, 16, 22,
41–2
Pollution beliefs, 267; the Iraqw,
228, 231, 235, 238–43, 247–9
Polygamy, 169, 179–80
Potash, B., 30(*16n*), 35, 73(*3n*), 80
Poverty, 16, 210
Power, 7, 17–18, 22, 49, 287–91;
the Akie, 135, 140; the Chewa,
83, 97; the Datooga, 188,
189–90, 199, 210–14; the Ihanzu,
48–9; the Iraqw, 225, 235, 246–
7; the Khoisan, 104, 123–6; the
Pogoro, 256–7, 262–3, 264, 269,
270, 273–4; the Turkana, 159,
162, 178–81, 181
Power, C. and Watts, I., 17, 22,
27–8, 35, 287; biographical
notes, viii–ix; ritual symbols,
43–4, 107, 110–12, 121–3, 126–8
Powers, M.N., 194, 221
Praxis, 3–28, 189
Prayers, 190, 193–4, 202–15, 227
Pregnancy, 20, 291; the Chewa, 88–
9, 94; the Datooga, 188–9, 194–
5, 213–17; the Iraqw, 237, 239–
40, 240–1, 243; the Pogoro,
263; the Turkana, 164, 168, 175,
179
Procreation and anthropological
theory, 6–7, 18–26
Protest marches, 187–8
Puberty, 17–18, 85–9, 111, 114,
256–7, 266, 273–4, *see
also* Female initiation; Male
initiation

Quarantine, 239–40, 241, 242–3
Quotidian praxis, 14–16, 19, 20

Radcliffe–Brown, A.R., 4, 28(*1n*),
35
Radcliffe–Brown, A.R. and Forde,
D., 73(*1n*), 80
Rain, 107–8, 123, 178, 228, 243–5;
the Akie, 139–40, 145; the
Chewa, 84, 95–6; the Ihanzu, 45,

46, 48, 52–3; and the maiden,
113–17
Rainmaking rites, 17–18, 45, 84,
117–18, 290; the Iraqw, 245; the
Khoisan, 105, 127
Rangeley, W.H.J., 41–2, 80
Rapp, R., 153, 183, 225, 252
Rappaport, R.A., 108, 125–6, 131
Rapport, N., 121, 127, 131
Rattray, R., 161, 183
Raum, O.F., 101, 131
Rebellion, rituals of, 17, 84, 101,
283
Regeneration, 7, 16–17, 22, 123,
178–9; the Akie, 138–9; the
Chewa, 84–5, 93–6
Reichel–Dolmatoff, G., 161, 184
Rekdal, O.B., 188, 211
Rekdal, O.B. and Blystad, A., 221–
2
Religion, 16, 41–2, 96, 156, 283, *see
also* Christianity; Spirit world
Richards, A., 11–13, 22, 29(*11n*),
30(*18n*), 35; ritual symbols,
41–2, 73(*1n*), 80, 84, 96–8
Richards, A.I., 101, 131, 262, 265,
280
Rigby, P., 17, 35; ritual symbols,
75(*10n*), 80, 135, 139, 152, 178,
184, 187, 222
Ritzenthaler, R.E., 41–2, 80, 187,
222
Robertson, C. and Berger, J.,
73(*3n*), 80
Rock paintings, 105–11, 117, 122
Rogers, S.C., 153, 184, 225, 252
Role reversal, 17, 22–4, 72,
101–128, 285, 290; the Akie, 139;
the Iraqw, 235–6; the Turkana,
172–3, *see also* transvestism
Roman Catholic Church, 161–2,
166, 181, 238–43, 248–9; the
Pogoro, 255–78
Rosaldo, M.Z., 153, 184, 225, 252
Rosaldo, M.Z. and Lamphere, L.,
153, 184, 225, 252
Rosenthal, J., 45, 81
Rushton, L., 255, 275–6, 280
Rwandans, the, 84

Saakse, J., 41–2, 81
Sacrifice, see Animal sacrifice
Sagilu, Chief (Ihanzu), 75(*14n*)
Saisee tororeita (ritual), 135,
138–43, 149–50
Sallnow, M.J., 278(*4n*), 280
Sanday, P.R., 161–2, 184
Sanders, T., 7, 21–2, 26–7, 30(*18n*),
36; ritual symbols, 44, 50,
76(*24n*), 81, 84, 98
Sargent, C., 194, 222
Schapera, I., 30(*18n*), 36, 73(*1n*),
81, 117, 120, 131
Scheper–Hughes, N., 255, 280
Schlegel, A., 227, 252
Schmidt, S., 108, 110, 114–15, 131
Schoffeleers, M., 84, 93, 98
Schwartz, A., 41–2, 81
Seasons, 94–6, 139–40, 164–5, 178,
192
Semen, 21, 111, 194, 230
Seniority, 12, 14
Serpent, Nyau, 91
Setréus, J., 222
Sex-strike hypothesis, 104
Sexual intercourse, 21–2, 83, 213,
290; the Iraqw, 239; the Pogoro,
261–7; the Turkana, 174
Sexuality, 13, 20–8, 183, 283–8,
290; the Chewa, 85, 89, 92, 95;
the Datooga, 205, 212; the
Khoisan, 103–4, 111; the
Pogoro, 263, 267–9, 276; the
Turkana, 174
Shasangirai (Pogoro funeral food),
272
Shepherd, G., 30(*17n*), 36
Shirala medicine, 264–5, 267, 269
Shona, the, 273–4
Shope, J.J., 47, 81
Shrine mediums, 273
Sierra Leone, 189
Silberbauer, G.B., 30(*18n*), 36, 41–
2, 81, 114, 131
Singer, M., 189, 222
Sky, 163–8, 174
Snow, L.F. and Johnson, S.M.,
194, 222
Snyder, K.A., 7–8, 18–20, 23, 28,

178, 225–50, 250(*7n/10n*),
250–1(*13*), 252; biographical
details, viii–ix; fertility and social
agency, 184, 187–8, 222
Social structures and
anthropological theory, 3–25
Solomon, A., 105–8, 112–13, 117,
121–2, 128(*n*), 131
Songs, 11–14; the Akie, 141–3; the
Chewa, 83–8, 95–6; the
Datooga, 187–90, 196–7,
204–11, 214–16; the Iraqw, 230–
1, 244–5; the Khoisan, 107, 114,
118; the Pogoro, 268, 270, 275;
the Turkana, 178
Speech-act theory, 125–6
Spencer, P., 75(*10n*), 81, 138, 139,
152, 178, 184, 187, 215, 222
Spirit world, 41–2, 213; the Akie,
133, 140–50; the Datooga, 189–
98, 202–4, 207, 214–17; the
Ihanzu, 50–69, 73; the Iraqw,
227–9, 231, 242–3; the Khoisan,
113–19, 121; the Nharo, 121; the
Pogoro, 256, 260–3, 269, 272;
the Turkana, 153, 159–69, see
also Deities
Star lore, 115, 168
Status, 154–60, 170; the Datooga,
188, 196; the Iraqw, 226, 233,
237, 247, 249–50
Stevens, L., 7, 18, 36
Stichter, S.B. and Parpart, J.L.,
30(*16n*), 36, 73(*3n*), 81
Stirrat, R.L., 255, 280
Stoll, R.P.A., 101, 132
Stoller, P., 190, 215, 222
StrapsAkie mythology, 144–7;
Turkana mythology, 163
Strathern, M., 24–6, 36; fertility
and social agency, 211, 222, 225–
6, 237, 252; ritual symbols, 43–4,
81, 153, 172, 181, 184
Strobel, M., 30(*16n*), 36
Structural-funcionalism, 157
Structuralist theory, 4, 15, 157; and
anti-structure, 289–92
Sun, 227
Sunseri, T., 43, 81

LONDON SCHOOL OF ECONOMICS
MONOGRAPHS ON SOCIAL ANTHROPOLOGY

1 & 2 The Work of the Gods in Tikopia
RAYMOND FIRTH
0 485 19501 1 (2nd edn in one volume) hb

14 Chinese Spirit-Medium Cults in Singapore (Second Edition)
ALAN J. A. ELLIOTT
With a new Preface by Sir Raymond Firth
0 485 19514 3 hb

17 Indigenous Political Systems of Western Malaya
J. M. GULLICK
0 485 19417 1 Rev edn hb

19 Political Leadership among Swat Pathans
FREDRIK BARTH
0 485 19619 0 pb

20 Social Status and Power in Java
L. H. PALMIER
0 485 19620 4 pb

22 Rethinking Anthropology
E. R. LEACH
0 485 19622 0 pb

24 Legal Institutions in Manchu China
A Sociological Analysis
SYBILLE VAN DER SPRENKEL
0 485 19624 7 Revised edn pb

28 Essays on Social Organization and Values
RAYMOND FIRTH
0 485 19628 X pb

33 Chinese Lineage and Society
Fukien and Kwantung
MAURICE FREEDMAN
0 485 19633 6 pb

37 Kinship and Marriage among the Anlo Ewe
G. K. NUKUNYA
0 485 19637 9 pb

38 Anthropology and Social Change
LUCY MAIR
0 485 19638 7 pb

39 Take Out Hunger
Two Case Studies of Rural Development in Basutoland
SANDRA WALLMAN
0 485 19539 9 hb

40 Time and Social Structure and Other Essays
MEYER FORTES
0 485 19540 2 hb

41 Report on the Iban
DEREK FREEMAN
0 485 19541 0 hb

42 The Political Structure of the Chinese Community in Cambodia
W. E. WILLMOTT
0 485 19542 9 hb

44 Political Systems of Highland Burma
A Study of Kachin Social Structure
E. R. LEACH
0 485 19644 1 pb

45 Pioneers in the Tropics
The Political Organization of Japanese in an Immigrant Community in Brazil
PHILIP STANIFORD
0 485 19543 3 hb

47 West Indian Migration
The Montserrat Case
STUART B. PHILPOTT
0 485 19547 X   hb

48 Land and Family in Pisticci
J. DAVIS
0 485 19548 8   hb

49 Beyond the Village
Local Politics in Madang, Papua
New Guinea
LOUISE MORAUTA
0 485 19549 6   hb

51 Metamorphosis of the Cassowaries
Umeda Society, Language and Ritual
ALFRED GELL
0 485 19551 8   hb

52 Knowledge of Illness in a Sepik Society
A Study of the Gnau, New Guinea
GILBERT LEWIS
0 485 19552 6   hb

53 White Nile Arabs
Political Leadership and Economic Change
ABBAS AHMED MOHAMED
0 485 19553 4   hb

54 Ma'Betisék Concepts of Living Things
WAZIR-JAHAN KARIM
9 485 19554 2   hb

55 Forest Traders
A Socio-Economic Study of the Hill Pandaram
BRIAN MORRIS
0 485 19555 0   hb

56 Communications, Social Structure and Development in Rural Malaysia
A Study of Kampung Kuala Bera
WILLIAM D. WILDER
0 485 19556 9   hb

57 Sacrifice and Sharing in the Philippine Highlands
Religion and Society among the Buid of Mindoro
THOAMS P. GIBSON
0 485 19559 3   hb

58 Ritual, History and Power:
Selected Papers in Anthropology
MAURICE BLOCH
0 485 19658 1   pb

59 Gods on Earth
The Management of Religious Experience and Identity in a North Indian Pilgrimage Centre
PETER VAN DER VEER
0 485 19510 0   hb

60 The Social Practice of Symbolization:
An Anthropological Analysis
IVO STRECKER
0 485 19557 7   hb

61 Making Sense of Hierarchy: Cognition as Social Process in Fiji
CHRISTINA TOREN
Fijian hierarchy and its constitution in everyday ritual behaviour
0 485 19561 5   hb

62 The Power of Love
The Moral Use of Knowledge amongst the Amuesha of Central Peru
FERNANDO SANTOS-GRANERO
0 485 19562 3   hb

63 Society and Politics in India:
Essays in a Comparative Perspective
ANDRE BETEILE
0 485 19563 1 hb

64 The Harambee Movement in
Kenya
Self-Help, Developmnet and Educa-
tion among the Kamba of Kitui
District
MARTIN J. D. HILL
0 485 19564 X hb

65 Hierarchy and Egalitarianism:
Caste, Class and Power in Sinhalese
Peasant Society
TAMARA GUNASEKERA
'fascinating' W W Reinhardt *Journal
of Social and Behavioural Sciences*
0 485 19565 8 hb

66 Leadership and Change in the
Western Pacific
Edited by RICHARD FEINBERG
and KAREN ANN WATSON-
GEGEO
Essays presented to Sir Raymond
Firth on the occasion of his 90th
Birthday.
0 485 19566 6 hb

67 The Art of Anthropology: Essays
and Diagrams
ALFRED GELL
0 485 19567 4 hb
0 485 19660 3 pb

68 Conceiving Persons:
Ethnographies of Procreation, Fer-
tility and Growth
Edited by PETER LOIZOS and
P. HEADY
0 485 19568 2 hb

69 Those who Play with Fire:
Gender, Fertility and Transformation
in East and Southern Africa
Edited by HENRIETTA L.
MOORE, TODD SANDERS and
BWIRE KAARE
0 485 19569 0 hb

70 Arguments with Ethnography:
Comparative Approaches to History,
Politics and Religion
IOAN M. LEWIS
0 485 19570 4 hb

For Product Safety Concerns and Information please contact our EU
representative
GPSR@taylorandfrancis.com
Taylor & Francis Verlag GmbH, Kaufingerstraße 24, 80331 München, Germany